BIG TRAILS

GREAT BRITAIN & IRELAND VOLUME 2

Vertebrate Publishing, Sheffield
www.v-publishing.co.uk

First published in 2021 by Vertebrate Publishing.

Vertebrate Publishing
Omega Court, 352 Cemetery Road, Sheffield S11 8FT, United Kingdom.
www.v-publishing.co.uk

A CIP catalogue record for this book is available from the British Library.

ISBN 978-1-83981-045-9 (Paperback)

Front cover: High Cup Nick on the Teesdale Way. © Andrew Locking – *andrewswalks.co.uk*
Back cover (left): Heading down from Pen y Fan on the Beacons Way. © Becky Angell @beckythetraveller
Back cover (right): Magnificent clifftop views with the Needles ahead on the Isle of Wight Coastal Path. © Clare Williams
Individual photography as credited.

Mapping contains OS data © Crown copyright and database right (2021) and Openstreetmap.org data © OpenStreetMap contributors.
Relief shading produced from data derived from U.S. Geological Survey, National Geospatial Program.
Cartography by Richard Ross, **Active Maps Ltd.** – ***www.activemaps.co.uk***
Ireland Way is a Registered Trademark – ***www.theirelandway.ie***

Cover design by Jane Beagley, Vertebrate Publishing.
Interior book design by **Ryder Design** – ***www.ryderdesign.studio***
Production by Cameron Bonser, Vertebrate Publishing.

Printed and bound in Europe by Latitude Press.

Vertebrate Publishing is committed to printing on paper from sustainable sources.

HEADING ALONG THE RIDGE OF THE BANNAU SIR GAER ON THE BEACONS WAY. ▶
© ANTHONY PEASE PHOTOGRAPHY

Orkney
Islands
Cape Wrath
Durness
Wick
Isle of Lewis
Stornoway
Outer Hebrides
Ullapool
Harris
North Uist
10
Moray Firth
North
Sea
Elgin
14
Skye
Inverness
Grantown-on-Spey
Aberdeen
South Uist
Barra
Vatersay
Mallaig
Cairngorms
Fort William
Atlantic
Ocean
Isle of
Mull
Oban
SCOTLAND
Perth
Dundee
Inner
Hebrides
Firth of Forth
Dunbar
Glasgow
Edinburgh
Lindisfarne
Ardrossan
Southern Uplands
01
Brodick
Isle of
Arran
Alnwick
Moffat
Cheviots
21
20
Ballycastle
Coleraine
Stranraer
Dumfries
Hexham
Newcastle-upon-Tyne
Tyne
Carlisle
NORTHERN
IRELAND
07
Penrith
22
Belfast
Whitby
Isle of
Man
Lake
District
Kendal
Yorkshire
Dales
North
York Moors
Scarborough
Douglas
Ulverston
Pennines
12
25
The
Wolds
Ballaghaderreen
Shannon
Inny
Drogheda
Leeds
Hull
Bradford
Galway
Dublin
Liverpool
Manchester
Sheffield
04
IRELAND
Anglesey
16
Bangor
Chester
ENGLAND
03
Lahinch
Wicklow Mts
Llŷn
Peninsula
Irish
Sea
13
19
Whitchurch
Peak
District
Trent
09
Shrewsbury
Leicester
King's
Lynn
Norwich
08
Limerick
Kilkenny
Tipperary
Plynlimon
Tralee
Waterford
Peterborough
Lowestoft
Killarney
Blackwater
Birmingham
Great
Ouse
Cambridge
Cardigan
WALES
Worcester
Severn
Wye
Cork
17
24
18
Bantry
Luton
Oxford
02
Cotswolds
05
London
Thames
Swansea
Chepstow
Cardiff
Reading
Rochester
Bristol
Bath
Canterbury
Minehead
North Downs
15
Dover
Exmoor
Calais
23
Southampton
Portsmouth
South Downs
Atlantic
Ocean
Exeter
Bournemouth
Brighton
Eastbourne
11
Isle of Wight
Newquay
Dartmoor
Plymouth
Channel
Falmouth
English
Penzance
Dieppe
Channel
Islands
Alderney
Cherbourg
Le Havre
Guernsey
06
Jersey
FRANCE
Paris

CONTENTS

THE TRAILS

INTRODUCTION

A Big Trail may be the biggest adventure you'll ever have. Paths have always connected us; paths take us to new places and show us the way home. They offer escape, adventure, an unimagined future. On a Big Trail, you will make friends, enjoy amazing panoramas, sit in silence under starry skies, and occasionally feel that reaching the end of the trail is impossible. Everyone has their own reasons for attempting a Big Trail, and everyone's experience on the trail is unique.

The idea for this book came about in the Refuge de Carrozzu, the second refuge on Corsica's GR20. A dozen shattered walkers and runners huddled together; half had decided to abandon the trail. Waiting for the rain to stop, we had plenty of time to talk and it was very clear that most of those on the trail had no realistic view of what they were letting themselves in for and also no perception of the wide range of amazing alternatives that are available throughout Europe. A Big Trail may be the biggest adventure you'll ever have. It may also be the worst trip you've ever taken – if you choose the wrong trail.

We believe that there is a Big Trail for everyone; Europe offers some of the best long-distance routes in the world. There are the iconic trails that we have all heard of, the trails that are mentioned in hallowed tones in every bunkhouse and campsite across Europe. There are also the trails that you've never heard of; the trails that are just as beautiful, just as challenging, just as diverting as the famous ones. This book describes the trails that you've always wanted to know more about, and the ones that you've never heard of before.

We are passionate about Big Trails. We walk and run them; we read about them; we talk to the people who know them best. We decided to research the very best long-distance trails across Europe, and find out all the information that you might want to know before you pick your next Big Trail. This book is packed full of practical information, beautiful photos, useful maps, facts and figures. There are trails in the mountains, trails around cities, trails along the coast, trails to walk in the summer, trails to run on the shortest days of the year. We hope that this book will help you find your next Big Trail. Be careful – you may find yourself yearning to complete them all.

ACKNOWLEDGEMENTS

We are grateful to the following photographers who have generously allowed us to reproduce their stunning images: Rudolf Abraham, Becky Angell, Jon & Thomas Barton, Ellie Berry, Maya Bimson, Jen & Sim Benson, Heidi Broennimann, Tracy Burton, Zana Benson, John Coefield, Paula Connelly, Rona Dodds, Adrian Hendroff, Amy Hunt, Kathi Kamleitner, Nik Langdon-Ward, Norman Lines, Andrew Locking, Adam Long, Claire Maxted, Jason McDonald, Audrey Menhinick, Anna Molan & Michael Fogarty, Dave Parry, Anna Paxton, Anthony Pease, Ellie Quinn, Jak Radice, Mark Rainsley, Kathy Rogers, Sarah Ross, Holly Stevens, Alan Ward, Andy Wasley, Paul & Helen Webster and Tom Wheatley. Thanks go to the following organisations who have helped us source the photography and provided information – many are tireless advocates for, and caretakers of, these Big Trails; Shropshire Way Association (www.shropshireway.org.uk), Walkhighlands (www.walkhighlands.co.uk), Wild Running (www.wildrunning.co.uk).

We are indebted to Kingsley Jones and Stephen Ross for allowing us to reproduce the Jones–Ross formula which has been used to calculate the trail timings in this book.

◀ LONSCALE FELL ON THE CUMBRIA WAY NEAR KESWICK.
© ANNA PAXTON

WHAT IS A BIG TRAIL?

A Big Trail is an adventure to be had on foot. It is a long-distance trail, suitable for walkers and runners, that requires several days or weeks to complete. This book presents the very best Big Trails in Great Britain and Ireland. The routes we have chosen for the Big Trails series are generally between 100 and 1,000 kilometres in length – although there are a few shorter trails that are simply too good not to mention, and some trails that form part of longer European routes. None of these trails require climbing or winter mountain skills (unless tackled out of season) and most are waymarked although you may still need to navigate, particularly in bad weather. Although some of these trails are more challenging than others, most are suitable for any walker or runner, with sufficient preparation, training and planning.

Every Big Trail is a unique adventure. Some climb over mountain ranges, and some follow the path of a river. Some offer sandy beaches, and some chalky ridges. You might enjoy Britain's freshest seafood, or discover Iron Age forts on high, grassy hills. Some traverse from coast-to-coast, some follow in the footsteps of saints and chieftains, some climb up and down over beautiful sea cliffs.

A Big Trail might reveal the landscape that inspired painters and poets, offer evenings of traditional music and camaraderie, or follow in the footsteps of the Celts, Romans, Saxons, Normans, all the other Europeans before you. The grassy machair offers a soft bed on remote paths best completed with a tent on your back. On other trails, Britain and Ireland's traditional pubs wait for you at the end of each day to offer a fireside to dry your boots beside, a hearty meal and a comfy bed. Some of these trails won't appeal to you. They will be too hilly, too flat, too boggy, too urban or just the wrong length. But whether you're a speedy runner, a mountain goat, a keen landscape photographer or a long luncher, this book has Big Trails to delight you.

THE GRASSY TRAIL LEAVING DETLING, ON THE NORTH DOWNS WAY. © SARAH ROSS

ABOUT THE ROUTES

Big Trails: Great Britain and Ireland Volume 2 provides descriptions of Big Trails in England, Scotland, Wales, Ireland and the Channel Islands. The most westerly route is **the Dingle Way**, an undiscovered treasure on Ireland's wild Atlantic coast, and the most easterly is the **North Downs Way**, over the rolling, green North Downs towards the Kent coast. The routes stretch from Speyside's whisky heartlands and the sandy beaches of Scotland's **Moray Way** to the **Channel Island Way** as it circumnavigates five islands nestled near the French coast.

At more than 500 kilometres, the **Beara-Breifne Way** is the longest route featured in this volume, passing through ten counties as it traverses Ireland from the Cork coast to Cavan. The shortest route – the **Burren Way** – reveals the beauty of the high Cliffs of Moher and the dramatic karst landscape of the Burren. The **Beacons Way**, which traverses the national park, is the hilliest route with approximately 6,000 metres of ascent and the **Severn Way**, which follows Britain's longest river from the Bristol Channel to its source on the slopes of Plynlimon, climbs an average of just four metres per kilometre.

The routes in this book pass through some of Europe's most beautiful national parks and stunning coastlines. The **Two Moors Way**, Devon's Coast to Coast, passes through Dartmoor and Exmoor and the **Cumbria Way** offers a low-level route across the Lake District. The **Hebridean Way** reveals sandy beaches on the ten islands of the Outer Hebrides, while the **Arran Coastal Way** encircles the island nicknamed 'Scotland in Miniature'. **St Oswald's Way** offers quiet moors before following Northumberland's beautiful coast.

THE TRAILS AT A GLANCE

- Seventeen trails are linear (including the **Beacons Way** and **Llŷn Coastal Path**), seven are circular or near circular and the **Shropshire Way** is a figure of eight.

- Four routes are National Trails (**Glyndŵr's Way**, the **North Downs Way**, the **Pembrokeshire Coast Path** and the **Yorkshire Wolds Way**). Two are Scotland's Great Trails (the **Arran Coastal Way** and **Southern Upland Way**) and the **Moray Way** combines sections of three Great Trails.

- Six trails are primarily through national parks (such as the Burren or Pembrokeshire Coast) but one (the **Peak District Boundary Walk**) encircles an entire national park.

- Three trails (**Arran Coastal Way, Channel Island Way, Isle of Wight Coastal Path**) encircle islands while the **Hebridean Way** traverses ten islands from south to north.

- Four trails follow in the footsteps of a historical leader (the **Beara-Breifne Way**, **Glyndŵr's Way**, **Lady Anne's Way** and **St Oswald's Way**) while three follow the course of rivers (the **Severn Way**, **Teesdale Way** and **Wye Valley Walk**).

OUR FAVOURITES

We think that every single Big Trail in this book is special, and there is something unique about every one of them that has earned them a place in *Big Trails: Great Britain and Ireland Volume 2*. But if you're not sure what to look at first, here are six of our favourites.

- With pretty seaside resorts, plenty of whisky distilleries and easy riverside paths linking charming towns, the **Moray Way** is Britain's ***Most Relaxed Trail***. Remember to keep your eyes peeled for dolphins and minke whales as you pass Moray's sandy beaches.

- The high **Beacons Way** which traverses the Brecon Beacons National Park and climbs some of Wales's remotest mountains is our ***Wildest Adventure***. It offers experienced hillwalkers the opportunity to enjoy the quieter western Beacons, and on a fine day presents stunning views across Snowdonia and the Welsh coast.

THE INGLIS MEMORIAL ON COLLEY HILL, NORTH DOWNS WAY. © MARK RAINSLEY

- The **Channel Island Way** encircles five of the Channel Islands. Three islands (Sark, Herm and Alderney) are small enough to run around in a few of hours, and Jersey, the largest, is just over seventy kilometres in circumference. With good weather, sea breezes and friendly villages, the Way is ***Great for Trail Running***. You can run in the morning, and still have time to explore each island before hopping on to your next ferry.

- Yorkshire is God's own country and the Yorkshire Dales, North York Moors and Yorkshire Coast attract droves of tourists, but few explore the green rolling hills between the moors and the sea. The **Yorkshire Wolds Way** is an ***Undiscovered Gem*** which leads you under the mighty Humber Bridge, past a deserted village, through green valleys and wildflower-edged fields to Yorkshire's high, bird-rich cliffs.

- The **Burren Way** is a little Big Trail that links two of Ireland's most scenic tourist destinations: the towering Cliffs of Moher and the other-worldly karst of the Burren National Park. It is a ***Great Weekend Escape***, short enough to be tackled in a long weekend, although you'll almost certainly want to stay longer to enjoy the seafood, traditional music and unique wildlife of the Burren.

- The **Capital Ring** is an opportunity to explore London's hidden green spaces on a trail that encircles the city, taking you under the mighty Thames, past an Olympic stadium and through the bluebells of Highgate Wood. With good public transport connections and plenty of cafes and parks en route, this is ***Perfect for All the Family***, a great big adventure to be tackled over weekends or school holidays.

HOW TO USE THIS BOOK

This book provides descriptions of twenty-five of the very best European long-distance trails in England, Scotland, Wales, Ireland and the Channel Islands. Each route description provides you with the following information.

- An overview of the route from start to finish.
- Useful information on how to get there, when to go and what to expect.
- Essential information on accommodation, weather and terrain.
- Highlights along the way – historical sites en route, wildlife to look out for, the best views.
- Interesting facts about the places you'll pass.
- A summary of route variations and detours.

This book is not intended to let you plan your next Big Trail adventure, but rather to inspire you. Whether you want a hilly challenge or a seaside amble, solitude or camaraderie, local beer, historic castles or ancient woods, this book has the trail for you. It includes iconic trails, such as the **Pembrokeshire Coast Path** and the **Cumbria Way**, but also undiscovered gems such as the **Isle of Wight Coastal Path**, which encircles the island beloved by Queen Victoria, and the **Teesdale Way** which takes you from the industrial landscape of Middlesbrough through green valleys to reach High Cup Nick. Each route description is accompanied by beautiful photography to give you a sense of what to expect on the trail.

The trails are presented in alphabetical order so that you can easily find the one you're interested in. But if you're not sure where to start, why not turn to the back of the book where you'll find our unique trail index that quickly allow you to find a trail based on where it is, how long is it (kilometres or days) or when to go?

In addition to detailed descriptions and inspiring photography, at the end of each trail a handy double page of the following essential information is provided.

- An overview map of the trail, which shows the route (and major variations), terrain, nearby towns and cities, and other local features.
- Trail length, and cumulative ascent and descent.
- An elevation profile of the route.
- Details of the start and finish, and how to get there, including information on the closest international air, rail or ferry connections.
- Days to complete the trail – for Walkers, Trekkers, Fastpackers and Trail runners, calculated using the Jones–Ross formula (information on the Jones–Ross formula and different trail users is provided on pages XVII–XVIII).
- Pros and cons to offer a quick insight into the trail.
- Information about the most common accommodation options available on or close to the trail.
- Details about trail characteristics and the paths that you will encounter on the trail.
- An indication of waymarking on the trail.
- A calendar showing months when the trail can be safely completed.
- How to find further information – details of Vertebrate Publishing's guidebooks and guidemaps, trail websites and other guidebooks or maps that will provide more detailed information if you want to plan a Big Trail adventure.

WHEN TO GO

Each route has a calendar indicating the best time to tackle the trail. Months (or half months) may be highlighted in the following colours.

Green – these are the best months to hit the trail. The entire route will be open; accommodation, food and public transport services will be operating at peak levels; normal weather conditions should not disrupt your trip.

Orange – it is generally possible to attempt the trail but it may require greater flexibility or better planning. Some accommodation may be closed; other tourist services may also operate over reduced hours, if at all. Parts of the trail may be closed or diverted, and weather may mean that you are forced to abandon the trail.

Red – you should not tackle the trail unless you have significant skills and experience; you may have to be completely self-sufficient on the trail in challenging weather conditions; you may require winter mountain skills and all accommodation may be closed.

LOOKING BACK TOWARDS THE VILLAGE OF ADRIGOLE, THE BEARA WAY. © ELLIE BERRY/TOUGH SOLES

ICONS USED IN THIS BOOK

ACCOMMODATION

The accommodation icons highlight the different accommodation options available along the length of the trail. If there are a number of hostels along the trail, but you may have to spend one night in a bed and breakfast, the hostel icon will be shown. If there are hotels at the start of a trail, but none on, or close to, the rest of the route, the hotel icon will not be shown.

Camping – there are campsites on or close to the route, or properties, such as hostels, that will permit camping nearby. This icon is generally not used to indicate wild camping, unless wild camping is legally permitted (or at least well-tolerated) and applicable to the route.

Bothies – these small, basic shelters are generally in mountainous or remote locations. Often they offer little more than a roof over your head – there may be no lights, toilet facilities or water, although some have a basic fireplace.

Hostels – budget accommodation is offered in shared dormitory rooms (and occasionally private rooms); often reduced rates are available to members of hostel associations. Although hostels vary greatly in the facilities they offer, the European hostelling movement grew out of walkers' and cyclists' need for affordable accommodation, so they are often located close to the trails and cater specifically for trail users.

Hotels – private rooms are offered, usually with en-suite facilities. In addition to breakfast, they will usually provide dining, and sometimes bar, facilities. They may offer additional services, such as laundry, a concierge and room service.

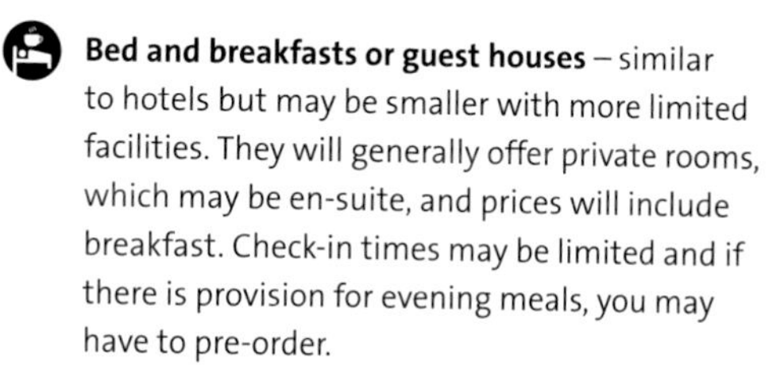

Bed and breakfasts or guest houses – similar to hotels but may be smaller with more limited facilities. They will generally offer private rooms, which may be en-suite, and prices will include breakfast. Check-in times may be limited and if there is provision for evening meals, you may have to pre-order.

TRAIL CHARACTERISTICS

The trail characteristics icons provide information on the challenges that a trail presents.

Exposed – these trails offer little protection from the weather. You may be exposed to torrential rain, hot sunshine or dangerous thunderstorms. Exposed trails are often in mountains, and sometimes on ridges or mountain edges, so may also involve the risk of steep drops.

Remote – these trails are distant from towns, villages and roads. If you need to abandon the trail in an emergency, it may be challenging and take some time to reach help.

Steep – these trails have sections of sharp ascent or descent. Some ascents may be laddered, or may involve minimal scrambling. This icon is used to indicate where a trail has ascents or descents which may be technically challenging, rather than to identify trails with a lot of ups and downs.

Forest – these trails have sections through forests. Forest sections may be slippery, particularly during autumn leaf fall, and may present trip hazards. Navigation may be more challenging in forest sections as landmarks on the trail are obscured.

PATHS

The path icons indicate what type of tracks and paths you will generally encounter en route; for example, a trail may have a short road section but the road icon is only shown if roads make up a significant part of the route or if a long road section is encountered.

Roads – sections of the trail follow roads. There may be a pedestrian walkway, but you may also find yourself on the main carriageway next to traffic (although generally not on busy or main roads).

Open countryside – the trail crosses open countryside, with little or no indication of a path. You may need a map and compass to follow the trail, and the route may be boggy, bouldered or covered with vegetation.

Hard paths – the trail follows well-defined stone or tarmac paths; these trails are often on forestry tracks, or on trails shared with horse riders and cyclists. Stony or rocky paths may be slippery in wet weather, and if the surface is rocky or potholed may present a trip hazard.

Grassy paths – the trail follows well-defined grassy paths, often across pastures, but sometimes through woods or by rivers. The paths may be muddy, and sometimes narrow.

WAYMARKING

The waymarking icons indicate how easy or difficult the navigation is on the trail.

The trail is clearly waymarked along its entire length. You may need to pay careful attention to the waymarking where paths cross, or where there are trail variations. In good weather conditions, you should be able to follow the waymarked trail with minimal reliance on a map, guidebook or GPS route (although you should always have alternative means of navigation for emergencies).

The trail has some waymarking but you will probably need to navigate using a map, guidebook or GPS route on some or all of the trail. Some sections may be missing waymarks; waymarking may be out of date or poorly maintained; the route may only partially follow a waymarked trail.

There is no waymarking or very little waymarking on the trail. Some non-waymarked trails may also be remote and/or exposed, and you should be cautious about attempting these without significant trail experience. You will need to rely on good navigational skills to safely follow these trails, or you might consider hiring a guide or joining an organised holiday.

WALK, TREK, FASTPACK, RUN

Everyone tackles a Big Trail at their own pace, but in order to give you an indication of how long the trail may take, we have identified four user groups: ***Walkers, Trekkers, Fastpackers*** and ***Trail runners***. The **Jones–Ross formula** has been developed that modernises and develops Naismith's rule to provide realistic timings for each user group.

All user groups move at different speeds and have a higher flat speed than ascent and descent speeds, but they also move at different rates in ascent and descent.

Walkers move at a flat speed of around five kilometres per hour and move at very similar speeds while descending and ascending.

Trekkers move at a flat speed of around six kilometres per hour and move more quickly while descending than they do while ascending.

Fastpackers, who typically run on some sections of routes and walk on others, move at a flat speed of around eight kilometres per hour and move more quickly while descending than they do while ascending.

Trail runners move at a flat speed of around ten kilometres per hour and move far more quickly while descending than they do while ascending.

The trail timings (in days) are calculated assuming an average of around eight hours travelling on the trail per day.

RUNNING THE CAPITAL RING NEAR BEVERLEY BROOK, RICHMOND PARK. © JEN & SIM BENSON

A shorter day length of six hours is used to calculate the trail timings for Walkers for routes that may be tackled outside the summer months, when daylight hours are more limited. The Jones–Ross formula assumes average speeds – heavy kit, adverse weather conditions, your particular strengths in ascent or descent and tired legs may all impact on your actual pace.

The trail timings provided in this book are intended to provide an indication of time taken to complete the trail, assuming full days on the trail and no rest days. You might choose to tackle a Big Trail differently by, for example, running the trail in the morning and enjoying the local area in the afternoon or taking advantage of baggage services to let you walk longer and further each day. The accompanying guidebooks and guidemaps from Vertebrate Publishing, when available, provide all the information you need to tackle each Big Trail however you prefer.
In a guidemap, the route is broken down into manageable sections, separated by timing points, allowing you to plan daily itineraries based on your user group, your own pace, and how long you want to spend on the trail each day. Each product provides information about food and accommodation at timing points, and suggested daily itineraries for each user group. As you follow the trail, you will quickly learn to adjust the timings provided by the Jones–Ross formula to fit your qualities of movement out on the trail.

The Jones–Ross formula in detail

Expressed in words, the Jones–Ross formula is:

$$\text{time} = \frac{\text{distance}}{\text{flat speed}} + \text{adjustment for ascent} + \text{adjustment for descent}$$

More precisely, it can be expressed as:

$$\underset{\text{(minutes)}}{\text{time}} = \frac{\text{distance (km)}}{\text{flat speed (km per hour)/60}} + \frac{\text{vertical ascent (metres)}}{\text{vertical ascent speed (metres per hour)/60}} + \frac{\text{vertical descent (metres)}}{\text{vertical descent speed (metres per hour)/60}}$$

The flat speeds and vertical ascent and descent speeds for the four user groups are shown in Table 1.

	Flat speed (km per hour)	Vertical ascent speed (metres ascended per hour)	Vertical descent speed (metres descended per hour)
Walker	5	425	450
Trekker	6	450	750
Fastpacker	8	600	1000
Trail runner	10	1000	2000

TABLE **1**

PLANNING FOR A BIG TRAIL

PREPARATION

PICK YOUR TRAIL

Choose the trail that's right for you. Do you like mountains or coastal views, solitude or camaraderie? Do you want to run the trail, walk a fast trail or take time to enjoy the scenery? How many rest days do you want?

TAKE IT EASY

If this is your first Big Trail, don't make it any harder that it needs to be. Consider baggage transfer services to keep your day pack light. There's no better start to the day than a hearty breakfast, cooked by someone else, that will keep you satisfied all morning, so why not treat yourself to a bed and breakfast or hotel?

TEST YOUR KIT

Everyone, from your mum to the sales assistant to the grizzled thousand-kilometre hiker, will tell you the easiest way to complete the trail and the best way to avoid blisters. None of them are quite right. Find out what kit works for you – trail shoes or boots, flapjacks or protein bars, what socks, walking poles or not. Don't take kit that you haven't tested out on a long-distance trail – it's never great finding that your waterproofs aren't waterproof, or your tent is missing a pole, but it's easier if you can go home and come back another day! It's not just about boots, rucksacks and technical t-shirts – work out what you like to eat on the trail, and how much water you need to carry. Always wear your boots or shoes in well.

TRAIN

Get as many kilometres under your belt as possible. Carry the kit you plan to take with you. Hit the trail even when it's raining, or windy, or foggy and, if you can, try to get out on the trail two or more days in a row. Every hard-won kilometre of practice will make your time on the trail easier, but there are things that you can squeeze into a lunch hour that will also help. Sessions on an exercise bike can increase your cardiovascular fitness and improve aerobic performance; circuit training and high-intensity interval training can quickly develop core strength that will be invaluable when you're carrying a heavy day pack on a tricky path.

DEVELOP SKILLS

Hone your map reading and navigation skills. Practise route finding when there is no clear path. Learn how to pay attention to the developing weather, and the signs that will indicate the driest path through a bog.

PLAN

Any Big Trail is a challenge, but you can make it easier if all you have to concentrate on each day is following the trail. Book accommodation in advance; find out where you can get food and water on the trail; know your escape routes and know how to get help in an emergency. It's useful to know where you might buy replacement walking poles, new waterproofs or more blister plasters, and where there are cash machines. Rest days are not only a chance to recover; they're an excellent opportunity to restock, sort out kit and check out reports on the trail condition and weather forecast.

RECOMMENDED KIT LIST

Kit can be highly subjective and vary depending upon the person, the season and the level of experience or comfort. These recommended kit lists for walking or trekking can be adapted by fastpackers and trail runners, and are endorsed by our equipment partner **Alpkit** – the ideal resource for sourcing equipment for your adventure. ***www.alpkit.com***

KIT LIST FOR WALKING OR TREKKING

Safety

- Map and compass
- Whistle
- Mobile phone and charger (with plug adaptor, if required)
- Head torch (and spare batteries)
- Trekking poles
- First aid kit and blister kit

- Winter equipment (if required – crampons/micro-spikes, gaiters, ice axe)
- Tick removal kit

Essentials

- Toiletries and wet wipes
- Travel towel
- Travel wash
- Sleeping bag liner
- Sleeping mask
- Ear plugs
- Camera
- Sunscreen
- Insect repellent

Food and drink

- Water bottle
- Knife
- Snacks

Clothing

- Rucksack
- Waterproof rucksack liner
- Walking boots or trail shoes
- Waterproof jacket
- Waterproof trousers
- Walking trousers and shorts
- Wicking top x2
- Insulating layer
- Socks and underwear x2
- Gloves and warm hat
- Sunglasses
- Sunhat

Paperwork

- Passport and visas/Photographic ID
- Bank card
- Cash
- Proof of travel/activities insurance
- European Health Insurance Card, if applicable

Extra gear for camping or backpacking

- Tent/bivouac bag
- Sleeping mat
- Sleeping bag
- Stove
- Cooking gear and utensils
- Food
- Trowel

HIKING WITH CHILDREN

A Big Trail is the perfect way to begin a lifetime's love affair with outdoor adventure and can be the holiday that your children never forget. But a bad day on the trail with a disgruntled child may be the longest hours you'll ever experience. Plan, practise and don't forget you're supposed to be having fun.

Pick the right trail – look for child-friendly accommodation, plenty of places to eat en route and have shorter days without too much ascent. If your child is a baby or toddler, will you carry them or do you need a buggy-friendly path? Is the path safe for children? What else is there to do on the trail?

Take a break – plan plenty of refreshment stops and rest days.

Make it easy – investigate where you can take public transport to shorten days or skip boring road sections; consider baggage transfer; book catered accommodation.

Know your child – don't overestimate how far they can walk; understand what they find difficult or when they get tired; work out what cheers them up.

Look after yourself – don't forget that you'll have to carry at least some of your child's kit as well as your own. Plan for a heavy day pack with their spare layers, lunch and waterproofs. Don't overestimate your pace when you're hand-in-hand with a recalcitrant child.

SAFETY AND RESCUE

Always carry a **mobile phone** on the trail in order to alert emergency services in the event of an accident. Phone signal may be intermittent, particularly in remote or mountain areas. An SMS message may connect when voice calling is unavailable, and some local rescue services provide the option to contact them by text.

Do not rely on a single form of navigation. Mobile signals may be intermittent; electronic devices may be broken or lose charge; waymarking may be vandalised. It is advisable to always carry a map, and consider downloading GPX files to your navigation device.

Emergency services: 112 is the single EU emergency number and will connect you to emergency services in every European Union country, including Great Britain and Ireland. **999** is the British and Irish emergency number. Both 112 and 999 will also work on the Channel Islands.

In Great Britain, the emergency services can also be contacted by SMS text – useful if you have low battery or intermittent signal. Although primarily aimed at deaf and speech impaired people, EmergencySMS is available to anyone, if your service provider supports it, but it requires registration; you can register by sending an SMS message, 'register' to 999 (the UK) or 112 (Ireland). It is particularly useful in areas of the countryside where mobile signal is too weak to sustain phone contact but a text message might be sent. **EmergencySMS should only be used when voice call contact with emergency services is not possible.**

Mountain and other countryside rescue services in Great Britain and Ireland are provided as part of national emergency services and by voluntary organisations. Organisations such as Mountain Rescue are charitable organisations, financed by public donation and reliant entirely on volunteers.

In event of needing to call for rescue, prepare the following information.

Your name – normally you are asked your full name, and sometimes your address. Your mobile number will show on the emergency operator's screen, but you may be asked to confirm it.

Where you are – make sure you know how to locate your UTM coordinates using your mobile phone or smartwatch.

Phone number – if you are low on battery, tell the operator and provide an alternative phone number of another group member.

What occurred – detail the event that occurred in terms of numbers involved, their ages, and injuries and how they were sustained. Provide any detail you feel pertinent, such as fractures, medication, or the time elapsed since the accident.

Rescuer details – you may be asked various details that the rescue teams might require, such as local weather.

Try and remain calm when providing this information, as your clarity and quality of the information is of vital importance to the rescue team.

DISTRESS SIGNAL

The International (European) distress signal is **six blasts** of a **whistle** evenly spaced over **one minute**, followed by **a break of one minute**. Then **repeat**. The response that confirms that your signal has been received is three blasts of a whistle over one minute followed by a break of one minute. At night, flashes of a torch in the same sequence can be used instead. **Always carry a torch and a whistle.**

INSURANCE AND EMERGENCIES

It is essential that anyone planning a Big Trail obtains adequate insurance for their trip. Standard travel insurance policies often provide cover for low-level hiking routes, but you may be required to pay an extra premium for mountainous or remote trails.

ENJOYING THE VIEWS OF CORN DU AND THE DRAGON'S BREATH. © ANTHONY PEASE PHOTOGRAPHY

THE
TRAILS

01

01 ARRAN COASTAL WAY – 103km

With its wooded slopes, granite ridges and sandy beaches, the island of Arran is nicknamed 'Scotland in miniature'. The 103-kilometre Arran Coastal Way, which encircles the island, offers a little of everything – from mossy paths through bluebell-rich woods and strolls along the beach to scrambles over boulders and tricksy, gorsy paths, as well as the occasional country road and the opportunity to climb Goat Fell, a Corbett and the island's highest mountain. The path is waymarked with a distinctive gannet symbol; gannets frequently swoop over the island on fishing excursions from their colony on the rocky Ailsa Craig.

The Calmac ferries from Ardrossan arrive in Brodick, and you can step from the ferry on to the Coastal Way. North of Brodick, there is a low-level route following forestry tracks that hugs the coastline, and in bad weather you might choose this option. However, most begin the Way by following the rocky path up to the granite peak of Goat Fell, Arran's highest mountain at 874 metres. The summit of Goat Fell offers views of the island's granite ridges stretching ahead of you, and seawards Arran's Holy Island, long a place of spiritual retreat. In the sixth century, St Molaise lived a hermit's life on Holy Island in a cave; the island is now host to a Buddhist Centre for World Peace and Health. You retrace your steps off the mountain to Corrie Burn; the bouldered path leads down to the coast near Corrie village and follows the coastal road to Sannox, or the village of the Sandy Bay, with its crescent beach.

North of Sannox, you will see a tall, white navigation mast – this is one of a sequence that defines Arran's Measured Miles, used to test that the ships built on the Clyde were up to specification, including Cunard's *TS Queen Mary* in 1936. A sandy path leads you above the pebble-dashed beach, still in the shadow of Goat Fell. You join a forestry path that circumvents the Fallen Rocks, giant sandstone boulders that fell from the cliffs in a landslide 300 years ago. At the end of a pebbled beach, you reach the whitewashed walls of the deserted croft, Laggan Cottage, which offers a sheltered spot to enjoy lunch while gazing out towards Bute and the distant Ayrshire coast.

A distinctive boulder at the top of the beach marks the Way – this is the eroded Cock of Arran rock; once a landmark for sailors, it was said to resemble a cockerel. Arran's unique geology makes it a magnet for geologists, and on Arran's north coast you pass Hutton's Unconformity, a junction of two rock layers which suggests that the earth is millions, not thousands, of years old. Now the north coast is more visited for its wildlife, which may include seals, herons and basking sharks. Near the Unconformity, at Newton Point, you'll first glimpse the shores of Loch Ranza.

By the shores of the Loch, you enter the pretty village of Lochranza. 'Arran Water', the illicit whisky, was considered one of Scotland's finest drams in the eighteenth and nineteenth centuries. In 1995 a new distillery opened at Lochranza, its stills being filled with the Scottish rainwater that filtered down through Gleann Easan Biorach from the hills. As you leave the village, you pass the ruined medieval Lochranza Castle, standing on a spit in the loch; if the castle is familiar, it is because it was the castle visited

◀ THE ROCKY PATH UP GOAT FELL ON THE ISLE OF ARRAN.
© KATHI KAMLEITNER – *WATCHMESEE.COM*

by Tintin in *The Black Island*. You follow in the steps of the island's postman on a challenging, slippery path through birch woodland and across ferny slopes, to reach the Twelve Apostles, Catacol's white cottages. These cottages were built after the Clearances, and each first-floor window is shaped differently so they can be recognised by island fishermen. However, the crofters were reluctant to turn from farming to fishing, and these long-empty houses gained the nickname 'hungry row'. You follow a long section of the coastal road before negotiating a rocky path beneath cliffs at the top of the shore.

The distinctive boathouse at Dougarie was once the Duke of Hamilton's sporting lodge but is now a popular wedding venue. You may want to leave the coast road to visit the nearby stone circles. The circle of fifteen stones at Auchagallon was probably built as a Neolithic burial cairn and there are at least six stone circles on Machrie Moor, near the deserted Moss Farm. This area of the island has a proliferation of Neolithic archaeology, and near the King's Cave you pass an ancient hut circle. King's Cave is rumoured to have been where the despondent Robert the Bruce learnt from a persistent spider not to give up in the face of adversity – the cave walls are etched with Christian and pre-Christian carvings.

You pass the high basalt columns at Doon to reach Blackwaterfoot, where you will have to walk across the golf course if the tide is too high to walk on the beach. A sandy path leads you towards Kilpatrick Point, where you will find the Preaching Cave. After the Clearances, the locals preferred to worship here as a Free Congregation.

Around the southern tip of the island, the beach route that takes you past Bennan Head and Dippen Head is not passable at high tide – a forestry track offers an inland detour, past the Giant's Graves chambered cairns and the Eas a' Chrannaig double waterfalls. The sandy beach at Lagg soon gives way to rocks, and boulders that must be scrambled over. You can explore the darkness of Black Cave, the island's largest cave, in the cliffs near Bennan Head. From the village of Whiting Bay, you can again choose either a waterfall route inland or follow the top of a beach. New boardwalk sections across the top of the pebbly beach make for drier feet and faster progress along the beach. Near Corriegills Point, the route again enters woodlands, on paths lined with bluebells and wild garlic in spring. You are now almost back at your starting point in Brodick.

The Arran Coastal Way is not a gentle stroll around a low coast. It often climbs over fern-lined paths, slippery underfoot, and even when it hugs the coast, you will find yourself scrambling over boulders or cursing the pebbles that seem to drag your feet backwards. At high tide, you may find yourself facing long stretches on the island's coastal road. However, the shores of this so-Scottish island will offer up deer, otters, seals, gannets and, if you're lucky, hen harriers and golden eagles. The island produces its own cheese, from the milk of five local dairy herds, and ice cream, as well as whisky and beer. There are plenty of rewards awaiting those brave enough to face Scotland's wild coastline, with its sometimes wild weather.

LAGGAN COTTAGE EN ROUTE TO THE COCK OF ARRAN. © *WALKHIGHLANDS.CO.UK*

HOLY ISLAND SEEN FROM LAMLASH PIER. © *WALKHIGHLANDS.CO.UK*

01 ARRAN COASTAL WAY: ESSENTIAL INFORMATION

TRAIL ESSENTIALS

Start: **Brodick, Isle of Arran, Scotland**
End: **Brodick, Isle of Arran, Scotland**
Distance: **103km**
Ascent/descent: **540m/540m**

HOW TO GET THERE

Brodick is served by ferries from Ardrossan harbour in Ayrshire. There is a direct rail link between Ardrossan and Glasgow, which is on the British mainline rail network. Glasgow is the closest international airport.

TIME TO COMPLETE

Walking: **4 days/23 hours**
Trekking: **3 days/20 hours**
Fastpacking: **2 days/15 hours**
Trail running: **2 days/12 hours**

PROS

- **Bus service** – several buses run along Arran's coast, including a clockwise and anticlockwise service that circles the island. You are never too far from the coastal road, providing an easy way back to the island's larger settlements for evening meals and accommodation.

- **Wildlife** – Arran is home to red deer, sea otters, hen harriers, gannets, golden eagles, basking sharks and seals. It is a stronghold of the red squirrel. You should be wary of getting too close to the red deer, Britain's largest land mammal, in autumn during rutting season.

- **Geology** – Arran straddles the Highland Boundary Fault, providing a huge geological variation across the small island, and highlights such as the folds of the North Sannox Grits, the red sandstone outcrop of the Kinnesswood Formation and the chlorite schist better known as Hutton's Unconformity. The ascent up Goat Fell takes you past Old Red Sandstone, and slate to the granite ridges that dominate the north of the island.

CONS

- **Weather** – the ascent up Goat Fell can be dangerous in poor visibility and you are strongly advised to take the lower-level alternative. Bad weather can make other sections of the route boggy, muddy and slippery. Weather can be unpredictable and occasionally disrupts ferry services to the island.

- **Tides** – beach sections of the route at Bennan Head and Dippen Head will be unpassable (and dangerous) at high tides. Some minor route diversions may have to be made on other parts of the routes – such as through the golf course at Blackwaterfoot – at high tide.

GOOD TO KNOW

The white Twelve Apostle cottages at Catacol have different shaped windows on their first floor. This was so that wives could signal, using oil lamps in the windows, to their fisherman husbands out at sea. The twelve cottages share thirteen chimneys.

FURTHER INFORMATION

www.coastalway.co.uk

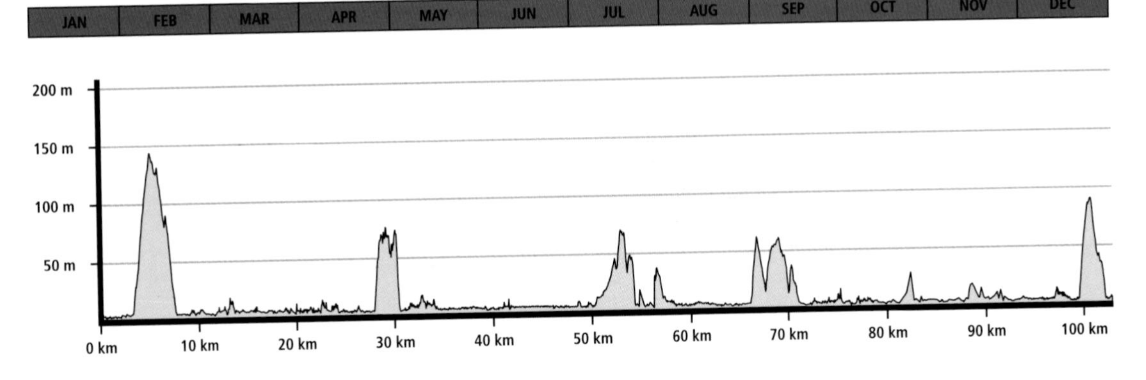

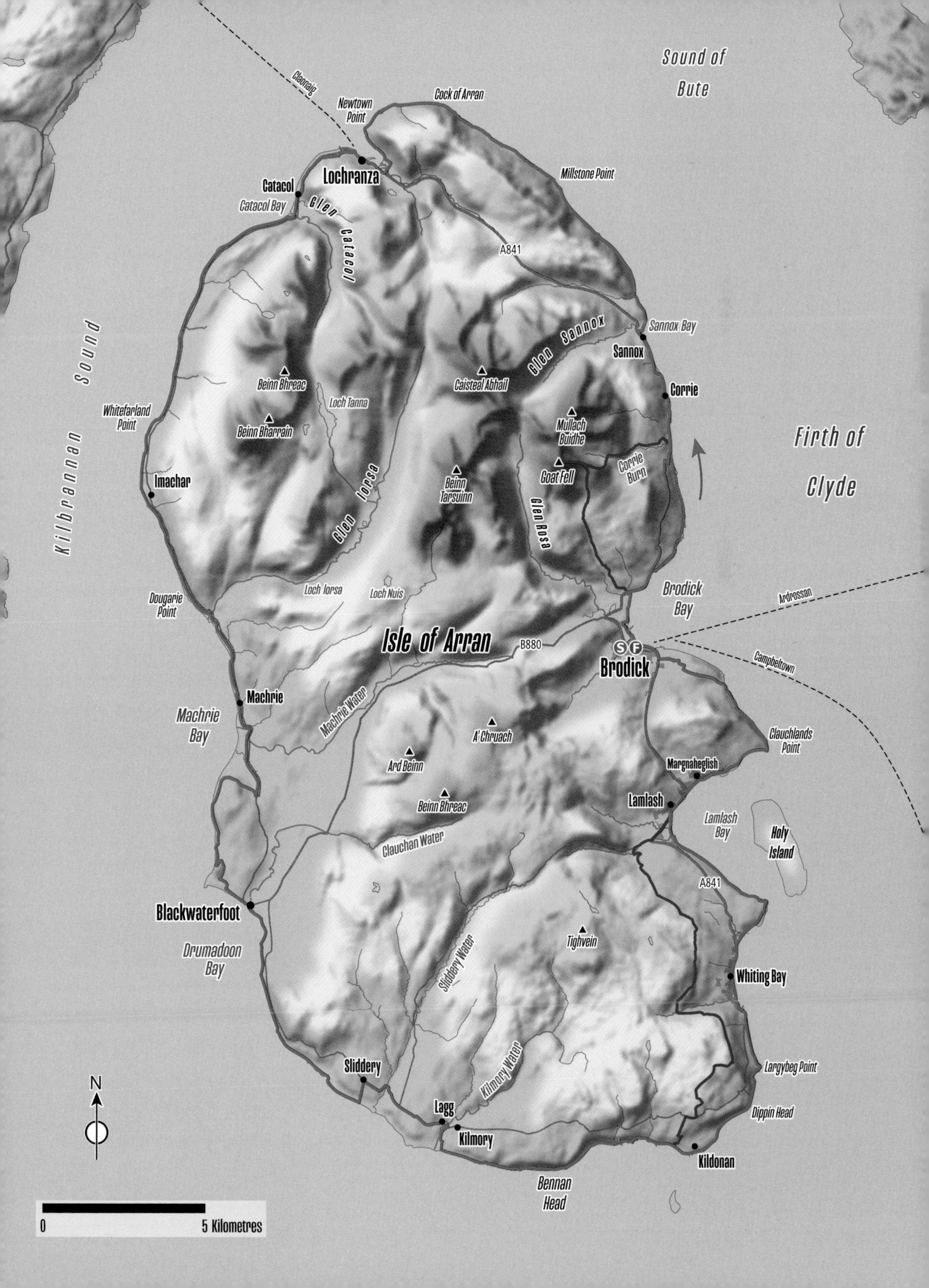

Sound of Bute
Cock of Arran
Newtown Point
Claonaig
Lochranza
Catacol
Catacol Bay
Glen Catacol
Millstone Point
A841
Sannox Bay
Glen Sannox
Sannox
Kilbrannan Sound
Beinn Bhreac
Caisteal Abhail
Corrie
Whitefarland Point
Loch Tanna
Beinn Bharrain
Mullach Buidhe
Firth of Clyde
Goat Fell
Corrie Burn
Imachar
Beinn Tarsuinn
Glen Iorsa
Glen Rosa
Clyde
Brodick Bay
Ardrossan
Loch Iorsa
Loch Nuis
Dougarie Point
Isle of Arran
B880
Brodick
Campbeltown
Machrie
Machrie Water
Machrie Bay
A' Chruach
Clauchlands Point
Ard Beinn
Margnaheglish
Beinn Bhreac
Lamlash
Lamlash Bay
Holy Island
Clauchan Water
A841
Blackwaterfoot
Tighvein
Drumadoon Bay
Sliddery Water
Whiting Bay
Kilmory Water
Sliddery
Largybeg Point
N
Lagg
Dippin Head
Kilmory
Kildonan
Bennan Head
0
5 Kilometres

02

02 BEACONS WAY – 155km

The Brecon Beacons National Park is a wild, green area in South Wales, encompassing high moorland, lush farmland and dramatic ridges. This is some of Wales's wildest country, and on fine days you can enjoy the views to the sea, the Midlands and towards Snowdonia. At other times, the mist and drizzle may challenge even the most proficient of hillwalkers. The 155-kilometre Beacons Way – which traverses the park from east to west – is not a route for novices, but is an adventurous trail for those who want to discover some of Wales's little-explored, remotest hilltops.

The Way begins in the pretty market town of Abergavenny, which the Cambrian Way also passes through – the Cambrian Way and Beacons Way often coincide through the Beacons, although the Cambrian Way tends to favour a higher, wilder route. The route begins with a steep, wooded ascent up the rocky Skirrid, or Holy Mountain. You can see the ruins of the medieval St Michael's Chapel near the summit.

You descend to the Skirrid Mountain Inn in Llanvihangel Crucorney, which claims to be one of the oldest pubs in Wales. While there was probably an inn here in the twelfth century, the current, reputedly haunted, building dates to the seventeenth century. A lane leads you up to the green moorland of Hatterall Ridge where you briefly meet Offa's Dyke Path. The trail has led north from Abergavenny but from the village of Llanthony, with its picturesque priory ruins that inspired J.M.W. Turner, you begin your east–west traverse of the Black Mountains and then the Beacons.

You leave Llanthony by a bracken-filled path that leads to a ridge walk along Bal Bach. You descend through green fields to Partrishow, where you will want to visit the eleventh-century St Issui's church, with its medieval wall paintings that include the skeleton Death holding an hourglass. You climb the grassy slopes of Crug Mawr and must climb again past the Iron Age hill fort on Table Mountain, also known as Crug Hywel, the hill that lends Crickhowell its name. This market town, which is only ten kilometres from your starting point in Abergavenny, hosts the Green Man Festival every August. The festival has a particular commitment to showcasing beers and ciders from independent Welsh breweries.

On the bracken slopes near Cwm Mawr you pass the memorial plaque to John Sansom, former secretary of the Brecon Beacons Park Society and creator of the Way. It is a steep climb to the summit of Cefn Moel, but you will be rewarded with views of the expansive Llangorse lake. You cross the Usk on the eighteenth-century Llangynidr arched-stone bridge, possibly the oldest bridge across the river. The Danywenallt youth hostel, in a converted Welsh farmhouse, is a short detour from the Way near Talybont reservoir.

The Way leaves the Black Mountains to climb the giants of the Brecon Beacons. It is a steep climb from the long, blue Talybont Reservoir along the edge of Craig y Fan Ddu. The Diving Board rock hangs over the escarpment edge on Fan y Big, a popular photo opportunity. The route technically skirts the edge of Cribyn, but few resist the lure of the

◀ WALKING ALONG THE FLANKS OF PICWS DU.
© ANTHONY PEASE PHOTOGRAPHY

distinctive peak. You do, however, climb to the summit of Pen y Fan, which at 886 metres is highest peak in South Wales. The Brecon Beacons youth hostel is close to the Storey Arms education centre, which is where you reach the road on your descent. This is the halfway point of the Way.

The western Beacons are wilder and more isolated than the touristy eastern sections. Should navigation on the ridge of Fan Llia prove difficult, there is a lower route along a Roman road. Another Roman road, Sarn Helen, leads you past the Maen Madoc standing stone. In Ogof Ffynnon Ddu National Nature Reserve, you can see the limestone pavement – the park is famous for its caves, and you pass the entrances to some. The area is also dotted with old quarries. You pass through Craig-y-Nos Country Park, once owned by opera singer Dame Adelina Patti, to reach the road.

A high ridge walk takes you across the Carmarthen Fans; over Fan Hir, Fan Brycheiniog – the highest point in the western Beacons (802 metres) – and Fan Foel. Your high path will offer good views of the sparkling Llyn y Fan Fach, associated with the legend of the Lady of the Lake. The route can be challenging navigationally even in good weather, and a poor weather alternative contours around the hills, then along the eastern side of Llyn y Fan Fawr, the highest natural lake in Wales.

After Llanddeusant, you take a high route over wild country, sometimes without a path to follow, and navigation may be challenging if visibility is low. On the rocky summit of Garreg Las, you pass two large Bronze Age burial cairns. The Way contours around Foel Fraith to protect the wild bird populations on the summit; you are likely to see the red kites that frequent these wild moors. The Beacons Way route was revised in 2016, and one change was that it was re-routed around some mountain summits with endangered wildlife habitats. You pass the now disused Black Mountain Quarries, where limestone was quarried for hundreds of years, to reach the medieval Carreg Cennen castle, perched high on limestone cliffs.

A gentler track leads you through the Carreglwyd Forest. You can enjoy a fine view of the mountains that you have left behind you from Y Garn Goch, where you find two Iron Age hill forts, Y Gaer Fach and Y Gaer Fawr, which is one of Wales's largest hill forts. There is also a more modern memorial to Gwynfor Evans, the first Plaid Cymru MP at Westminster. The Way finishes in Bethlehem, a village that has to run a part-time Post Office in winter to deal with the flurry of Christmas cards wanting the village's postmark. A carved oak bench marks the official end of the Way, but most carry on another five kilometres to the railway station at Llangadog.

The Beacons Way is a challenging route across some of Wales's wildest mountains, and is not always waymarked, particularly on its higher sections. In bad weather with poor visibility navigation may be challenging, and all but the most experienced of runners or walkers would be sensible to opt for the bad weather alternatives in those conditions. Its rewards, however, are spectacular views, stunning ridge walks and the chance to explore some of the quieter mountains of the western Beacons, as well as the iconic Pen y Fan. The Beacons Way is challenging in warmer months, and will be a very wild, possibly snow-drenched, challenge in winter. It is not a route for the novice walker but this high green path from the Holy Mountain to Bethlehem should be a pilgrimage for anyone who loves mountains.

HEADING TOWARDS GRAIG CERRIG GLEISIAD. © ANTHONY PEASE PHOTOGRAPHY

CROSSING HATTERALL HILL ON THE WALES–ENGLAND BORDER. © TRACY BURTON

02 BEACONS WAY: ESSENTIAL INFORMATION

TRAIL ESSENTIALS

Start:	**Abergavenny, Monmouthshire, Wales**
End:	**Bethlehem, Carmarthenshire, Wales**
Distance:	**155km**
Ascent/descent:	**5,870m/5,860m**

HOW TO GET THERE

Abergavenny has a direct rail service to Cardiff, although the service to Bristol requires a change at Newport. Cardiff and Bristol are the closest international airports.

Bethlehem is poorly served by public transport and most Beacons Way-ers continue on to Llangadog, where there is a train station offering services to Cardiff via Swansea. Cardiff is the closest international airport.

TIME TO COMPLETE

Walking:	**10 days/58 hours**
Trekking:	**6 days/47 hours**
Fastpacking:	**5 days/36 hours**
Trail running:	**4 days/25 hours**

PROS

- **Youth hostels** – some of the earliest YHA hostels to open were Welsh, and there are three YHA hostels close to the Beacons Way (Llangattock Mountain Bunkhouse, Danywenallt and Brecon Beacons) as well as a number of independent hostels and bunkhouses.

- **Carmarthen Fans** – Pen y Fan and Cribyn in the eastern Beacons are well-known and popular with day walkers, but the Carmarthen Fans in the western Beacons, in the Black Mountain range, are an undiscovered treasure and offer you a wild, high ridge walk with spectacular views.

- **Four for one** – although commonly referred to as the Beacons, the trail through the Brecon Beacons National Park actually encompasses four mountain ranges: the Black Mountains, Fforest Fawr (once a royal hunting ground), the Beacons and the Black Mountain.

CONS

- **Navigation** – route-finding may be tricky, particularly in the Black Mountain range. The trail does not always follow a well-defined path and you should be confident in navigating with a compass, particularly in bad weather.

- **Route** – changes were made to Sansom's original route in 2016, and you should be wary of outdated maps or guides.

- **Accommodation** – when the Way emerges from the hills on to the road, you may find yourself some distance from the closest village and may have to arrange a taxi or pickup from your accommodation provider. Accommodation options are limited, and may often be booked up in advance in the summer.

GOOD TO KNOW

According to legend, a beautiful woman rose from the waters of Llyn y Fan Fach and agreed to marry a local farmer on condition that he promised not to strike her. He broke his promise, striking her three times, but her sons would visit her at the lake and she taught them herbal medicine. These were the first in generations of physicians from Myddfai, that were active from the thirteenth to eighteenth centuries.

FURTHER INFORMATION

www.breconbeacons.org/things-to-do/walking/the-beacons-way

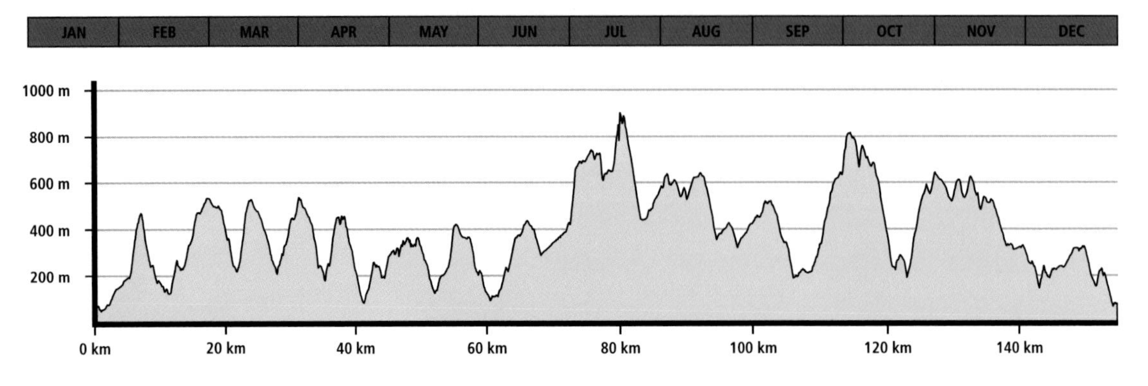

ENGLAND
WALES
Brecon Beacons National Park
Black Mountains
Black Mountain
Hay-on-Wye
Llandovery
Llangadog
Bethlehem
Trichrug
Llandeilo
Carreg Cennen Castle
Llanddeusant
Usk Reservoir
Llyn y Fan Fach
Fan Foel
Llyn y Fan Fawr
Fan Brycheiniog
Twyn Swynd
Foel Fraith
Glyntawe
Fan Gyhirych
Fan Nedd
Fan Llia
Fan Frynych
Storey Arms
Fan Fawr
Pen y Fan
Corn Du
Cribyn
Fan y Big
Libanus
Brecon
Llangorse Lake
Tor y Foel
Talybont Reservoir
Bwlch
Cefn Moel
Cwmdu
Usk
Llangynidr
Waun Fach
Chwarel Y Fan
Llanthony Priory
Bal Bach
Hatterrall Hill
Partrishow
Llanbedr
Crug Hywel
Crickhowell
Llanvihangel Crucorney
Skirrid
Abergavenny
Brynmawr
Ebbw Vale
Blaenavon
Tredegar
Merthyr Tydfil
Ystradfellte
Penderyn
Brynaman
Ammanford
Ystradgynlais
Pontardawe
Swansea
Aberdare
Treorchy
Maesteg
Tonypandy
Pontypridd
Bargoed
Blackwood
Caerphilly
Abertillery
Pontypool
Cwmbran
Usk
Newport
A483
A482
B4302
A40
A470
A479
A4069
A4067
A4059
A4221
A474
A465
M4
A4077
B4560
A4048
A467
A4043
A4042
A472
A469
N
0
10 Kilometres

03 BEARA-BREIFNE WAY – 578km

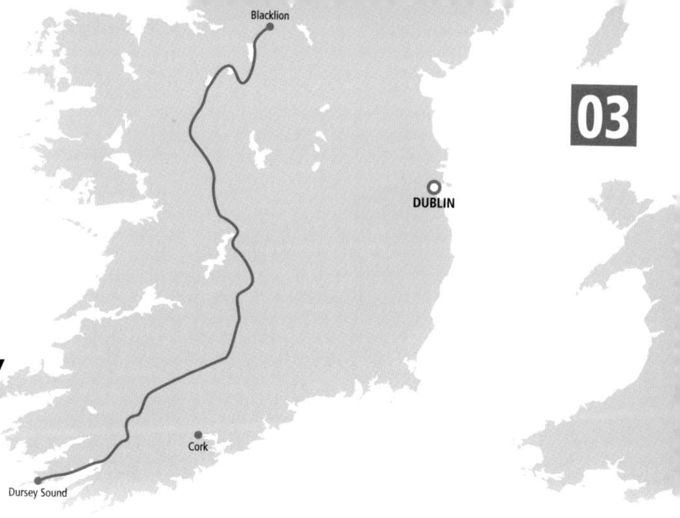

03

Blacklion

DUBLIN

Cork

Dursey Sound

On 31 December 1602, Donal Cam O'Sullivan Beare, Ireland's last prince, set off on an epic march across the whole of Ireland. The 578-kilometre Beara-Breifne Way, Ireland's longest waymarked National Trail, follows in O'Sullivan's footsteps. It starts from Ireland's south-west tip on the wild Beara Peninsula and travels through the heart of the country, finally reaching its end at Blacklion, near the border with Northern Ireland. It follows rugged coasts, climbs hills and snakes through shaded forests on its way. One thousand men, women and children followed O'Sullivan on his march. Fourteen days later, when he reached safety at O'Rourke's Castle, only thirty-five remained with him – most went back home. A warmer welcome awaits you today, as you follow the path that meanders through Ireland's rural landscape between small villages.

The trail begins at Dursey Sound, by the cable car that sways across the sea to Dursey Island. The route begins on the Beara Way – the Beara-Breifne Way connects sections of other local trails to make its path across Ireland. While you might choose to follow the Beara Way along either the southern or northern coast of the Beara peninsula, the southern route is more direct. You take a rugged path that climbs through the rocky remains of abandoned copper mines, before descending to Castletownbere. Once a treaty port, it is now one of Ireland's biggest fishing ports, and a great place to enjoy the freshest local seafood. The Way follows a high, and often boggy, pass through the Caha Mountains to reach Glengarriff, a village renowned for traditional Irish music.

You leave Glengarriff by briefly following the busy N71 road around the top of Bantry Bay, before turning off to cut across high moorland to reach Kealkill, where you join the Sli Gaeltacht Mhuscrai. The ruins of O'Sullivan's castle, Carriganass, which fell to the English in 1601, can be seen on the Way just outside Kealkill. You climb forestry tracks over Conigar to follow a high route offering spectacular views of Gougane Barra, a glacial valley and loch. Although this section is largely on forestry tracks and quiet roads, you may encounter muddy and boggy trails in these remote hills.

The path takes the North West Cork Way from Millstreet, the smallest town to ever host the Eurovision Song Contest (in 1993). The only place that O'Sullivan and his 1,000 followers could safely ford the Blackwater, Ireland's second largest river, in winter was near Millstreet, but the creators of the Beara-Breifne Way negotiated the construction of a pedestrian bridge so that you can keep your feet dry. Quiet country roads lead you through shady woodland to Newmarket and on to Lismore.

Near St John's Bridge, you leave the road-centric North West Cork Way and join the Ballyhoura Way. You can see the ruins of one of Ireland's finest Norman castles at Liscarroll, once the stronghold of O'Sullivan's enemies, the Barrys. In the lush green fields between Liscarroll and Churchtown, you might stop for a tea and a slice of cake at the Donkey Sanctuary. At the small village of Churchtown, you can visit actor Oliver Reed's grave; he lived here for the last few years of his life, and when he died in 1999 his wake lasted for ten days.

◀ CROSSING THE BEARA PENINSULA ABOVE CASTLETOWNBERE.
© ELLIE BERRY/TOUGH SOLES

QUARTZ CAIRN ON THE LOWER SLOPES OF HUNGRY HILL, WITH BANTRY BAY IN THE BACKGROUND. © JON BARTON

A stony trail leads you over the Ballyhoura Mountains; you have finally left the first county on the Way and reached County Limerick. In County Tipperary, you are in the shadow of the Galtee Mountains as you follow the Glen of Aherlow and contour around Slievenamuck, to reach the lofty statue of Christ the King. You turn north to follow roads to Tipperary.

The route takes the short Multeen Way on quiet country roads between Tipperary and Donohill. You then enjoy grassy footpaths and tracks through the pastured Golden Vale and over the Red Hills to Milestone, where you join the Ormond Way. This trail begins through farmers' fields but prefers the roads; the Ormond Way is a recently established trail, and its route may change. Past Templederry there is a pleasant, if often overgrown, section by the banks of the River Nenagh.

You reach the halfway point of the Beara-Breifne Way near Toomevara. Passing the crumbling tower of John O'Kennedy's Lackeen Castle and crossing the mighty Shannon, which marks the border between Tipperary and Galway, you leave the Ormond Way for the Hymany Way in Portumna. The Hymany Way follows the grassy banks of the wide Shannon until Meelick Weir, which lies next to the fifteenth-century Meelick Church, the oldest Roman Catholic church still in regular use in Ireland. You take a road-heavy route to Clonfert, past the small sixteenth-century Brackloon Castle, and then a ferny path through woods.

You pass the site of the 1691 Battle of Aughrim, possibly the bloodiest battle fought on Irish soil; between five and six thousand died in William of Orange's decisive victory over James II's forces. The route crosses the M6 motorway, which was controversially routed through the battlefield in 2005, to take a grassy path through farm fields. After woods, bog and long grass, the Hymany Way meets the Suck Valley Way in Ballygar.

You will encounter plenty of cows on the Suck Valley Way's soggy paths through farmland. The Suck Valley Way roughly follows the course of the River Suck, a tributary of the Shannon; it occasionally leaves the farms for woods, and sometimes follows country lanes. Near Ballinlough, you leave Galway for Roscommon. On a long road section

THE BEARA WAY NEAR ADRIGOLE, OVERLOOKING BANTRY BAY. © THOMAS BARTON

you pass Lough O'Flynn, a popular brown trout fishing spot but also a haven for the endangered European eel, to reach Loughglynn and the Lung or Lough Gara Way. The Lough Gara Way is a forty-five-kilometre slog along sometimes busy roads; hopefully a better route may be negotiated as the Beara-Breifne (and Ireland) Way gain more momentum. The highlight of the section is the ruined Moygara Castle.

In contrast, the Miners Way from Ballinafad offers you some of the best countryside walking on the whole trail. On green tracks through rolling hills, the Way curves and contours through an expansive landscape with panoramic emerald views. A detour on the Historical Trail will take you to Carrowkeel, a unique megalithic complex with caves, cairns and passage tombs to explore. Leaving the high ridges and cliff-lined paths behind you, you follow a shoreline path around Lough Meelagh. Green paths through peat bogs lead you to Leitrim.

O'Sullivan's march ended here at O'Rourke's Castle, of which very little remains, but the Way continues to Blacklion. The Leitrim Way, which follows the canal out of Leitrim, is currently under redevelopment; unless you enjoy road walking, you might choose instead to remain on the Miners Way, on the opposite shore of Lough Allen, to Dowra.

The final twenty kilometres are on the Cavan Way. The Way follows muddy paths next to the River Shannon, to the river's source at the Shannon Pot, before returning to the roads. The Way still has surprises to delight you with – a shady path through the wooded Burren leads you to a collection of Neolithic tombs. All that remains is for you to cross the Giant's Leap to reach Blacklion, nestled between the two MacNean loughs, on the Irish border.

If you complete the Beara-Breifne Way you have crossed a country, passed battlefields and castles, followed the long Shannon, climbed hills and crossed bogs, seen Ireland's green farmland and tramped its long, quiet roads. If that is not enough for you, you can continue on along the Ulster Way to reach the Northern Irish coast, and the Giant's Causeway on the Ireland Way and get a certificate of completion from the Ballycastle Tourist Information Office.

03 BEARA-BREIFNE WAY: ESSENTIAL INFORMATION

TRAIL ESSENTIALS

Start:	**Dursey Sound, County Cork, Ireland**
End:	**Blacklion, County Cavan, Ireland**
Distance:	**578km**
Ascent/descent:	**6,790m/6,750m**
Also known as:	**Part of the Ireland Way**

HOW TO GET THERE

Dursey Sound is not served by public transport. In summer, a Ring of Beara bus service runs. At other times of year, Glengarriff and Castletownbere are served by Bus Éireann. Glengarriff has bus connections to Cork, and in summer to Killarney – both of which have rail stations. Cork has an international airport and ferry services to France and Spain.

Blacklion is served by Bus Éireann Expressway 66 which stops at Sligo, with its rail station. Belfast's international airports are the closest, but Dublin is easier to reach by rail. There are ferries to England, Wales and Scotland at Dún Laoghaire, Larne and Belfast.

TIME TO COMPLETE

Walking:	**24 days/147 hours**
Trekking:	**15 days/120 hours**
Fastpacking:	**12 days/90 hours**
Trail running:	**9 days/68 hours**

PROS

- **Ireland's history** – as well as passing historical sites associated with O'Sullivan's march, you will also discover more about the Great Hunger of the potato famine, the Williamite Wars and the fight for Irish independence, as well as Ireland's Neolithic past.

- **Scenery** – from the wild Atlantic coast to the emerald Galtee Mountains and the horizons of the Arigna hills, the Beara-Breifne Way explores the most varied and beautiful landscapes in Ireland.

- **Collaboration** – Irish trails are collaborative by necessity. The Beara-Breifne Way combines sections of local trails, negotiated with local landholders, often by ramblers with a passion for the local countryside. The communities through which the Way passes have an investment in the route, and you will discover local knowledge as you travel along.

CONS

- **Roads** – some sub-trails on the Beara-Breifne Way are almost entirely road, and while most of the roads are quiet country lanes, some are busy regional roads with no footpaths and very little verge.

- **Immature** – the Beara-Breifne Way is an opportunity to traverse an entire country, from its wild coast through its green mountains and farmland. However, this is a new route and not all sections are well worn in. Some sections may be improved as negotiations with landowners continue and as investment in the route continues.

GOOD TO KNOW

Ireland does not enjoy extensive public rights of way or rights to roam. All land is either in private or State ownership, and most public rights of way relate to on-road, not off-road, access. Off-road routes tend to be permissive rights of way, which means there may be limitations on their use (for example, frequently dogs are not permitted) and permissions may change if the land changes ownership. An initiative that has seen considerable improvements to Ireland's trail network, the Walks Scheme, was launched in March 2008 by Minister Éamon Ó Cuív; participating landholders receive a payment for the development, maintenance and enhancement of National Waymarked Ways.

FURTHER INFORMATION

www.bearabreifneway.ie; www.theirelandway.ie

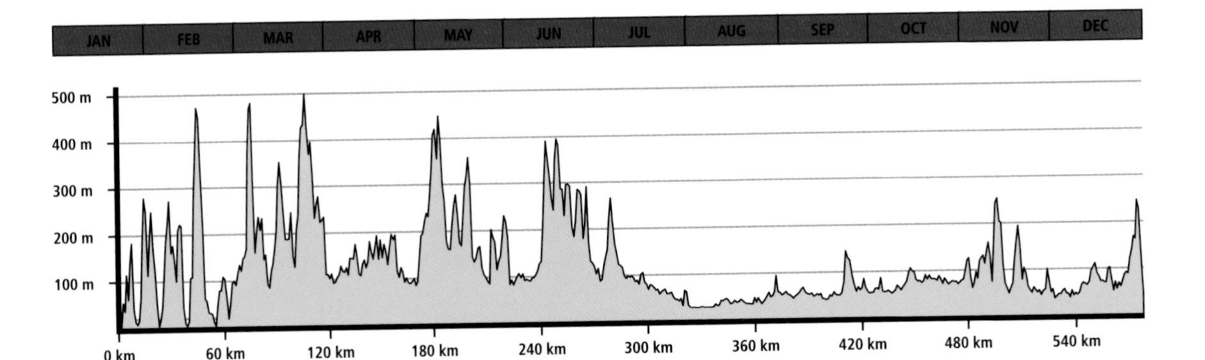

Atlantic Ocean
Giant's Causeway
Portrush
Ballycastle
Castlerock
Coleraine
Londonderry/ Derry
A2
A44
A29
A26
Dungiven
A6
Larne
A5
The Sperrins
Ballymena
Strabane
Draperstown
M2
Gortin
N15
Drumlegagh
NORTHERN IRELAND
Lough Neagh
Belfast
Pertigo
Omagh
Ballyshannon
Lower Lough Erne
A5
M1
Belleek
A4
Enniskillen
Armagh
Sligo
N16
Belcoo
Blacklion
Lough Allen
Dowra
Cuilcagh
Newry
N2
Castlebaldwin
Ballyfarnan
Drumshanbo
Ballinafad
Leitrim
Cavan
Boyle
N3
Ballaghaderreen
Irish Sea
Westport
N17
Castlerea
N5
N4
Claremorris
M3
M1
Ballymoe
Lough Ree
IRELAND
Creggs
Ballygar
Suck
M2
Athlone
Lough Corrib
M4
M6
Dublin
Athenry
Ballinasloe
Galway
M6
M50
Clonfert
Brosna
Shannon
Banagher
N11
Portumna
M7
M18
Wicklow
Ballingarry
Lough Derg
Cloughjordan
M9
Nenagh
Nore
Barrow
Toomevara
Silvermines
Shannon
Limerick
M7
Milestone
Slieve Felim Mountains
Slaney
M11
Tipperary
N20
Wexford
Galtee Mountains
Waterford
Churchtown
Tralee
Liscarroll
Ballyhoura Hills
Rosslare Harbour
Newmarket
Buttevant
N25
Killarney
N72
Blackwater
Bride
Millstreet
N20
M8
Coniga
Lee
N22
Cork
Caha Mountains
Kealkill
Slieve Miskish Mountains
Bantry
Atlantic Ocean
Castletownbere
Dursey Island
N
0
50 Kilometres

DUBLIN

04 BURREN WAY – 80km

The eighty-kilometre Burren Way allows you to enjoy two of Ireland's best natural wonders – the towering Cliffs of Moher, a spectacular section of Ireland's Wild Atlantic Way, and the other-worldly landscape of limestone karst in the Burren. On the coast, you may glimpse puffins, dolphins or basking sharks. Thriving in the cracks of the Burren's pavements, you may spot purple orchids or sunny Irish eyebrights. Although this trail suffers perhaps more than any other Irish Way from the necessity of following the road, the views will distract you from the tarmac underfoot.

The Burren Way begins in the small seaside resort of Lahinch. Avid golfers might want to enjoy a round at one of the town's two courses, the Old Course and the Castle Course. Watch out for the goats that roam across the links – they apparently are reliable weather forecasters, preferring to linger near the clubhouse when bad weather is approaching. The Burren Way begins by taking a sandy path behind the Old Course, but you soon find yourself on the first of many long road sections on the trail.

The Way passes the village of Liscannor to join the stunning coastline of the Cliffs of Moher at Hag's Head, where a rock outcrop resembles a sea-witch's head. The nineteenth-century watchtower on the promontory stands on the site of a much older fort, or moher, that gave the cliffs their name. More than one and a half million people visit the cliffs each year, but on the remoter sections, you will enjoy breathtaking views of the precipitous, striated cliffs without the crowds.

The cliff path is sometimes stony, sometimes grass, but clings close to the high edge and is usually unfenced. The cliff edges are unstable and prone to rockfalls, so you should not leave the paths. The high, exposed trail is often swathed in sea mist or buffeted by gusty breezes, and even in the best of weather may be challenging for those who suffer from a fear of heights. The cliffs are an amazing haven for birds, and you may see Atlantic puffins, fulmars, kittiwakes and peregrines. Most visitors to the cliffs congregate near the award-winning, underground Visitor Centre, which is nearly six kilometres from Hag's Head. If you want to explore this popular attraction, which was built from local Liscannor stone in 2007, you may wish to time your arrival early. Your admission fee also allows you to climb O'Brien's Tower, built as an early tourist attraction by politician and landowner Cornelius O'Brien. On a sunny day, the tower offers fantastic views towards Galway's coastline and the Aran Islands.

The Way follows the cliffs as they descend towards the colourful village of Doolin, renowned as a centre for traditional Irish music, which you can enjoy in the local pubs. You can also take a boat trip from the village, which will allow you to visit the Aran Islands, or to view the cliffs from the sea. The Way rejoins the roads at Doolin. You may choose to follow the road spur to visit the spa town of Lisdoonvarna, where you can taste wild Irish salmon, smoked at the town's Burren Smokehouse.

Near Craggagh, you have a choice – the main route turns inland, but you can continue to follow the li

◀ ON THE EDGE OF THE CLIFFS OF MOHER.
© MOLAN/FOGARTY

LOOKING SOUTH, BACK TOWARDS HAG'S HEAD. © MOLAN/FOGARTY

coast past Fanore's sandy beaches and the lighthouse at Black Head, County Clare's most northerly point. This northern loop offers the opportunity to see a fine section of the Burren's karst landscape. The inland route skirts Slieve Elva, the highest point in the Burren, and then on past the pre-Famine ruins, firstly of a shebeen, or illegal drinking den, and further on the Formoyle Chapel. Just past the ruins of the old ring fort, Cathair an Ard Rios, the main route meets the end of the Black Head loop. On this section, the Burren Way follows ancient green roads, built for drovers, through some of Ireland's most flower-rich landscapes – you may see one of the twenty-four species of orchids known to grow in the Burren, as well as heather, hoary rock-rose and gentians. Another spur leads to Ballyvaughan, a pleasant harbour village with plenty of restaurants, pubs and bed and breakfasts for the weary walker.

After crossing the N67 national road, the Way follows another country lane as it snakes through the green, stone-strewn landscape of the Burren. Among the scattered farmhouses, you pass the ruins of Cathair Mhic Neachtain, which was the Brehon Law School of the scholarly O'Davorens during the fifteenth and sixteenth centuries. The land then begins to rise, offering you a hint of what is to come. The Way crosses the R480 main road near the Poulawack cairn but you will have to detour approximately two kilometres north if you want to see the Poulnabrone dolmen. This large tomb, sat amidst limestone pavement, was excavated in the 1980s as part of conservation work – the remains of more than thirty people were discovered underneath it.

You are entering the heart of the Burren now, where wide, grey limestone pavement provides shelter for wildflowers, although the rocks also attract slippery moss. There is a spur that takes you into the national park. There are seven waymarked loops and if you explore no other, it is worth taking one of the routes that leads you to the summit of Mullaghmore for its spectacular views across the Burren area, particularly the swirled neighbouring summit of Slieve Rua.

The main route continues down a singletrack country lane, past the swirls of the limestone hills and the Bronze Age Parknabinna wedge tomb. At the crossroads where the

LOOKING OUT FOR THE TURN-OFF TO FANORE. © MOLAN/FOGARTY

route crosses the R476 road, the grey stone walls of Leamaneh Castle stand. Built in the fifteenth century by Toirdhealbhach Donn Ó Briain, one of the last high kings of Ireland, it was also home to the flame-haired Maire Rua (Red Mary), famous for her fierce temper and numerous husbands, although there is little evidence for most of the legends associated with her.

Another narrow, stonewalled lane leads you through green fields, past farmhouses and around the shores of Inchiquin Loch, a popular fishing spot for its wild brown trout. You may be able to make out the crumbling walls of the O'Brien's Inchiquin Castle on the north shores of the lake. The Way finishes in the small village of Corofin, the childhood home of artist Frederic William Burton, who painted Ireland's favourite painting *Hellelil and Hildebrand, The Meeting on the Turret Stairs*.

The long road links, exposed cliff sections and slippery Burren make this trail a poor choice for families with younger children. This is, however, the perfect trail for those who want to experience some of the most dramatic and unusual scenery that Ireland has to offer. It is also one of the richest trails on which to explore Ireland's past. As much of the trail is on-road, you will be able to enjoy some of the best views that Ireland has to offer without worrying about getting your feet wet – if the mist holds off.

04 BURREN WAY: ESSENTIAL INFORMATION

TRAIL ESSENTIALS

Start:	**Lahinch, County Clare, Ireland**
End:	**Corofin, County Clare, Ireland**
Distance:	**80km**
Ascent/descent:	**1,130m/1,150m**

HOW TO GET THERE

Lahinch has regular daily bus services to Ennis and Galway, which both offer bus connections to the closest international airport at Shannon. Both Ennis and Galway are on the Irish rail network.

Corofin has infrequent bus services to Ennis, and you may need to take a taxi or drive fourteen kilometres to Ennis, where bus connections can be made to Shannon International Airport.

TIME TO COMPLETE

Walking:	**4 days/22 hours**
Trekking:	**3 days/18 hours**
Fastpacking:	**2 days/14 hours**
Trail running:	**2 days/10 hours**

PROS

- **Orchids** – at least twenty-four of Ireland's thirty native orchids can be seen in the Burren, including the fly orchid, bee orchid, butterfly orchid and the rare sword-leaved orchid.

- **The Cliffs of Moher** – the towering, striated rock faces were voted Ireland's favourite tourist attraction in 2019 and 2020, and the cliffs are perhaps Ireland's most spectacular scenery.

- **History** – the earliest indications of human inhabitation of Ireland were discovered in County Clare, and the Burren Way allows you to explore ring forts and tombs; the Burren is dotted with National Monuments. You will also pass castles and churches.

CONS

- **Road** – approximately three-quarters of the trail is on roads, albeit quiet country lanes with infrequent traffic. Some of these narrow country lanes give little leeway to the walker who encounters a car.

- **Quiet** – the Burren area is one of Ireland's least-populated areas. There are few towns and only small villages, with limited accommodation and food, and the region is poorly served by public transport.

- **Weather** – western Ireland is prone to rain and mist. The Cliffs of Moher are exposed and tricky to negotiate in bad weather and the limestone karst is extremely slippery underfoot when wet.

GOOD TO KNOW

The Way passes the ruins of Leamaneh Castle, once home, and now haunted by, Maire Rua or Red Mary. According to folklore, Mary married twenty-five times, killing her husbands when they displeased her, before being starved to death herself in a tree. Mary did make three astute marriages to protect herself, her children and estate in turbulent times. She received a royal pardon for a murder allegedly committed during the Confederate Wars. It is unclear whether there is any truth to the legend that she sent enemies to their death over the Cliffs of Moher on horseback, but Leamaneh does mean 'Horse's Leap'.

FURTHER INFORMATION

www.discoverireland.ie/clare/the-burren-way

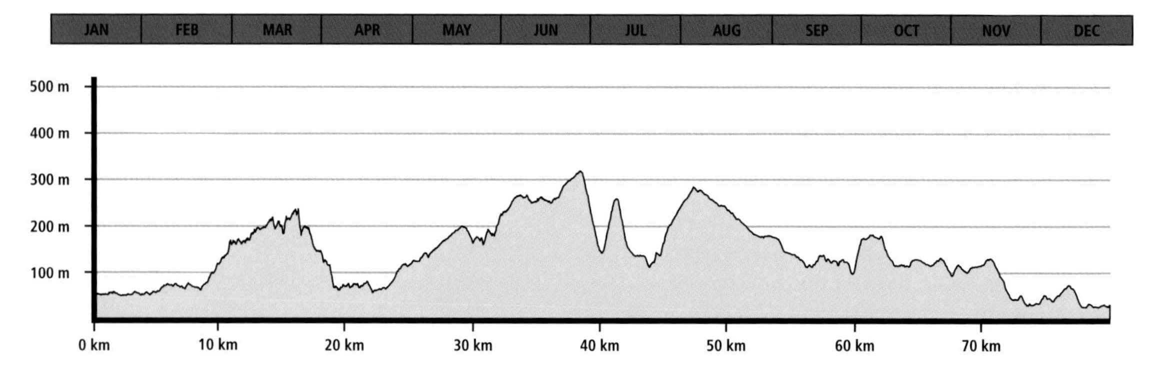

Galway Bay
Atlantic Ocean
Black Head
Doughbranneen
R477
Gleninagh Mountain
Cappanawalla
Fanore
Caher
N67
Ballyvaughan
Moneen Mountain
Abbey Hill
Slieve Oughtmama
Turlough Hill
Slievecarran
R477
Slieve Elva
N67
Gortacare Mountain
Doonmore
The Burren
N67
R480
Carran
Lisdoonvarna
Doolin
Aille
Burren National Park
N67
Kilfenora
R476
O'Brien's Tower
Knockardakin
Cliffs of Moher
Killinaboy
Lough Cullaun
Inchiquin Lough
R460
Dealagh
Lickeen Lough
Corofin
Liscannor
Lahinch
Ennistymon
Craggaunboy
Lough Atedaun
N85
R476
Inagh
Liscannor Bay
IRELAND
R476
N67
Inagh
N
N85
Milltown Malbay
R460
Ennis
0
5 Kilometres
R474

05

05 CAPITAL RING – 120km

The 120-kilometre Capital Ring was one of two routes proposed by the London Walking Forum, the other being the longer London LOOP (see our first volume of British Big Trails). The Ring is a loop through London's suburbia. Although it has more than its fair share of pavement plodding along London's quieter residential streets, it will also reveal the green paths through the capital's parks, woods, allotments and playing fields.

The route begins at the Woolwich foot tunnel, which provides the vital river crossing needed to close the circle. The foot tunnel was built in 1912, but the nearby Woolwich Free Ferry has operated for 800 years. Little remains of Woolwich Dockyard, once one of the most important in Europe, save for two cannons from the Gun Drill Battery. You begin by passing the Thames Barrier, constructed in the 1970s to protect London from flooding.

The Ring offers a pleasant meander through Charlton Park, past Charlton House, a fine Jacobean house built for Sir Adam Newton in 1612. After crossing Woolwich Common – once home to Charlton Athletic Football Club – you enter the deciduous Oxleas Woods, climbing to the eighteenth-century folly of Severndroog Castle, which was restored in 2014. This viewpoint is the highest point on the Capital Ring.

From Falconwood, the trail joins the Green Chain Walk. The Green Chain Walk provides approximately eighty kilometres of linked paths through the green spaces of south-east London. Your route through Eltham, birthplace to Bob Hope, takes you under an avenue of horse chestnuts in Eltham Park. You pass a medieval brick structure, the Conduit Head, which controlled the supply of water to Eltham Palace. The Palace, which the Ring now takes you past, was a popular royal palace in the fourteenth century, but was ransacked by Oliver Cromwell. The Courtald family subsequently renovated it, turning it into an art deco masterpiece – their pet lemur enjoyed free run of the house.

The route here takes paths through parks before popping out on to roads. The mast of Crystal Palace looms large on the horizon, making navigation straightforward. The glass-domed Crystal Palace was built to host that celebration of Britishness, the Great Exhibition of 1851, but was burnt down in 1936. The Victorian dinosaurs, however, remain in the Palace grounds. The path climbs up to the pretty Norwood Grove park, which offers panoramic views of the distant London skyline. On Streatham Common the Ring passes close to the Rookery, a hidden ornamental garden which also has a cafe.

Between Streatham and Wimbledon, the Ring spends a lot of time on London's streets, although it does cross Tooting Bec Common – close to Tooting Bec Lido, one of Britain's oldest and largest open-air swimming pools – and Wandsworth Common. On leaving Wandsworth Common the route passes Wandsworth Prison, which once housed Oscar Wilde and from where Great Train Robber Ronnie Biggs escaped.

◀ HIGHGATE WOOD.
© SHUTTERSTOCK/I WEI HUANG

After Wimbledon Park, neighbour to the famous tennis courts, you cross the wooded Wimbledon Common where you can visit the Wimbledon Windmill Museum. The nineteenth-century flour mill is a rare example of a British hollow-post mill. Robert Baden-Powell lived here in 1902, while he was writing *Scouting for Boys*. The windmill is next to the London Scottish Golf Club, one of Britain's oldest golf courses.

You enter Richmond, the largest Royal Park, near Spankers Hill Wood and cross the Pen Ponds. You are likely to encounter deer but should avoid the antlered males, particularly during rutting season. You may choose to make a small detour to the summit of King Henry's Mound, where on a clear day you should enjoy views of St Paul's dome on the skyline, as well as the Surrey Hills and Windsor. When you exit the park you join the Thames Path to reach Richmond Lock and cross the river.

The Ring passes Capability Brown's gardens at Syon House before reaching the Grand Union Canal at Brentford Lock. Just before the six locks of the Hanwell Flight, the trail turns to join the River Brent. As the trail under the stone bridge sometimes floods you may have to leave the path to join Uxbridge Road, but you will walk under the towering Wharncliffe Viaduct, one of Isambard Kingdom Brunel's early projects. The route continues to follow the river through Brent Lodge Park, nicknamed Bunny Park for its zoo, and Paradise Fields, a wetland nature reserve.

From the top of Horsenden Hill (eighty-four metres), site of an Iron Age settlement, you may be able to see the Chilterns. After the oaks of Horsenden Woods, another climb faces you at Harrow on the Hill. The Ring takes a permissive path through the grounds of Harrow School, and you encounter the only stile en route as you leave the grounds to reach Watford Road. A brambly path winds behind the hospital.

The grassy fields of Fryent Country Park, often grazed by horses, are some of London's more rural spots. From the trig point, near the ponds on the summit of Barn Hill, you may be able to see Wembley and its arch. The Welsh Harp reservoir is a feeder reservoir for the Grand Union Canal, but it was also a popular spot for racing, fairs, ice skating and other entertainment. It was a nudist spot in the 1920s, a practice that was ended by the Sunbathing Riots in 1930. The trail returns to the Brent, and then traverses green parkland by Mutton Brook.

As you cross the busy Finchley Road you may be able to glimpse the *La Délivrance* sword-wielding, naked lady, locally nicknamed 'Dirty Gertie'. A commemoration of the World War I First Battle of the Marne, it was donated to Finchley by Lord Rothermere, who insisted it be placed here so that he could see it when driving to visit his mother. Another statue awaits of the archer at East Finchley station – the Ring passes through the ticket hall.

The bluebelled Highgate Wood was once part of the ancient forest of Middlesex. The Parkland Walk, which follows the line of an old railway, is London's longest nature reserve. After Finsbury Park, you follow New River, not a river but an aqueduct built in 1613 to supply water to London. A good towpath along another man-made water feature, the Lee Navigation, leads you back towards Woolwich. You leave the waterway by the stadium built for London's 2012 Olympics but then follow yet another water feature, taking the grassy Greenway above the route of the Northern Outfall Sewage Embankment. This was one of Joseph Bazalgette's achievements – the Abbey Mills Pumping Station was built to return the subterranean sewage to the surface. After Beckton Park, the Ring rejoins the Thames Path to return to Woolwich.

You will often find yourself on London's grey streets as you follow the Capital Ring, but you will also discover green corridors along quiet waterways, ancient woodlands, hilltop views and historic buildings. You may encounter foxes, squirrels, herons, deer and even dinosaurs along the Ring. Whether you're a Londoner or a tourist, the Capital Ring can show you that you are never far from a muddy adventure, even in one of the world's busiest cities.

SEVERNDROOG CASTLE. © SHUTTERSTOCK/FOTOSIN

THE 'DINOSAURS' IN CRYSTAL PALACE PARK. © JOHN COEFIELD

05 CAPITAL RING: ESSENTIAL INFORMATION

TRAIL ESSENTIALS

Start: **Woolwich, London, England**
End: **Woolwich, London, England**
Distance: **120km**
Ascent/descent: **690m/690m**

HOW TO GET THERE

Woolwich can be reached by rail via the Woolwich Dockyard train station or Woolwich Arsenal, which is also on the Docklands Light Railway. The Woolwich Free Ferry and the foot tunnel offer connections across the Thames. London has international connections via its airports and the Eurostar train service, from St Pancras international rail station.

TIME TO COMPLETE

Walking: **5 days/27 hours**
Trekking: **3 days/23 hours**
Fastpacking: **3 days/17 hours**
Trail running: **2 days/14 hours**

PROS

- **Accessible** – most of the Ring is wheelchair and pushchair friendly. There are alternative accessible routes for difficult sections, and the urban nature of the route means that it is possible to bypass problematic paths.

- **Sports** – the Ring is the perfect route for avid sports fans, passing many of London's most iconic sporting venues. It passes numerous football stadiums, including West Ham's new home at the London (formerly Olympic) Stadium, and Wembley is only a small detour from the trail. It also passes one of London's oldest golf clubs, the world-famous All England Lawn and Croquet Club, better known as Wimbledon, and Hackney Marshes, which holds a Guinness World Record for the largest number of football pitches in the world.

- **Transport** – each section of the Ring starts and ends near public transport links. It is close to underground stations but also well served by buses and trains, and starts and ends at a free ferry. This makes it easy to stay in one location and avoid the necessity of carrying large rucksacks or arranging baggage transfers.

CONS

- **Opening times** – parks on the route may close at dusk, and East Finchley station – which the route passes through – also closes overnight, as do some sections through residential developments. Sections may also be closed for events and on public holidays, particularly Christmas Day.

- **Roads** – the Capital Ring has more than its fair share of tarmac sections on residential roads. Although the notorious crossing point on Finchley Road has been much improved, there are dangerous crossings on busy roads to negotiate.

GOOD TO KNOW

The woods and parkland of Wimbledon Common and Richmond Park are perhaps the prettiest parts of the Capital Ring, but it is also rich in interesting buildings. Wimbledon Windmill is a rare hollow-post flour mill, and Richmond's White Lodge, once George II's Hunting Lodge, is now home to the Royal Ballet School. Pembroke Lodge, now a popular wedding venue, was once home to the local mole-catcher. The obelisks in the Old Deer Park mark a meridian line, used by the King's Observatory. The Old Deer Park was host to the first World Scout Jamboree in 1920.

FURTHER INFORMATION

tfl.gov.uk/modes/walking/capital-ring

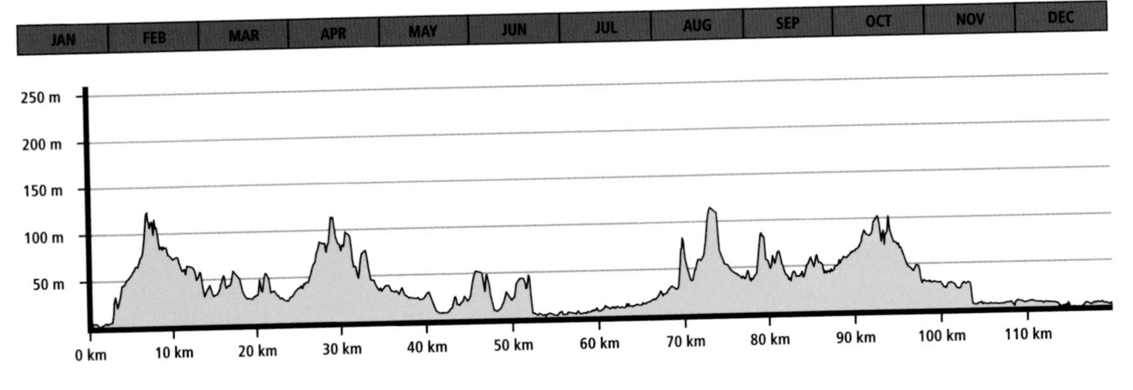

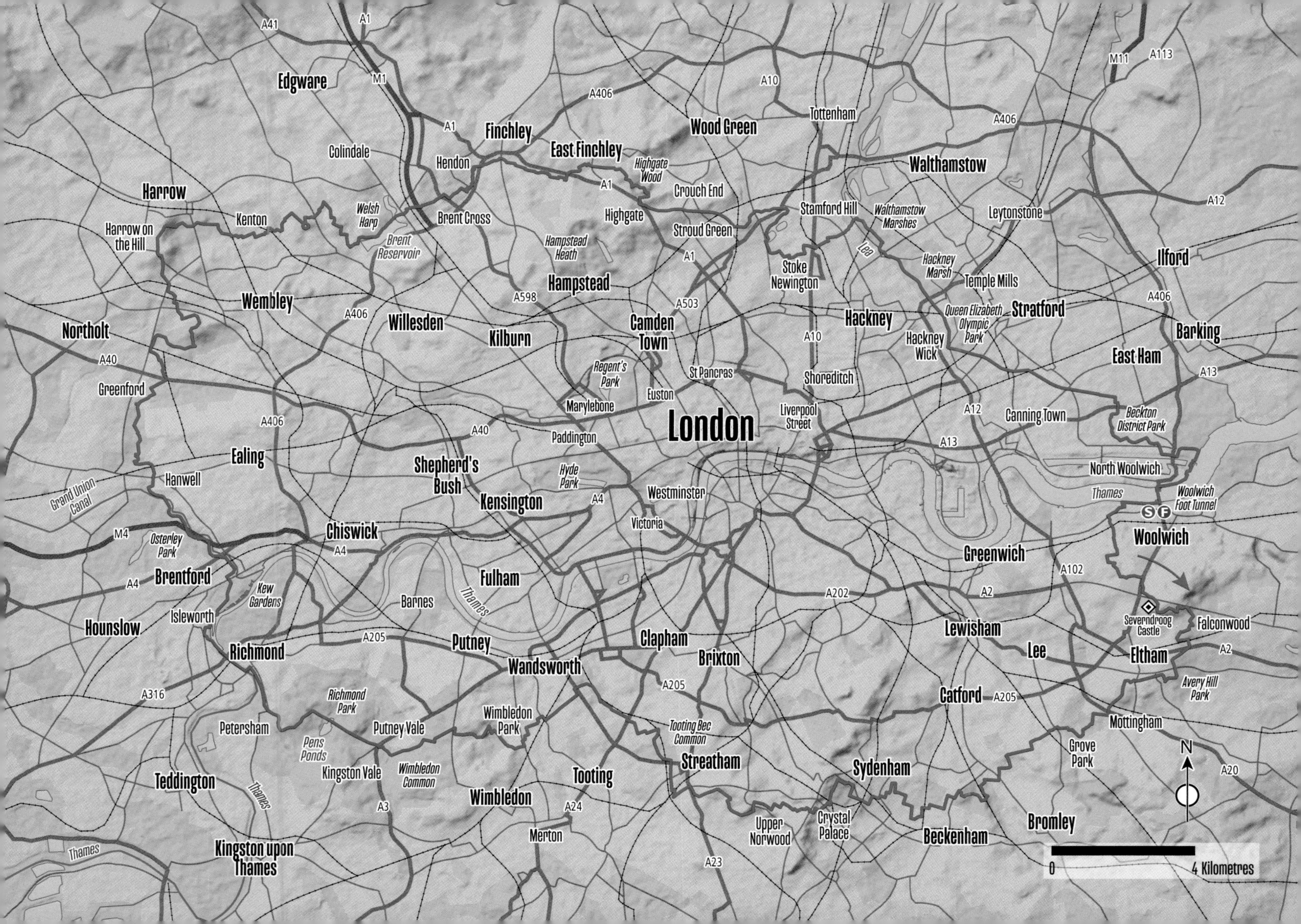
London
Edgware
Finchley
East Finchley
Wood Green
Tottenham
Walthamstow
Colindale
Hendon
Harrow
Harrow on the Hill
Kenton
Welsh Harp
Brent Reservoir
Brent Cross
Highgate Wood
Crouch End
Highgate
Stroud Green
Stamford Hill
Walthamstow Marshes
Leytonstone
Ilford
Hampstead Heath
Hampstead
Lea
Stoke Newington
Hackney Marsh
Temple Mills
Wembley
Willesden
Kilburn
Camden Town
Hackney
Queen Elizabeth Olympic Park
Stratford
Barking
Northolt
Hackney Wick
East Ham
Regent's Park
St Pancras
Shoreditch
Greenford
Euston
Marylebone
Liverpool Street
Canning Town
Beckton District Park
Paddington
Ealing
Shepherd's Bush
Hyde Park
Hanwell
Grand Union Canal
Westminster
Kensington
North Woolwich
Thames
Woolwich Foot Tunnel
Victoria
Chiswick
Woolwich
Osterley Park
Greenwich
Brentford
Fulham
Kew Gardens
Barnes
Hounslow
Isleworth
Lewisham
Severndroog Castle
Falconwood
Richmond
Putney
Clapham
Brixton
Lee
Eltham
Wandsworth
Richmond Park
Catford
Avery Hill Park
Wimbledon Park
Tooting Bec Common
Mottingham
Petersham
Putney Vale
Pens Ponds
Grove Park
Streatham
Sydenham
Kingston Vale
Wimbledon Common
Teddington
Tooting
Wimbledon
Upper Norwood
Crystal Palace
Bromley
Merton
Beckenham
Kingston upon Thames
N
0
4 Kilometres
A1
A41
M1
A406
A10
M11
A113
A12
A598
A503
A40
A13
A4
M4
A205
A202
A102
A2
A316
A3
A24
A23
A20

06 CHANNEL ISLAND WAY – 165km

The Channel Island Way winds its 165-kilometre path around five of the Channel Islands – Jersey, Guernsey, Herm, Alderney and Sark. It's an opportunity to experience the distinctive, and differing, culture of these small British Crown Dependencies, nearer to France than England. The Channel Island Way is the perfect choice for you if you want to enjoy car-free walking, dark, starry skies, clifftop views and sandy beaches.

You can step off the ferry and straight on to the Way at Guernsey's bustling St Peter Port. The Way follows the La Vallette promenade out of the town, past tunnels built into the cliffs by Germans for fuel supply. A steep-stepped climb up to Les Terres Point offers fine views back across the bay. The Channel Islands are some of Britain's most heavily fortified shores, and you're never far from a tower or arsenal – up here it is the Clarence Battery, built in 1780. The Way takes you through shady bluebell woods before emerging on to scrubby clifftops, with views across to first Herm then Sark. The coastline here is rugged, and the trail climbs up and down and around steep coves.

The fifty-five-kilometre Way around Guernsey favours the green clifftops, although there are paths and roads down to sandy beaches. You pass many forts and towers; one of the more striking being the square chunks of the German L'Angle observation tower, through which you can peer seawards after climbing the five levels to the top. Towards the north-west of the island, the path descends towards Portelet Bay where you might choose to stop for an ice cream at the fishing harbour.

If the tide is out, you can avoid the road by following the long sands of L'Eree beach. While the Way attempts to cling to the coast, you will sometimes find yourself cutting a corner on tarmac because no footpath exists. It is easy to be distracted as the Way passes loophole towers, forts and magazines, but pay attention at Fort le Marchant – if a red flag is flying, the shooting range is active and you will need to follow a diversion. Marinas and harbours, busy with bobbing boats, mark your return to St Peter Port where you'll need to board a boat to continue your trail.

Jersey is the largest of the Channel Islands – its coast path is just over seventy kilometres. St Helier is the largest urban area on the island and you face a long walk out of town, your path often parallel to the A4 main road. The thirteenth-century Mont Orgueil Castle was the island's primary defence until Elizabeth Castle was built in 1594. The route then leaves the more urban areas behind to pass quieter coves and bays. Archirondel Tower was one of the last loophole towers to be built on the island (in 1792), but if you can climb the narrow spiral staircase, you can now stay in the self-catering accommodation.

A prehistoric dolmen stands on Jersey's north-east corner. You face a serious of tough ascents and descents, sometimes stepped, through clefts in the cliff on the north coast. A short detour will take you to the crater of the Devil's Hole, with the waves crashing against the cliffs. It is guarded by a horned statue – the original figurehead was washed from a wrecked French ship. On the western coast, the eighteenth-century La Rocco Tower stands on a rocky

◀ LA COUPÉE, THE NARROW ISTHMUS BETWEEN GREAT SARK AND LITTLE SARK. © MARK RAINSLEY

shale outcrop – it is cut off by the sea at high tide. The sea near the white lighthouse at La Corbière is dangerous, and a memorial on the headland commemorates the successful rescue of 307 from the *Saint-Malo* in 1995. The southern coast offers a return to St Helier via curved, sandy bays, backed by gentle wooded slopes. At low tide at St Aubin, you can walk across the causeway to the fort, built on the islet by Henry Cornish in 1542.

Alderney is the Channel Island closest to France, and as a result was heavily fortified by slave labourers, many of whom died during the German occupation. The seventeen-kilometre coastal walk around this small island visits many of these fortifications. Some have been repurposed – one is now a wildlife bunker, with information on birds and plants. Near the sea stacks at Fourquie, you might make a short detour from the route to visit the site of the Lager Sylt Nazi concentration camp. Back en route, you pass the Telegraph Tower on Alderney's highest point, built in 1811 to communicate with the other islands.

You are never far from the next German fortification, but Forts Clonque and Tourgis are Victorian fortifications. The sandy northern beaches of Saye and Braye are popular swimming spots, but you should not pause for a dip at Platte Saline due to a dangerous undertow. Near Braye, you'll pass the Channel Islands' only working railway, although only a few trains run on weekends and bank holidays. The short railway ends near the Odeon observation tower and the Mannez Lighthouse. Your route back to the capital of St Anne takes you past the Nunnery, now believed to have been a Roman fortification, and the ruins of the Tudor fort, Essex Castle.

Sark is an island divided in two, with Great Sark and Little Sark connected by the narrow isthmus of La Coupée. The Guernsey ferry arrives at Maseline Harbour and a steep climb up Harbour Hill will take you to the sixteen-kilometre Way and on towards Hogs Back, where a commando raid came ashore in 1942. The concrete road across the narrow ridge of La Coupée was built by German prisoners of war in 1945. The Way does a small loop around the southern cliffs of Little Sark, past abandoned lead and silver mines before making a gorsy return.

ABOVE: SAYE BAY AND ALDERNEY LIGHTHOUSE, AT ALDERNEY'S NORTHERNMOST POINT. © MARK RAINSLEY
BELOW: THE SWINGE CHANNEL, FROM ALDERNEY. © MARK RAINSLEY

Your loop on Great Sark continues through The Village, where you pass the Anglican church, village hall and La Seigneurie, traditional home of Sark's Seigneur or feudal lord, and also the location of the Isle of Sark Brewing Co. The Way follows footpaths across the high, scrub-covered clifftops of northern Sark before heading back towards The Village and harbour. Sark is the world's first Dark Sky Island, in part because it has no street lights.

The tiny car-free island of Herm is six kilometres in circumference. The island was not always car free – one previous tenant was Sir Percival Perry, chairman of the Ford Motor Company. If you head south from the steps or harbour you will reach the high cliffs of the southern island, and may see a puffin at Puffin Bay. Northern Herm has beautiful beaches, and you reach by the soft sands of Belvoir Bay there is a small ice cream kiosk. A footpath leads you to Shell Beach and the north-east corner of the island.

The obelisk of Pierre aux Rats guides you along the northern coast – this was built as a daymark for fisherman after quarrymen removed a Neolithic monument from the spot. At Oyster Point, the island's most north-westerly point, you can enjoy views across the azure sea back towards Guernsey. At low tide, you can walk barefoot on the beach back towards the harbour, but higher tides may force you on to the footpath at the back of the beach. If you have time to spare before your return ferry you could make the short detour into Herm village, to enjoy a pint at the Mermaid Tavern.

MONT ORGUEIL CASTLE WITH THE HARBOUR TOWN OF GOREY IN FRONT. © ELLIE QUINN/THE WANDERING QUINN TRAVEL BLOG

06 CHANNEL ISLAND WAY: ESSENTIAL INFORMATION

TRAIL ESSENTIALS

Start:	**St Peter Port, Guernsey**
End:	**Herm village, Herm**
Distance:	**165km – Guernsey 55km/Jersey 71km/ Alderney 17km/Sark 16km/Herm 6km**
Ascent/descent:	**2,560m/2,560m**

HOW TO GET THERE

St Peter Port is served by ferries from Portsmouth and Poole, and St Malo (as is St Helier on Jersey). There are airports on Jersey and Guernsey, offering flights to the UK mainland. Alderney airport offers flights to Guernsey and Southampton on the UK mainland.

Herm has a ferry service from Guernsey. There are ferry services from Guernsey to all the Channel Islands, although private boat companies also offer chartered connections between the islands.

TIME TO COMPLETE

Walking:	**10 days**/15 hours (Guernsey), 20 hours (Jersey), 5 hours (Alderney), 5 hours (Sark), 2 hours (Herm)
Trekking:	**7 days**/12 hours (Guernsey), 16 hours (Jersey), 4 hours (Alderney), 4 hours (Sark), 2 hours (Herm)
Fastpacking:	**6 days**/9 hours (Guernsey), 12 hours (Jersey), 3 hours (Alderney), 3 hours (Sark), 1 hour (Herm)
Trail running:	**5 days**/7 hours (Guernsey), 9 hours (Jersey), 2 hours (Alderney), 2 hours (Sark), 1 hour (Herm)

PROS

- **Beach cafes** – the Channel Island Way offers kilometres of sandy beaches, and these are well served by beachfront cafes and kiosks where you can enjoy locally produced ice cream or fresh seafood.
- **Mild weather** – nearer to France than England, the Channel Islands enjoy slightly warmer weather than the British Mainland.
- **Unique culture** – the Channel Islands have their own unique culture and their own language, although English is spoken everywhere. Influenced by their proximity to France and the rest of mainland Europe, they have also been shaped by their complex history.

CONS

- **Route finding** – the Way is not consistently marked, and in some sections is more a suggestion than a well-established route. You will need maps of the islands and good navigational skills.
- **Expensive** – with ferry or air travel to the islands, and travel between the islands, this is not the cheapest long-distance trail to complete. Accommodation, which is limited, and food can be slightly more expensive than in the rest of Britain.
- **Tidal** – at low tide, stretches of the Way can be enjoyed barefoot on sandy beaches. It is easy to be cut off by the islands' tides and particular care should be taken if visiting La Corbière lighthouse – in 1947, the assistant lighthouse keeper drowned trying to save someone stranded on the causeway and visitors still find themselves in trouble here.

GOOD TO KNOW

In June hundreds of walkers gather in St Helier to try and complete a circuit of Jersey's coast path in twenty-four hours to raise money for charity, during the annual Island Walk.

FURTHER INFORMATION

www.visitchannelislands.com; The Channel Island Way (Perry's Guides, 2011; currently out of print).

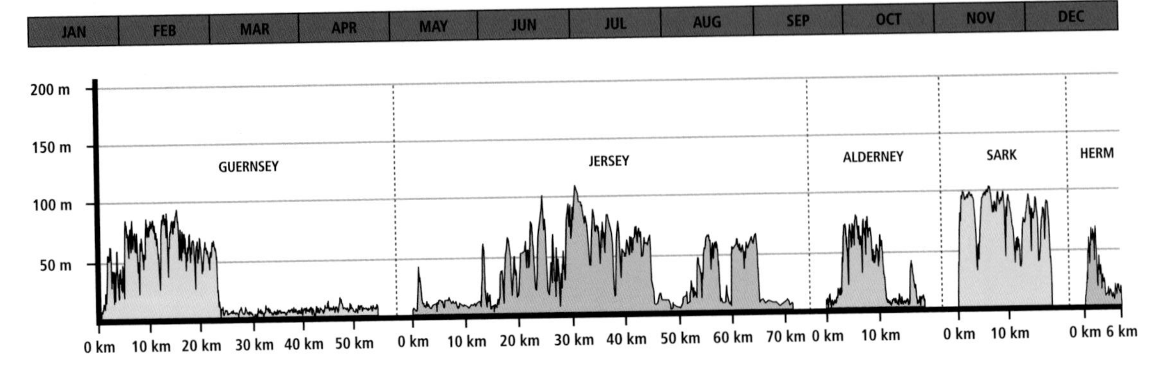

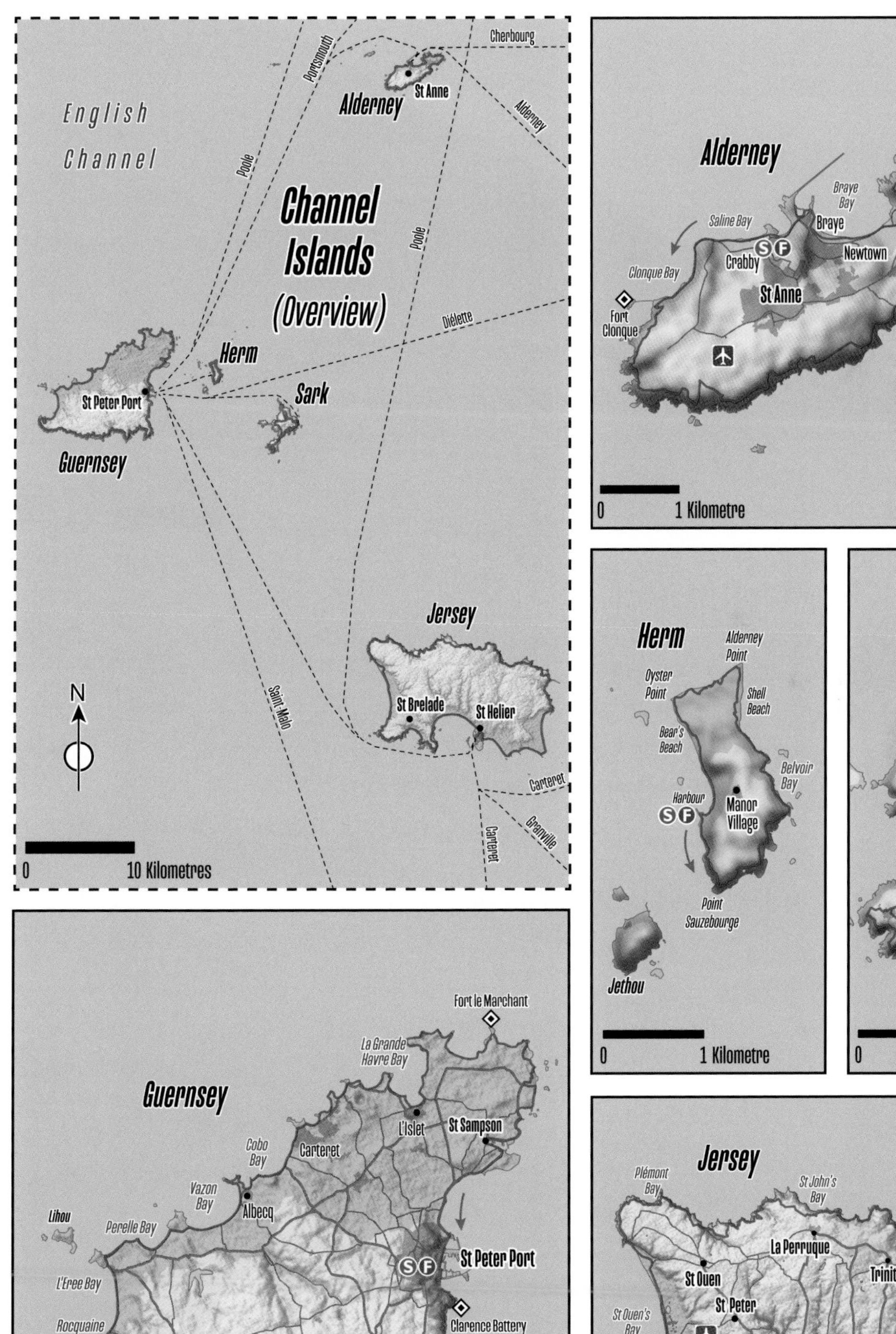

English Channel
Channel Islands (Overview)
Cherbourg
Portsmouth
Alderney
St Anne
Poole
Poole
Diélette
Herm
Sark
St Peter Port
Guernsey
Jersey
St Brelade
St Helier
Saint-Malo
Carteret
Carteret
Granville
N
0
10 Kilometres
Alderney
Corblets Bay
Braye Bay
Saline Bay
Braye
Crabby
Newtown
Longis Bay
Clonque Bay
St Anne
Fort Clonque
Essex Castle
0
1 Kilometre
Herm
Alderney Point
Oyster Point
Shell Beach
Bear's Beach
Belvoir Bay
Harbour
Manor Village
Point Sauzebourge
Jethou
0
1 Kilometre
Sark
Great Sark
Sark Village
Harbour
Hogs Back
La Coupée
Little Sark
0
1 Kilometre
Guernsey
Fort le Marchant
La Grande Havre Bay
L'Islet
St Sampson
Cobo Bay
Carteret
Vazon Bay
Albecq
Lihou
Perelle Bay
St Peter Port
L'Eree Bay
Rocquaine Bay
Clarence Battery
Portelet
Fermain Bay
L'Angle Tower
Saints Bay
0
3 Kilometres

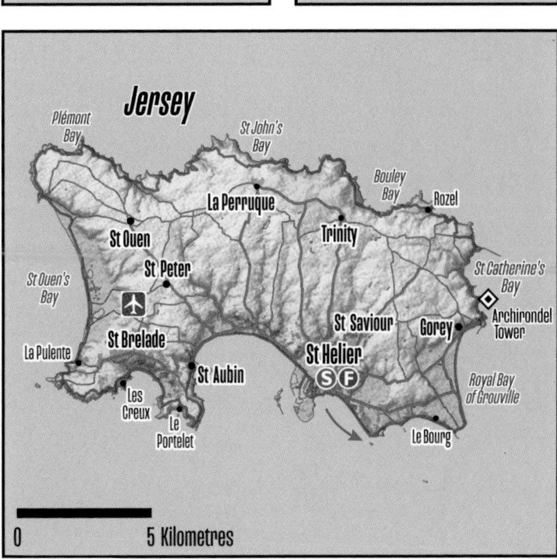

Jersey
Plémont Bay
St John's Bay
Bouley Bay
Rozel
La Perruque
Trinity
St Ouen
St Peter
St Catherine's Bay
St Ouen's Bay
Archirondel Tower
St Saviour
Gorey
St Brelade
La Pulente
St Helier
St Aubin
Royal Bay of Grouville
Les Creux
Le Portelet
Le Bourg
0
5 Kilometres

07

Carlisle
Keswick
Ulverston

07 CUMBRIA WAY – 115km

The 115-kilometre Cumbria Way leads through the Lake District, offering a gentle route through some of England's most dramatic scenery. Although there are some challenging climbs, and most will choose to detour to explore some of Wainwright's favourite fells, the Cumbria Way is the perfect trail if you want to explore some of England's wildest countryside without getting lost. The Way generally follows good paths, often stone or gravel, and is clearly waymarked.

The quiet coastal town of Ulverston was the birthplace of comedian Stan Laurel. It owed its commercial success to the construction of a short, deep canal in the eighteenth century that connected the town to the nearby Morecambe Bay. A cairn and compass mark the start (or end) of the Cumbria Way at The Gill. You follow a quiet road, and then farm tracks, out of town towards the Lake District. You enter the national park near Gawthwaite and encounter your first lake at Beacon Tarn. The Old Man of Coniston looms on the horizon, but you should turn to admire the blue view across Morecambe Bay behind you.

After the high Blawith Fells, you follow the course of Torver Beck to reach Coniston Water, famous for Donald Campbell's water speed records set in his *Bluebird* boat. Campbell's last record attempt on Coniston Water ended in tragedy in January 1967, when he crashed and died – the wreckage of *Bluebird* was finally recovered in 2001, and donated by Campbell's daughter to the Ruskin Museum. A lakeside path, sometimes muddy, sometimes sheltered by trees, leads you past the sixteenth-century Coniston Hall into Coniston – many make their first detour, up on the mine-scarred Old Man, here. Coniston, its wealth built on copper and slate, was home to Victorian philosopher and critic John Ruskin, who is buried in the town's churchyard and who lends his name to the town's museum.

Should you stay on trail, the path leads you through the dappled beauty of Tarn Hows woods. The clear blue tarns are a man-made beauty spot, created during the nineteenth century when a beck was dammed. Near the wooded Tongue Intake Plantation you might choose an easy detour to the pretty waterfall of Colwith Force. En route you pass another waterfall, Skelwith Force, near the village of Skelwith Bridge. You take a riverside path along the river Brathay to Elterwater.

The valleys of Great Langdale and Langstrath, which the Way now takes you through, are some of the quietest, and most remote, of the Lakes. Under grey, stony cliffs, you pass the iconic Old Dungeon Ghyll hotel, a favourite climbers' haunt, although the campsites along the valley offer cheaper accommodation. Much of Great Langdale is owned by the National Trust – historian G.M. Trevelyan bought Old Dungeon Ghyll, Stool End, Wall End, Low Millbeck and Harry Place farms and donated them to the Trust. The valley path, following the course of the beck through Great Langdale, leads you under the shadow of the imposing hills. Depending on the paths you choose to follow to Caldbeck, Stake Pass is one of the highest points on the Way. As you tackle the challenging climb over the pass, you should look back to enjoy long views down the dramatic Great Langdale. You descend to another stunning valley, the

◀ ON THE CUMBRIA WAY NEAR KESWICK.
© ANNA PAXTON

quiet Langstrath. This isolated, roadless valley is one of the Lake District's hidden treasures, which you follow until you reach the tourist hotspot of Smithymire Island. As you reach Borrowdale, renowned as one of the Lake District's most beautiful valleys, you will meet with the Coast-to-Coasters.

You pass through the tourist-friendly town of Rosthwaite to reach Derwent Water at Brandlehow Bay. The low, flat lakeside paths through the wooded paths by the lake are popular and well-maintained, although the lofty path over the bumpy summit of the Cat Bells is one of the easier high-level deviations from the route. The bustling market town of Keswick, with its pencil museum, lies at the head of Derwent Water.

The trail takes you on good tracks over the shoulder of Lonscale Fell. A rocky path contours along the valley above the Glenderaterra Beck in the shadow of Skiddaw and the long dragonback ridge of Blencathra. The grey walls of Skiddaw House Hostel, tucked into the hillside in a small copse of trees, have been a welcome sight for weary walkers. Skiddaw House Hostel is the highest hostel in Britain, at 472 metres. The house was built as a game-keeper's residence and shooting lodge, and later provided a lonely shelter for shepherds and farmers.

You face a choice of a challenging, exposed climb over High Pike, the highest point on the Cumbria Way at 658 metres, or a lower-level alternative past the Whitewater Dash waterfalls. In bad weather, the lower, western route is a safer choice for all but the most experienced of hillwalkers. There is little in the way of shelter on this remote section of the Way, although the high path does take you past the Great Lingy Hut bothy. The eastern route over High Pike, a favourite peak of local resident and mountaineering legend, Sir Chris Bonington, is a rare opportunity to bag

LOOKING DOWN OVER CONISTON WATER FROM THE WALNA SCAR ROAD. © JOHN COEFIELD

a Wainwright and experience some hillwalking on the Cumbria Way, although there are plenty of hillwalking opportunities should you detour from the official route.

The rolling hills of the Lakes, the grey-green moorland and bracken and heather, give way to greener farmland as you reach Caldbeck and the edge of the Lake District. The Way follows the course of the River Caldew, as it flows from the heights of Skiddaw down to Carlisle. Nine kilometres of cycle path connect Dalston to Carlisle, where the Cumbria Way reaches its end at the Old Town Hall in the city's Market Place – although not the most attractive section of trail, this is an easy conclusion and offers a quick way to traverse Cumbria's flatter farmland. Whether you walk the Way north to south or south to north in part depends on whether you want this long, uninteresting stretch of cycleway as your introduction or your easy finish to the Way.

Although the Cumbria Way is a gentle introduction to the Lake District, you will still find your daily distances dictated by the sparsely scattered towns and villages along the route. While the Way contours around the hillsides rather than taking a high path over them, you will still discover that the wind and rain can blast along a long valley as well as over the hilltops. You can attempt the Way at any time of year, and are unlikely to encounter severe weather, but hostels and other accommodation may close over winter, and public transport runs to a reduced timetable. The Cumbria Way traverses the Lake District National Park, and while it is a route that is perfect for running, it is perhaps best enjoyed at leisure. The Way leads you past some of the Lakes' most iconic peaks, and you should allow yourself time to divert from the trail to explore them.

ABOVE: THE ZIGZAGGING MAIN PATH UP SKIDDAW. © JOHN COEFIELD
BELOW: ON THE CUMBRIA WAY NEAR YHA SKIDDAW HOUSE HOSTEL. © ANNA PAXTON

07 CUMBRIA WAY: ESSENTIAL INFORMATION

TRAIL ESSENTIALS

Start:	**Ulverston, Cumbria, England**
End:	**Carlisle, Cumbria, England**
Distance:	**115km**
Ascent/descent:	**2,060m/2,070m**

HOW TO GET THERE

Ulverston has a rail station, and connects to the West Coast Main Line at Carnforth or Kendal. The closest international airport is at Manchester.

Carlisle is on the West Coast Main Line, offering fast connections to Glasgow and Manchester. Carlisle's airport only offers British and Irish flights – more destinations are served by Newcastle, as well as Glasgow and Manchester international airports.

TIME TO COMPLETE

Walking:	**5 days/32 hours**
Trekking:	**4 days/27 hours**
Fastpacking:	**3 days/20 hours**
Trail running:	**2 days/15 hours**

PROS

- **Good underfoot** – the Way favours stony tracks, broad bridleways and rocky paths over muddy trods or tarmac roads.

- **Hostels** – at Coniston, Keswick and Skiddaw, you have the opportunity to enjoy a budget stay in some of England's best youth hostels.

- **Views** – from the vista over Morecambe Bay, to the long line of Great Langdale, or the knobbly ridge of Blencathra, the Way offers some of the best-loved views in England.

CONS

- **Wainwrights** – if you love the Lakes because you like to bag Wainwright's summits, this trail – which prefers the valley bottoms over the hill tops – is not for you, although it is easy to leave the route and head for the hills.

- **Busy** – the Way takes you through some of them most popular areas in the Lakes, and should you visit in summer, you are likely to encounter many other tourists in Borrowdale, Coniston and Keswick, and the lakeside paths around Derwent Water may be thronged with daytrippers.

GOOD TO KNOW

Every September, trail runners gather to run the Cumbria Way Ultra – Jacob Snochowski holds the men's course record (twelve hours fifteen minutes) and Sabrina Verjee the women's (thirteen hours forty-five minutes), although steadier runners have twenty-seven hours to complete the Way.

FURTHER INFORMATION

www.keswick.org/what-to-do/walking-routes/the-cumbria-way; *The Cumbria Way* (Cicerone, 2015).

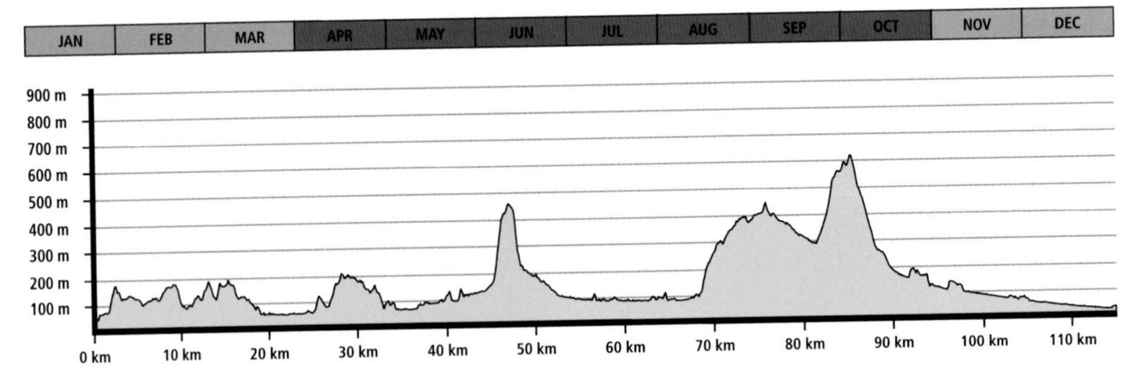

Solway Firth
Silloth
Carlisle
Brampton
Cummersdale
Dalston
Buckabank
Wigton
A596
A595
A69
Eden
M6
A6
Sebergham
Caldbeck
Ellen
Fell Side
Nether Row
B5305
Maryport
A591
Orthwaite
High Pike
Caldew
ENGLAND
Knott
Cockermouth
Embleton
A66
Workington
Skiddaw
Bassenthwaite Lake
Skiddaw House Hostel
Blencathra
Troutbeck
Penrith
Threlkeld
Pooley Bridge
Portinscale
Keswick
A595
Derwent Water
Borrowdale
Grasmoor
Great Dodd
Ullswater
Whitehaven
Crummock Water
Buttermere
Grange
Thirlmere
Glenridding
Dale Head
Helvellyn
Patterdale
Rosthwaite
Ennerdale Water
High Stile
Stonethwaite
Lake District
Haweswater Reservoir
Pillar
Fairfield
Great Gable
Glaramara
National Park
High Street
Harter Fell
Seatallan
Old Dungeon Ghyll
Great Langdale
A592
Scafell Pike
Chapel Stile
Ambleside
Wast Water
Elterwater
Skelwith Bridge
Swirl How
Hawkshead
Windermere
The Old Man of Coniston
Coniston
Coniston Water
Kendal
A593
High Nibthwaite
Broughton in Furness
Tottlebank
Staveley-in-Cartmel
N
A590
Kirkby-in-Furness
Broughton Beck
Milnthorpe
Newbiggin
Grange-over-Sands
Ulverston
Kirkby Lonsdale
0
10 Kilometres
Barrow-in-Furness
Carnforth

08

08 DINGLE WAY – 182km

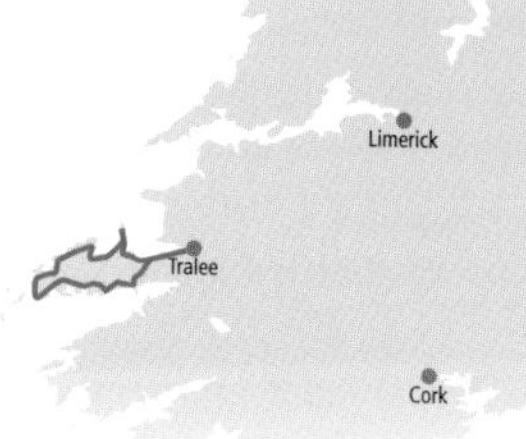

The 182-kilometre Dingle Way traces a coastal path around Ireland's most westerly peninsula. Long a popular filming location, the Dingle peninsula offers picture-perfect sandy beaches, a backdrop of high green mountains and turquoise seas. The trail, on country roads, boreens or unpaved roads and good paths, is only occasionally boggy or tricky. You are never too far from a warm welcome in the next village pub.

The Dingle Way starts in Tralee, Kerry's county town and internationally renowned for the annual Rose of Tralee competition, a celebration of young Irish (and Irish descent) womanhood. You follow the ship canal towards the Tralee Bay, passing the Blennerville Windmill, the largest working windmill in Ireland. In the shadow of the Slieve Mish mountains, you climb on quiet country roads out on to rocky paths that cut across the boggy hillside, fording glacial streams on stepping stones.

Approaching Camp, you pass the ruins of the early Christian church, Killelton Oratory – this section of the Dingle Way is also called the Kerry Camino, as you follow in the footsteps of Kerry's patron saint, St Brendan. The Way now follows quiet country lanes as you enjoy views of the megalithic fort, the highest promontory fort in Ireland, that clings close to the top of the giant Caherconree mountain. This was the fort of magician Cú Roí – for whom the mountain is named – and it is said that he would spin the fort around to confound his enemies searching for the entrance. He was allegedly killed when a kidnapped maiden poured milk into the stream that rises nearby to signal that the fort was undefended – the Way crossed the Finglas, or white river, near Camp.

You climb to cross a high saddle between Corrin and Knockbrack, before descending past a conifer plantation. Ireland, the Emerald Isle, has the lowest forest cover in Europe, in large part due to historical clearances for agriculture and the demand for wood in shipbuilding and industry. The Way offers views towards the Slieve Mish mountains and the wild Atlantic, and now you descend towards the shore. You can briefly enjoy the sandy Inch Beach – a five-kilometre-long strand which has often been used as a film set, perhaps most famously in *Ryan's Daughter* – before the Way takes you inland again to Annascaul.

You will find Kerry's own south pole, or South Pole Inn at least, in Annascual. Dedicated to its former owner, Tom Crean, the pub is rammed full to the rafters full of memorabilia relating to the explorer, who participated in Scott's doomed British Antarctic Expedition and Shackleton's narrow escape on the *Endurance*. He was awarded the Albert Medal for walking alone more than fifty kilometres across the Ross Ice Shelf to save Edward Evans's life during Scott's expedition.

The Way follows a narrow country lane through undulating farmland to Minard Castle on Kilmurry Bay, the Bay of Stones. The sandstone Fitzgerald castle was irreparably damaged by Cromwell's troops in 1650. You may choose to make a short detour down steps to visit the horseshoe Holy Well of Tobar Eoin Baiste. You continue to follow road and boreens, crossing by the high-arched medieval Garfinny bridge to reach Dingle, the only town on the peninsula. The route through the town passes the

◄ HIKING TOWARDS INCH BEACH.
© HEIDI BROENNIMANN, SWITZERLAND, *WWW.EARLYMORNING.CH*

Dingle Distillery, which distils whiskey, vodka and gin. Established in 2012, the distillery released its first cask whiskey to market in 2016, and in 2017 released a rare Single Pot Still, a uniquely Irish whiskey that is distinguished by its use of unmalted, in addition to malted, barley.

After Dingle, the trail leaves the road behind it, preferring instead muddy paths fringed with fuchsia. You walk along the sandy beach at Ventry Bay and then climb around the flanks of Mount Eagle. You pass the famine cottages, where you can learn more about impoverished rural life during the potato famine, and also watch demonstrations of working sheepdogs. Within the walls of the Dunbeg Iron Age ring fort, you can view an even more basic home; clocháns, or beehive huts, are believed to have been home to early Christian hermit monks.

As you reach Ireland's most westerly tip, you enjoy good views of the Blasket Islands, which were once home to fishing communities, but the final residents were evacuated to Dunquin on the mainland in 1953. Peig Seyers, the great *seanchaí* or storyteller, made Great Blasket her home for fifty years after her marriage to an islander. Charles Lindbergh made his first European landfall here at the Dingle peninsula on the first solo transatlantic flight. As you follow the Dingle Way up the rugged western peninsula, the peaks of the Three Sisters appear on the horizon.

You contour around the flanks of Cruach Mhárthain, passing the site of 'Kirrary', the temporary village built for the filming of David Lean's film *Ryan's Daughter*. It is on this, Ireland's most westerly coast, that St Brendan is believed to have set off on his voyage to discover the Promised Land of the Saints – some claim that Brendan was actually the first European to reach America. In the shadow of Mount Brandon, Ireland's highest mountain outside of the MacGillycuddy's Reeks, you walk on the beach before turning inland at Feothanach. You climb to a high pass below Brandon's summit, passing the carved Arraglen Ogham Stone which is the highest point on the Way. There is a bad weather alternative that takes advantage of a lower, disused road.

ABOVE: FOLLOWING THE WELL-MARKED PATH ALONG THE ATLANTIC COAST. © HEIDI BROENNIMANN, SWITZERLAND – *WWW.EARLYMORNING.CH*
BELOW: THE VIEW SOUTH-WEST AT BRANDON BAY. © *ADRIANHENDROFF.COM*

The route reaches the coast again at Brandon and follow country lanes to Cloghane. You encounter a gentler section of the Way as you follow the beach around Brandon Bay. The sand leads you up the finger of the Maharees peninsula to Scraggane, a small fishing port and popular surfing and diving destination. You return down the spit, past rock pools and marram grass dunes, to Castlegregory. A country road and another beach section bring you back to Camp. The Dingle Way officially begins and ends in Tralee, but many choose not to revisit the eighteen-kilometre spur from Camp to Tralee which you completed on your outward journey.

Like most Irish trails, the Dingle Way suffers from being forced too often on to the road, but it compensates for this with sandy beaches, mountain views and fascinating historical sites. It is well waymarked and, except when it climbs over the saddle of Mount Brandon, does not offer any challenging ascents. The Blasket Islands and Maharees peninsula are renowned birdwatching spots, and you may see dolphins, basking sharks and whales in the foaming Atlantic. The Dingle Way may be attempted at any time of year, although tourist facilities may be reduced over the winter months. Summer guarantees long days, but not necessarily sunny weather.

The Dingle peninsula has always attracted more than its fair share of voyagers and adventurers, perhaps because there is so much to discover. Each turn and wiggle in the Way reveals another stunning view, a fascinating archaeological site or a deserted sandy beach.

LOOKING DOWN ONTO BEENAMAN AND BRANDON CREEK FROM THE DINGLE WAY AT CNOC NA MBRISTI. © *ADRIANHENDROFF.COM*

08 DINGLE WAY: ESSENTIAL INFORMATION

TRAIL ESSENTIALS

Start:	**Tralee, County Kerry, Ireland**
End:	**Tralee, County Kerry, Ireland**
Distance:	**182km**
Ascent/descent:	**2,720m/2,720m**

HOW TO GET THERE

Tralee has bus services to nearby Kerry's Farranfore airport, although Shannon and Cork airports offer more international flights. Tralee has a railway station and is well served by Bus Éireann services.

TIME TO COMPLETE

Walking:	**8 days/49 hours**
Trekking:	**5 days/40 hours**
Fastpacking:	**4 days/30 hours**
Trail running:	**3 days/22 hours**

PROS

- **Gaeltacht** – the Dingle peninsula is one of a handful of the Gaeltacht, or predominantly Irish language, areas and has a rich Gaelic literary tradition. Language summer schools are available if you want to learn Gaelic.

- **Marine wildlife** – the western coast, near the Blasket Islands, is a great place for whalespotting (humpback, minke, fin and killer whales) but you may also see blue fin tuna, basking sharks and bottlenose dolphins. Sadly, Dingle's beloved dolphin, Fungie, who had been a regularly visitor to the harbour for thirty years, has disappeared, although a sculpture of him can be seen on the harbour front.

- **Beaches** – the Dingle peninsula boasts some of Ireland's longest sandy beaches and offers you the opportunity to walk along several of them, although this can make for tiring progress.

CONS

- **Roads** – nearly half of the Dingle Way is on roads. While most of the roads are quiet country lanes, on occasion you may encounter a tourist minibus or coach bowling around the bends, on their way to a Wild Atlantic Way viewpoint.

- **Dogs** – as the Way passes through farmland, with the permission of landowners, dogs are not permitted on the Dingle Way.

GOOD TO KNOW

In May 1976, explorer Tim Severin and his crew set off from Brandon Creek in a curragh, made from tanned oxhides wrapped around an oak frame, to recreate Brendan's legendary sixth-century voyage to America. The curragh reached America in June 1977, proving conclusively that it is possible to make a transatlantic voyage in the type of boats that were used in the sixth century. Severin's *The Brandan Voyage* provides an account of his adventure.

FURTHER INFORMATION

www.dingleway.com

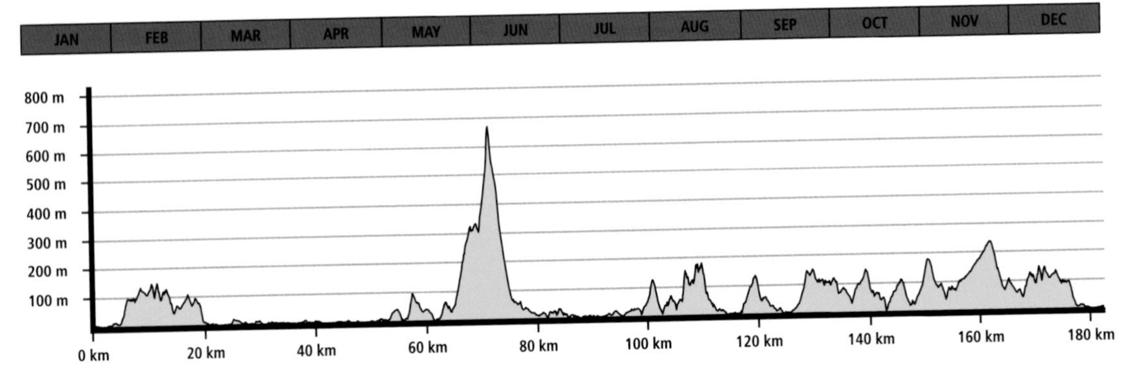

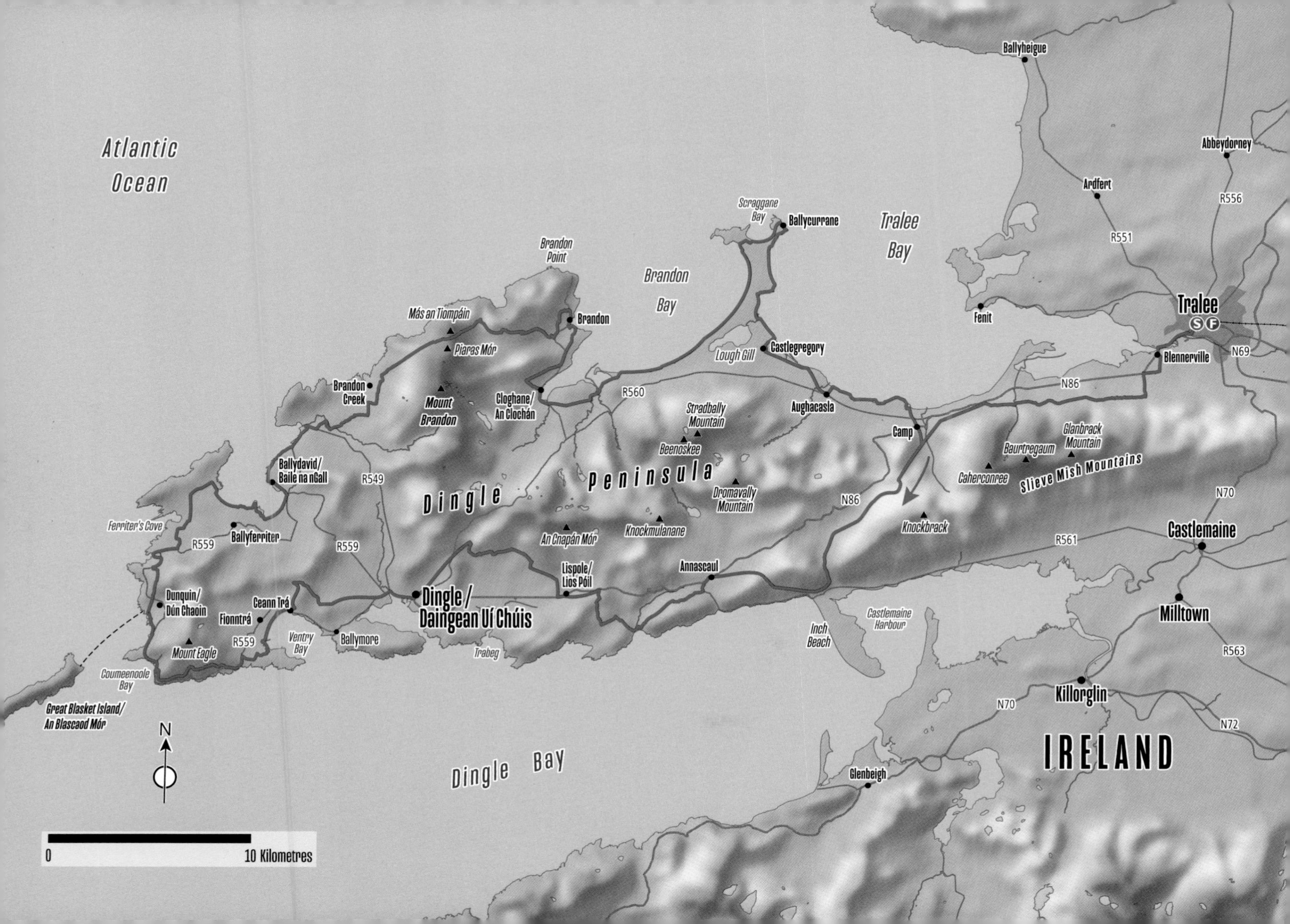
Atlantic Ocean
Tralee Bay
Brandon Bay
Dingle Bay
Dingle Peninsula
IRELAND
Tralee
Ballyheigue
Abbeydorney
Ardfert
Fenit
Blennerville
Castlemaine
Milltown
Killorglin
Glenbeigh
Slieve Mish Mountains
Glanbrack Mountain
Baurtregaum
Caherconree
Knockbrack
Camp
Aughacasla
Castlegregory
Lough Gill
Ballycurrane
Scraggane Bay
Brandon Point
Brandon
Más an Tiompáin
Piaras Mór
Mount Brandon
Brandon Creek
Cloghane/ An Clochán
Stradbally Mountain
Beenoskee
Dromavally Mountain
Knockmulanane
An Cnapán Mór
Lispole/ Lios Póil
Annascaul
Inch Beach
Castlemaine Harbour
Dingle / Daingean Uí Chúis
Trabeg
Ballymore
Ventry Bay
Ceann Trá
Fionntrá
Mount Eagle
Dunquin/ Dún Chaoin
Ballyferriter
Ballydavid/ Baile na nGall
Ferriter's Cove
Coumeenoole Bay
Great Blasket Island/ An Blascaod Mór
R556
R551
N69
N86
N70
R561
R563
N72
R560
R549
R559
N
0
10 Kilometres

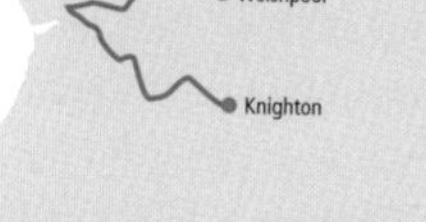

09 GLYNDŴR'S WAY – 217km

The 217-kilometre Glyndŵr's Way meanders through the Mid Wales county of Powys in a horseshoe shape. Named for Wales's legendary nationalist prince, the trail does not follow in his footsteps but travels from town to village, offering on its way pastures, moorland and forest. In the towns and villages on this route through Wales's green heart, you will encounter again and again the story and history of Owain Glyndŵr. Although the route never climbs mountains, it wanders up and down Powys's hills, each ascent offering fine views down lush valleys.

Glyndŵr's Way starts at the clock tower in Knighton and begins, as it continues, with a hill, climbing up the High Street, also known as The Narrows. Knighton, a market town since the thirteenth century, is on the English–Welsh border and is only the town on the line of Offa's Dyke. It is not long before the route escapes the town's roads and near Garth, joins a grassy path. You climb first Garth Hill, and then Bailey Hill, an early indication of the Way's fondness for ups and downs.

You take the Way through the sleepy village of Llangunllo and then up bracken-lined paths over the heathered Beacon Hill Moor and Stanky Hill. A broad track takes you down to Felindre. You follow grassy trods and farm tracks through pastures to climb to Castell-y-Blaidd, or the Castle of the Wolf, a horseshoe Norman ringwork on a hilltop.

You contour through moorland above the meanders of the River Ithon to reach Abbeycwmhir, named for its abbey. The twelfth-century Cistercian Cwmhir Abbey was once Wales's largest, although never completed; its abandonment probably linked to Glyndŵr's uprising. You can visit the ruins of the abbey, believed to be the burial place of Llywelyn ap Gruffydd, the last sovereign Prince of Wales. The village also has a traditional, family-run pub, the Happy Union, easily identified thanks to the unique pub sign depicting a man wearing a leek-bedecked hat, riding a goat.

You climb a wooded track over Y Glog and then face a short road section. This hilly section offers long views over valleys, easy walking on forestry tracks and some country roads. The next town en route is Llanidloes. A market town since the thirteenth century, its half-timbered Old Market Hall is the last such surviving building in Wales. Glyndŵr was not the only Welshman to rebel against injustice; in 1839, local flannel weavers seized control of Llanidloes for five days during a Chartist uprising, demanding the right to political representation via the ballot box.

The Way coincides briefly with the Severn Way as well as the Sarn Sabrina, a circular walk that celebrates Sabrina, the nymph associated with the river. Near the Clywedog dam, you pass the abandoned Bryntail lead mine – mining was an important local industry in the nineteenth century. The reservoir formed by damming Clywedog was controversial at the time of its construction because Welsh farmland was flooded to provide water to the English Midlands. Now Llyn Clywedog, whose shores you contour above, is a popular sailing spot. The Way turns on to tracks to pass through the edge of Hafren Forest.

◀ THE TRACK FROM GLASLYN, LOOKING TOWARDS THE SUMMIT OF FOEL FADIAN.
© JOHN & MAYA BIMSON

Following in the tracks of lead-laden horse carts, you reach the now-deserted mining town of Dylife. In its Victorian heyday 1,000 people lived here, but little remains today other than the seventeenth-century Star Inn. You leave Dylife, via a drovers' road, to Penycrobren, once the site of a Roman fort. In the early eighteenth century, Sion y Gof was executed for murder after the bodies of his family were discovered in a mineshaft. Penycrobren, or Gallows Hill, is reputedly to be the spot where he was hanged on a gibbet that, as local blacksmith, he had had to build himself.

The heathery moorland around the lake of Glaslyn is a nature reserve. You contour around the slate slopes of Foel Fadian, a perfect spot to see red kites. A hilly moorland section, with plenty of climbing, leads you to Machynlleth via the Roman Steps. The market town of Machynlleth was the seat of Glyndŵr's parliament in 1404; the site of the historic parliament is now occupied by the Owain Glyndŵr Centre, a museum that examines Glyndŵr's life. Machynlleth is the point on the Glyndŵr's Way's horseshoe where you turn back eastwards.

You walk through fields of sheep to reach Penegoes, and then climb to an up-and-down, brackened moorland section. The trail here through forests, farms and fields passes closes to towns and villages, but they require a detour. You pass through the large forest of Dyfnant to emerge by Lake Vrynwy, a reservoir built in the 1880s to supply Liverpool with water. The route is gently descending from the higher hills towards its conclusion. You follow the River Vyrnwy through forests towards Pontrobert. In a small copse, you pass the small, isolated Dolobran Friends Meeting House – still in use today, this was probably the first purpose-built Quaker's Meeting House in Wales. The Way takes a meandering route to its end through woods and by lakes.

There is one final climb up Broniarth Hill, with its Iron Age hill fort, but you can enjoy views of the green Vale of Meifod. Glyndŵr's Way ends by the Montgomery Canal in Welshpool – the canal was built to transport agricultural produce from the upper Severn Valley. A short detour from the Way's end, the red gritstone walls of the thirteenth-century Powis Castle survived the sacking of the town in Glyndŵr's rebellion.

Glyndŵr's Way, a National Trail, is waymarked not only with the white acorn but also with the golden dragon that flew on Glyndŵr's standard. Most tourists are drawn to Wales's mountains or coastline so you may well be lucky enough to have Powys's lush hills to yourself. This does however mean that the trail is not well-provided for with respect to accommodation and other tourist facilities. You may have to leave the trail to find the nearest bed and breakfast or shop. Although the Way is a horseshoe, it is reasonably straightforward to turn it into a circular route by following the Severn Way from Welshpool to Melverley and then the Offa's Dyke Path to Knighton. You can walk or run the Way at any time of year, although facilities will be even more limited outside summer months and you may encounter snow on the hilltops in winter.

Glyndŵr's Way is not restricted to following a river, a coastline or a wall. It is free to choose the greenest hills, quiet nature reserves, shady forests and undulating pastures. From Llywelyn to Glyndŵr, the Chartists and 'Rebeccas', Mid Wales has always had a rebellious streak, and Glyndŵr's Way is the perfect trail for those who want to stand out from the crowd and do something a little different.

THE VIEW FROM PENYCROCBREN, ACROSS DYLIFE, WITH THE PENNANT VALLEY IN THE DISTANCE. © JOHN & MAYA BIMSON

THE HEATHERY MOORLAND AROUND GLASLYN. © JOHN & MAYA BIMSON

09 GLYNDŴR'S WAY: ESSENTIAL INFORMATION

TRAIL ESSENTIALS

Start:	**Knighton, Powys, Wales**
End:	**Welshpool, Powys, Wales**
Distance:	**217km**
Ascent/descent:	**6,100m/6,190m**

HOW TO GET THERE

Knighton has a train station (which is actually just across the border in England) on the Heart of Wales Line. There are connections to Birmingham with its international airport, via Shrewsbury.

Welshpool is on the Cambrian Railway Line with direct connections to Birmingham, and its international airport.

TIME TO COMPLETE

Walking:	**12 days/72 hours**
Trekking:	**8 days/58 hours**
Fastpacking:	**6 days/45 hours**
Trail running:	**4 days/31 hours**

PROS

- **Quiet** – the Way is one of the least walked of England and Wales's National Trails. It has all the benefits of a National Trail – well-maintained paths, good waymarking, plenty of information – but you can often enjoy the green paths in solitude.

- **Rural** – you will pass through a rural, heavily agricultural landscape, particularly of upland sheep grazing, that is little changed in centuries.

CONS

- **Ups and downs** – for a route that offers no mountains to conquer, the Way has a lot of ascent and descent. Often you reach one valley to climb up yet another hill.

- **Accommodation** – bed and breakfasts and campsites are limited, and many will close over the winter months.

GOOD TO KNOW

Owain Glyndŵr was the last Welsh Prince of Wales (although Llywelyn ap Gruffydd was the last sovereign Prince). From 1400 to 1415 he led the Welsh revolt against English rule in Wales, ultimately unsuccessfully. The revolt had fizzled out by 1415, but no one knows what happened to Glyndŵr; legend says that, like Arthur, he will return in the nation's hour of need. Although now revered as a hero of nationalism, the rebellion began as a protest against injustices such as unfair taxation.

FURTHER INFORMATION

www.nationaltrail.co.uk/en_GB/trails/glyndwrs-way

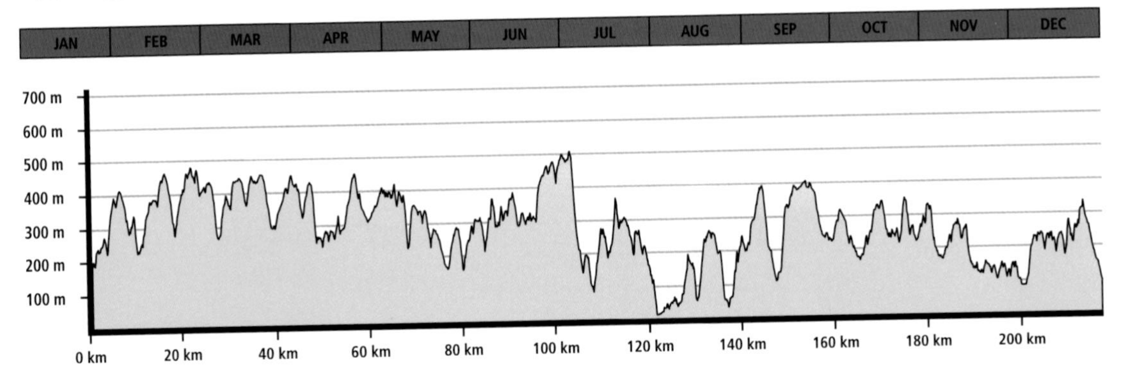

Llyn Tegid/
Llanuwchllyn
Snowdonia
National Park
Cyrniau Nod
Llangynog
Oswestry
A494
Aran Fawddwy
Lake Vyrnwy
Glasgwm
Llanwddyn
Abertridwr
Llanfyllin
A495
Dolgellau
Dinas Mawddwy
Dyfnant
Forest
Efyrnwy/
Vyrnwy
Arddleen
A483
Mallwyd
A458
Foel
Dolanog
Pontrobert
Meifod
Dyfi/
Dovey
A458
Welshpool
Llanfair Caereinion
Castle Caereinion
Glantwymyn
Nant yr Eira
Machynlleth
Commins Coch
Llanbrynmair
Penegoes
Manafon
Hafren/
Severn
A470
Pennant
Carno
Montgomery
Foel Fadian
Glaslyn
Dylife
Staylittle
Caersws
Newtown
Sarn
Ceri
A489
Nant-y-moch
Reservoir
Clywedog
Reservoir
Trefeglwys
Stepaside
Bishop's Castle
Y Fan
Dolfor
Plynlimon
Hafren/Severn
A470
Shropshire Hills
AONB
Llanidloes
A483
A44
Felindre
Clun
Cwmbelan
Llangurig
A470
ENGLAND
Llanbadarn Fynydd
Beacon Hill
Cambrian Mountains/
Elenydd
Teme
A488
A470
Pool Hill
Bwlch-y-Sarnau
Garn
A4113
Knighton
WALES
Abbeycwmhir
Llangunllo
A483
A488
Llanddewi Ystradenni
B4343
Rhayader
A44
Presteigne
Claerwen
Reservoir
N
Llandrindod
Kington
0
10 Kilometres
Builth Wells

HEBRIDEAN WAY

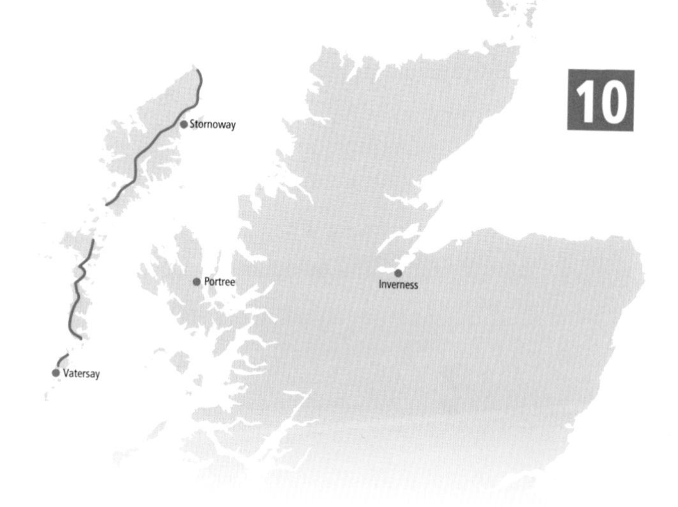

10 HEBRIDEAN WAY – 249km

The 249-kilometre Hebridean Way begins at the southernmost of the inhabited islands, Vatersay, curving over ten islands across peatland, beaches and gentle hills to reach Lewis. It sometimes follows quiet country roads or good tracks, but also takes waymarked, pathless routes across open moors. The long, golden coasts of the Hebrides are some of Scotland's most beautiful, and although the summits are low you will still enjoy spectacular views over the stunning islands. You follow in the footsteps of the people who walked these paths long before the roads existed to discover hidden histories and quiet countryside.

Although the route technically starts at Vatersay's community hall, you should first visit the beaches next to the hall. The Way crosses Vatersay on a singletrack road, taking a route that contours around the bumps in the landscape, to reach the causeway to Barra. After the causeway you leave the road behind to climb over the open moorland of Beinn Tangabhal – the hilltop offers spectacular views back over Vatersay. It is a short detour from the route to visit the promontory ruins of the Iron Age fort Dun Ban. You continue along the rocky coast to reach the hotel by the sandy beach at Halaman Bay, where you join the road briefly before turning on to a good track.

You emerge on to the road near Barra's airport, the world's only airport that uses a tidal beach as its airstrip. After your first ferry crossing, you do not spend long on the tiny island of Eriskay, where Bonnie Prince Charlie landed to begin his Jacobite uprising. The island is famous now for its association with Compton Mackenzie's novel *Whisky Galore* about a shipwrecked boat shedding its cargo; the writer lived on Barra in the 1930s. The Way follows off-road tracks along the western coast to reach the causeway to South Uist.

You follow the road to reach the southern end of Polochar beach, a strand that runs up South Uist's western shore for more than thirty kilometres. You take a grassy path through the machair, next to the golden sands. Near a tall aerial you pass the remains of the prehistoric Cladh Hàlainn roundhouses; four skeletons dating from around 1,000BC, the only known British prehistoric mummies, were discovered here during archaeological excavations in 2001. If the tide is out, you can walk along the beach. The route skirts the edge of the golf course. Where the route meets the road, you can detour to Kildonan, reputedly Flora MacDonald's birthplace, where there is a cafe.

You pass Rubha Aird a'Mhuile, South Uist's most westerly point, where evidence of Viking settlements has been uncovered. You continue on grassy tracks and good trails past the ruins of Caisteal Ormacleit. Next to the ruins of a thirteenth-century monastery you reach a traditional, thatched crofter's cottage, now Howmore Hostel, one of three Hebridean hostels run by the Gatliff Trust. The route follows good tracks, with the occasional road section, past Loch Druidibeag – you can see the ruins of Dun Raouill, a seventeenth-century fort, on an island in the loch. The route here has been much improved; although sometimes there is no clear path across the moor, boardwalk has been laid over tricky sections. You emerge on the road under the gaze of the granite Our Lady of the Isles statue.

◀ A SIGNPOST MARKING THE HEBRIDEAN WAY ON THE MOORLAND NEAR LOCH DRUIDIBEAG, SOUTH UIST. © KATHI KAMLEITNER – *WATCHMESEE.COM*

CRANNAG AND TRÀIGH MHÒR, BARRA. © ADAM LONG

The route skips the causeway across Loch Bi; built in the eighteenth century, it is the oldest causeway in the islands. Instead you take on a challenging route across blanket bog; the worst sections have been boardwalked or bridged. You rejoin the road to cross the South Ford causeway to reach Creagorry on Benbecula, a small village with a supermarket. You follow the western coast along sandy beaches and dunes before traversing to the island's east to climb Ruabhal. The summit of the small hill offers you stunning views across South and North Uist. You descend the boggy hillside across open countryside with no path to follow, to reach the North Ford causeway.

The causeway merely places a foot on Grimsay on its way to North Uist. The island is rich in prehistoric sites, and the Way follows good tracks across the peatlands and past lochs to reach a stone circle at Croanabhal and a chambered cairn at Langais.

Following the road from Lochmaddy, you turn on to a path to contour around Blathaisbhal. You pass a line of standing stones, Na Fir Bhreige, reputedly three faithless husbands from Skye turned to rock. A boggy trek back to the roads briefly follows, before tackling the water-laden, otter-rich shores of Bàgh Teileam – the worst sections are boardwalked. You climb to near the summit of the Beinn Mhòr or Big Hill, which tops out at 190 metres. After this you return to the road by Loch an Sticir. The ruins of Dun an Sticir, a seventeenth-century fortification built in the remains of an Iron Age fort, sit on an islet in the loch; if you want to risk wet feet, it is possible to teeter across the stepping-stone causeway to inspect it.

After crossing the causeway to Berneray you take the half-kilometre road trip to the ferry terminal. You arrive on Harris near the Clachan store, and take a road past Loch na Moracha. There follows a turf path through the glen and, after a brief road stretch, a challenging up-and-down route through heathery bog. From Seilebost, you follow the coffin road over the Bealach Eorobhat pass, originally used to carry coffins from the rocky east to the sandy west. The Scholar's Path, a good path once used by schoolchildren, is followed past crystal-clear lochs to reach Greosabhagh. The route generally follows the road north along Harris's west coast, occasionally cutting the corner on a firm path or track, to reach Tarbert.

ABOVE: THE PRINCE'S BEACH ON ERISKAY WHERE BONNIE PRINCE CHARLIE FIRST SET FOOT ON SCOTTISH SOIL. © KATHI KAMLEITNER – *WATCHMESEE.COM*
BELOW: THE CAUSEWAY BETWEEN BERNERAY AND NORTH UIST. © *WALKHIGHLANDS.CO.UK*

You take a pleasant path that gently climbs past Lochannan Lacasdail and then rejoin the road. A grassy, often muddy, path takes you over the pass between Gormul Màraig and Cleit Ard to reach the Scaladale outdoor activity centre, where you cross to Lewis. A rare forest, planted in the 1970s, is passed before you climb up the small Griamacleit to enjoy more views and descend to the old road, running parallel to the modern road. You follow a good, sometimes turf, path across soggy moorland and up the shores of Loch Stranndabhat to reach the long village of Baile Ailein.

You follow the main road, sometimes on a parallel track, for five kilometres to Laxey. You face a tough, and sometimes pathless, section over the undulating Lewis peatlands. After reaching the road at Acha Mòr, Lewis's only inland village, you follow a track towards Stornoway. The route passes the ruins of shielings, summer shelters for shepherds. While the Way officially concludes at Lews Castle in Stornoway, most continue up the coast, picking up the Heritage Trail to reach Lewis's most northerly point, the Butt of Lewis.

Although the Way may be tackled in either direction, the blustery wind is likely to be against you should you attempt to travel north to south. While you are never safe from storms and high winds, these are particularly frequent in winter and spring. With little public transport and limited accommodation, it is challenging, although possible with advance planning, to complete the Hebridean Way between October and March unless you are prepared to wild camp. The Hebridean Way is not the easiest trail to complete, but it offers a unique opportunity to explore these beautiful, remote islands.

10 HEBRIDEAN WAY: ESSENTIAL INFORMATION

TRAIL ESSENTIALS

Start: **Vatersay, Scotland**
End: **Stornoway, Isle of Lewis, Scotland**
Distance: **249km**
Ascent/descent: **2,750m/2,730m**

HOW TO GET THERE

To reach **Vatersay** there are flights from the Scottish mainland to Barra (which land on the beach) and a ferry service from Oban, which has a train station. Vatersay is approximately twenty kilometres from the ferry port. If you are planning to take a car on to the islands, you must book your ferry crossings in advance.

Stornoway offers ferry connections to Ullapool. There are bus and coach services to Inverness, which has a train station.

TIME TO COMPLETE

Walking: **10 days/62 hours**
Trekking: **7 days/52 hours**
Fastpacking: **5 days/38 hours**
Trail running: **4 days/29 hours**

PROS

- **Machair** – the grassy plains of the machair, found by the beaches, are a unique environment. The fertile ground is rich in flowers, such as the sea bindweed, harebell, gentian and orchids. The flowers in turn attract bumblebees, butterflies and birds.

- **Sandy beaches** – from the wide curves of Harris's Luskentyre to the solitude of Berneray's long West Beach to the flower-bedecked Halaman Bay on Barra, the Outer Hebrides offers some of the sandiest, and quietest, beaches in Great Britain.

- **Seafood** – the Outer Hebrides are famous for their seafood, particularly shellfish – which is still landed and processed on the islands. You can enjoy langoustines, lobsters, scallops, crabs and mussels. You can also try peat-smoked salmon from North Uist's Hebridean Smokehouse.

CONS

- **Bad weather** – the islands are susceptible to violent storms and strong winds, blowing in from the Atlantic with little warning at any time of year. This not only makes the exposed paths dangerous and causeway crossings impossible but may leave you stranded on the islands if the seas are too rough for ferries.

- **Accommodation** – bed and breakfast accommodation is limited on the islands, and books up quickly in the summer.

- **Detours** – facilities – such as shops, cafes and accommodation – are extremely limited on the islands, and you may have to add a few kilometres on to your daily distance to reach them.

GOOD TO KNOW

South Uist's Askernish golf course was designed by Tom Morris in 1891, who had also created world-renowned courses at Muirfield, Prestwick and Carnoustie. The course was lost in the 1920s, buried under grazing and the dunes, until Gordon Irvine visited on holiday in 2005 and recognised the outline of the old course, sparking a restoration. Another unexpected disappearance happened on Benbecula in 1980; trained bear Hercules disappeared during the filming of a Kleenex advert. He was safely rescued, a lot thinner, after being spotted swimming in the sea by a crofter three weeks later.

FURTHER INFORMATION

www.visitouterhebrides.co.uk/hebrideanway/walking

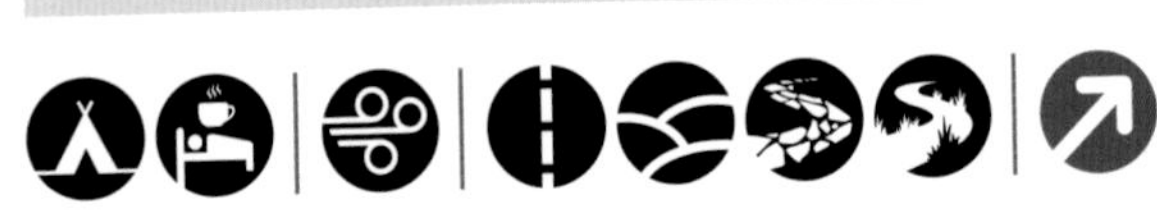

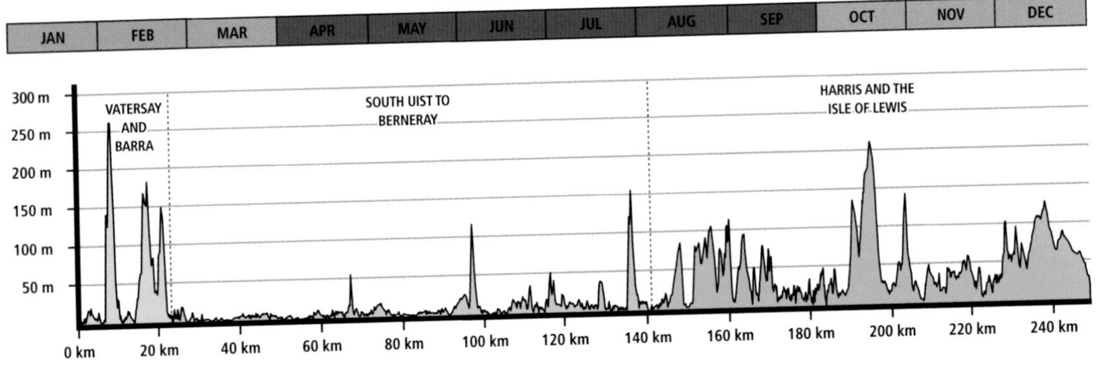

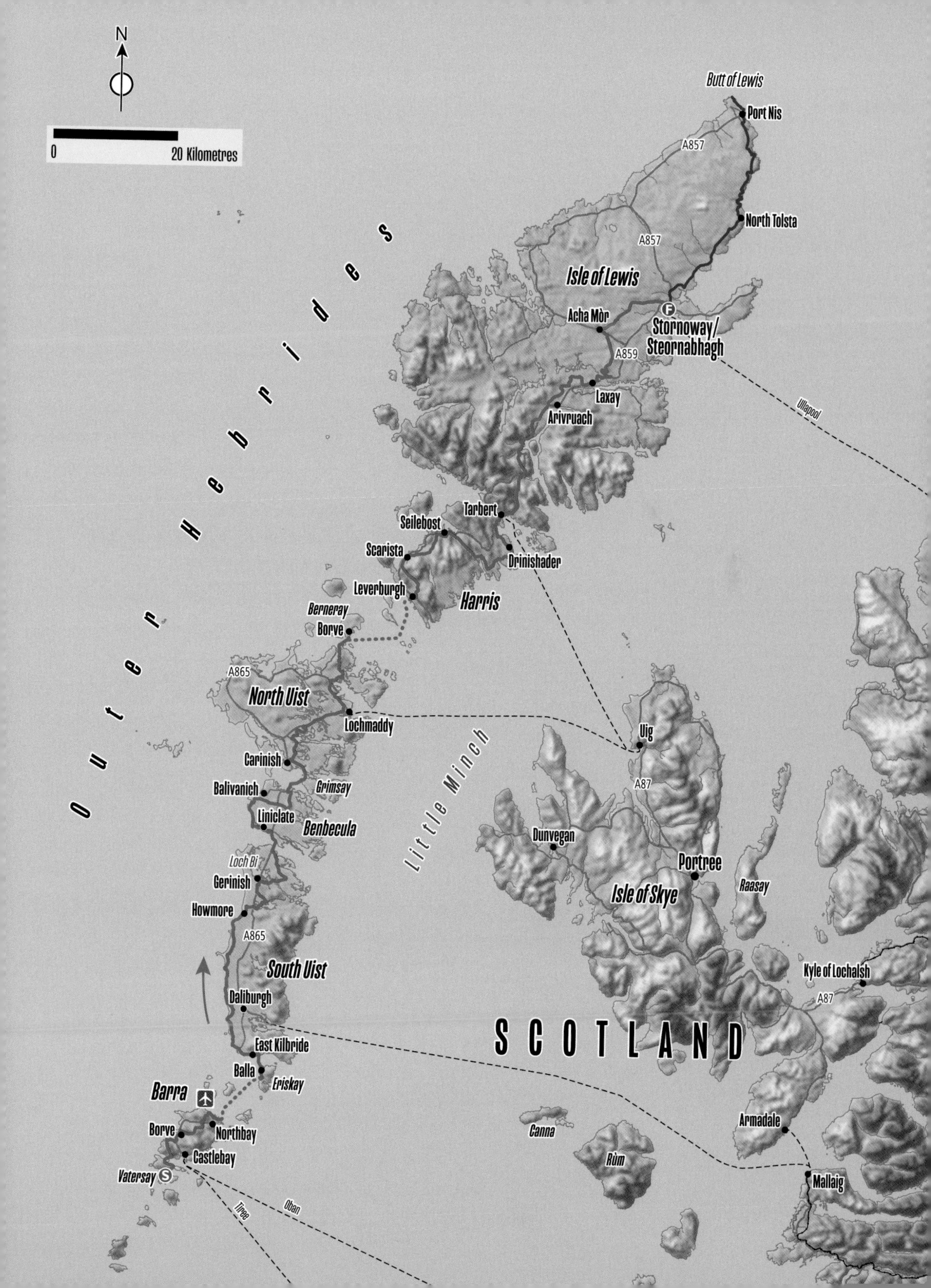

N
0
20 Kilometres
Outer Hebrides
Butt of Lewis
Port Nis
A857
North Tolsta
A857
Isle of Lewis
Acha Mòr
Stornoway/
Steornabhagh
A859
Laxay
Arivruach
Ullapool
Tarbert
Seilebost
Scarista
Drinishader
Leverburgh
Harris
Berneray
Borve
A865
North Uist
Lochmaddy
Uig
Little Minch
Carinish
Balivanich
Grimsay
Liniclate
Benbecula
A87
Dunvegan
Loch Bi
Gerinish
Portree
Isle of Skye
Raasay
Howmore
A865
South Uist
Kyle of Lochalsh
Daliburgh
A87
SCOTLAND
East Kilbride
Balla
Eriskay
Barra
Borve
Northbay
Castlebay
Vatersay
Canna
Rùm
Armadale
Mallaig
Tiree
Oban

11

11 ISLE OF WIGHT COASTAL PATH – 113km

SOUTHAMPTON
Lymington
PORTSMOUTH

Just one and a half kilometres from Southern England, the Isle of Wight is a runner's and walker's delight, offering an incredible diversity of landscape in just 380 kilometres square. The 113-kilometre Isle of Wight Coastal Path encircles the island, beginning in the popular sailing town of Cowes and passing beaches, grassy downs, crumbling cliffs and island beauty spots. Although the coastal path is a well-established route, it is likely to see some alterations to create an improved trail for the England's Coast Path project; these should be well waymarked.

The Isle of Wight has always been a maritime island – it was a popular entrepôt for goods (and people) travelling between Europe and America – and Cowes still bustles with boats. As you leave Cowes, you will pass the popular Island Sailing Club and possibly the world's most exclusive sailing club, the Royal Yacht Squadron, who use Henry VIII's defence fort, Cowes Castle, for their clubhouse. The Path leaves the road behind near Thorness Bay but this section of the route is subject to frequent erosion, resulting in diversions.

After a stroll along the sandy beach, you turn through the holiday park at Thorness Bay to head inland towards quiet Newtown, one of the island's oldest settlements. Newtown was once an important harbour but the silting of the natural bay barred larger vessels. You take a shady path to follow the River Newtown back towards the coast at Hamstead Lodge. The trail meanders through Bouldnor Forest, a nature reserve, before reaching Bouldnor cliff – the remains of a Mesolithic village were discovered submerged off the coast here in 1999, when a diver observed a lobster clearing its seabed burrow of worked flint.

After Yarmouth – where car ferry passengers arrive on the island – you follow a Military Road to the forts Victoria and Albert, built to defend against a nineteenth-century French attack that never happened. Fort Victoria is now a country park, with a reptilarium and planetarium. Headon Warren offers one of your last opportunities of a view across the Solent towards the mainland, and you can see Henry VIII's Hurst Castle built on a shingle spit stretching into the sea. The Path takes you past one of three Bronze Age barrows on the warren.

At the Isle's westerly corner, you reach the old mining area of Alum Bay, now more famous for its striped sands in twenty-one different hues – the sands owe their spectrum of colours to different levels of oxidised iron compounds. At the end of Alum Bay, you reach the Needles, the Isle of Wight's iconic chalk stacks, and the lighthouse at the end of them. As you turn on to the south-west coast, you are taking a high grassy path in the footsteps of Tennyson on the trail named for him – the Poet Laureate decided to buy a family home here in the 1850s, and a monument has now been erected to him on the Tennyson Down.

You'll also pass the home of his neighbour, Julia Margaret Cameron, who bought her home, Dimbola, after visiting Tennyson and turned the ramshackle chicken coop into a photography studio, later becoming one of Victorian England's most important portrait photographers.

◀ DESCENDING TENNYSON DOWN TOWARDS FRESHWATER BAY.
© MARK RAINSLEY

THE JAGGED CHALK STACKS OF THE NEEDLES AND THEIR LIGHTHOUSE. © JASON MCDONALD

On the south of the island, the Path favours the clifftops and green downs, which provide you with panoramic views. The clay cliffs have often been eroded by rivers, creating steep-sided chines, or gorges, that must be either be climbed through or walked around.

After the quiet, gorsey cliff paths, you may be surprised to encounter a giant pirate at the entrance to Blackgang Chine, the UK's oldest amusement park. It was opened by the Dabell family, who still own it, in the 1840s – Queen Victoria visited in 1853 to delight in the skeleton of a beached whale, one of their first attractions. Past the park's entrance, the Path turns towards St Catherine's Lighthouse and again follows grassy paths on the clifftop. You descend to the seaside village of St Lawrence before facing another climb towards the aptly named Steephill Cove.

The Path follows the sea wall through Ventnor, the popular Victorian resort that gained the name 'the English Mediterranean', but quickly climbs again to visit the Bonchurch landslip. The landslip is a rocky, woody gorge in the cliff that owes its appearance to landslides in the early nineteenth century. You can choose to make a small detour to the Devil's Chimney, if only for the tearooms, where you can make a stepped descent through a deep, dark rock cleft. Back on the Path, you should hope for sunshine if you sit on the mossy boulder of the Wishing Seat. You descend into Shanklin via the Appley Steps.

The Path from Shanklin follows the clifftop promenade but at low tide you can also walk along the beach to Sandown. You pass the Isle of Wight Zoo to begin another climb towards the island's south-eastern headland of Culver Down where the Earl of Yarborough monument stands. This granite obelisk was erected in 1849 by public subscription in memory of Charles Anderson-Pelham, founder of the Royal Yacht Squadron. It originally stood at a higher point nearly a kilometre further west, but had to be moved stone by stone in the 1860s to make way for the Bembridge Fort.

Verdant clifftop paths gradually descend towards Bembridge, famous for its harbourside houseboats. You follow the line of the sea wall at the top of pebbly beaches to reach Ryde, and stroll along the town's long esplanade, past the pier and above expansive sandy beaches. You leave Ryde on

NEWTOWN NATIONAL NATURE RESERVE, A CRISP DAWN OVER THE ESTUARIES OF NEWTOWN. © TOM WHEATLEY

the shady, wooded Ladies Walk as it cuts through the golf course. On a quiet cycle track, you pass the stunning Belgium red-brick Quarr Abbey. Rebuilt in 1912, the abbey hosts a working Benedictine monastery, founded by French monks exiled from Solesmes – and a tearoom.

Near the pretty village of Wootton, you pass the site of the 1969 Isle of Wight Festival, headlined by Bob Dylan – the modern festival takes place at Newport. Between Wotton and Cowes, the Path is forced to follow a road route inland to circumvent the Osborne estate. Queen Victoria, who adored the Isle of Wight, built Osborne House in the style of an Italian palazzo in 1845, and died there in January 1901. The house, gardens and private bathing beach are now open to the public. You must take the Floating Bridge chain ferry to reach Cowes from East Cowes.

The Victorians loved the Isle of Wight, and its charms are still evident. The Isle of Wight enjoys a milder climate than most of the United Kingdom, making it the ideal destination for winter as well as summer walking. The Isle of Wight Coastal Path enables you to enjoy an ice cream in the charming seaside resorts, explore the wooded clefts of the southern coast, pass monasteries and royal houses, and marvel at multicoloured cliffs. Although the island is small, the Path leads you to the quietest parts of the isle's coast and the scenery changes each time you turn a corner.

11 ISLE OF WIGHT COASTAL PATH: ESSENTIAL INFORMATION

TRAIL ESSENTIALS

Start:	**Cowes, Isle of Wight, England**
End:	**Cowes, Isle of Wight, England**
Distance:	**113km**
Ascent/descent:	**1,290m/1,290m**

HOW TO GET THERE

Cowes is served by ferries from Southampton; ferries also serve the Isle of Wight from Portsmouth, Southsea and Lymington, arriving at Fishbourne, Ryde and Yarmouth. The closest international airports are London Gatwick and Heathrow; all the mainland ferry ports are on the English rail network.

TIME TO COMPLETE

Walking:	**5 days/29 hours**
Trekking:	**3 days/24 hours**
Fastpacking:	**3 days/18 hours**
Trail running:	**2 days/14 hours**

PROS

- **Coastal views** – from dramatic cliffs to views along England's southern coast and the iconic sea stacks, the Needles, the Isle of Wight offers an incredible variation of dramatic coastal views in a little over 100 kilometres of coastal walking.

- **Chines** – the deep-sided gorges, eroded by rivers into the Isle of Wight's southern coast, are a unique island feature. Once associated with smugglers, they are not only a haven for wildlife but also offer a window into the geology of the island, and as they crumble they reveal dinosaur fossils.

- **Seaside resorts** – the Isle of Wight's southern seaside resorts – Sandown, Shanklin and Ventnor – are perfect for swimming, and retain their Victorian charms. Ryde boasts a seafront esplanade walk, and the world's oldest amusement pier.

CONS

- **Road sections** – although the Path generally avoids the roads, the concluding section from Ryde to Cowes is almost entirely on the road. While this may make for an easy finish for runners or fastpackers, trekkers or walkers may spend all or most of their last day by a road. Road sections are likely to be reduced or removed when England's Coast Path is completed on the island.

- **Erosion** – the dramatic coastal scenery of the Isle of Wight owes much of its charm to erosion but that also means coastal paths may become impassable. Natural England's plans for England's Coast Path on the island includes provision for rolling back paths in the event of erosion.

- **Events** – the Isle of Wight is a popular destination for events, particularly in summer. You may find it difficult to book ferries or accommodation during the Walking Festival, Cowes Week, the Round the Island Race and the Isle of Wight Festival.

GOOD TO KNOW

One of the UK's biggest walking festivals, the Isle of Wight Walking Festival, takes place over two weeks in May every year. The Festival offers you the opportunity to brush up on skills, learn more about the island's history and legends, and discover local wildlife. The festival opens with the Isle of Wight Challenge, an ultra that challenges participants to run (almost) the entire coastal path in twenty-four hours; another highlight is Walk the Wight, crossing the island from Bembridge to Alum.

FURTHER INFORMATION

www.visitisleofwight.co.uk/things-to-do/walking/coastal-path

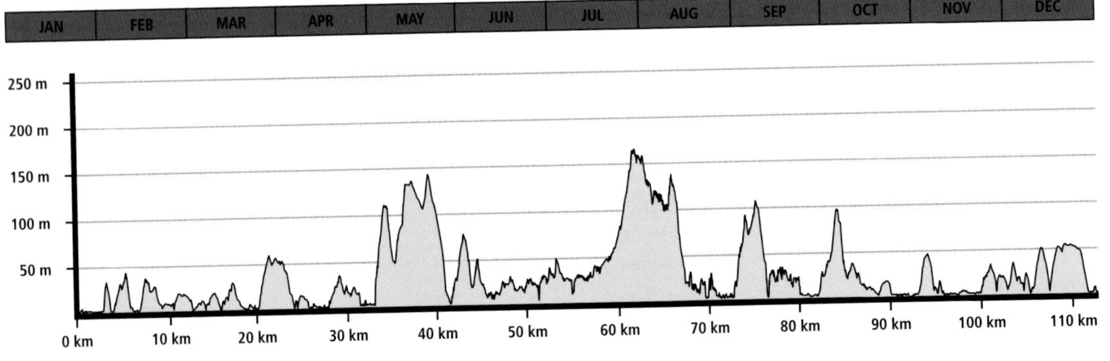

ENGLAND
The Solent
English Channel
Isle of Wight
Lymington
A337
Milford on Sea
Keyhaven
Gosport
A32
Portsmouth
Southampton
Cowes Roads
Gurnard Bay
Cowes
East Cowes
Gurnard
Osborne Bay
Thorness Bay
Northwood
Whippingham
Ryde Roads
Fishbourne
A3021
A3020
Medina
A3054
Binstead
Ryde
Wootton
Seaview
Newtown
Porchfield
Bouldnor
A3055
Fort Albert
Norton
Yarmouth
Ningwood
Shalfleet
Newport
St Helens
Colwell Bay
Carisbrooke
Bembridge
Totland
Freshwater
Newbridge
B3401
Brading
Totland Bay
The Run
Tennyson Monument
Easton
B3399
Blackwater
Yaverland
Whitecliff Bay
Alum Bay
Brighstone Forest
Freshwater Bay
Culver Down
A3056
The Needles
Compton Bay
Brook
Sandown
Brighstone
Shorwell
Sandown Bay
Godshill
Shanklin
St Martin's Down
Brighstone Bay
Chale Green
Wroxall
Luccombe
Stenbury Down
Atherfield Point
Chale
St Catherine's Down
Whitwell
Chale Bay
Niton
Ventnor
St Lawrence
St Catherine's Point
N
0
5 Kilometres

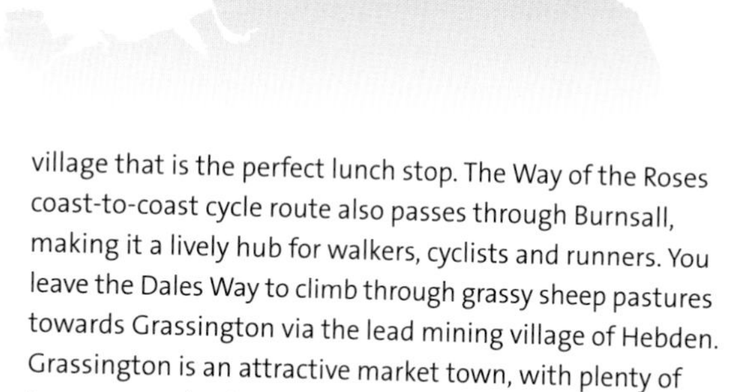

12 LADY ANNE'S WAY – 154km

In the seventeenth century, when men very much held the reins of power, the intelligent and independently minded Lady Anne Clifford forged her own path. The 154-kilometre Lady Anne's Way leads from her birthplace in Skipton across the grassy Yorkshire Dales and through the quiet beauty of the Eden valley, to her final resting place in Appleby-in-Westmorland and on to Cumbria's former capital, Penrith. The Way traces a green track between the castles, houses and churches that she restored, across the expansive northern Clifford estates. Although Lady Anne's Way sometimes traverses the wild, rugged moorlands of the Yorkshire Dales, it is not a route for the peak baggers or wilderness junkies. It is instead a route that celebrates paths long trodden between communities, that reveals the rich histories and outstanding beauty of Northern England.

Lady Anne's Way starts in the market town of Skipton, at one of the best-preserved medieval castles in England, in parts thanks to Anne's restoration after the Civil War. The route climbs out of Skipton, around the golf course, to contour on the gentler slopes of the Dales, past Embsay and Eastby. You may glimpse the steam trains on the heritage railway, puffing towards Bolton Abbey. On the heathered open access moorland of Barden Fell, dogs are only permitted on lead and on public rights of way. Barden Tower, damaged during the Civil War, is the next of Lady Anne's restorations en route.

The trail joins the Dales Way to meander along the pleasant banks of the Wharfe to Burnsall, a pretty Dales village that is the perfect lunch stop. The Way of the Roses coast-to-coast cycle route also passes through Burnsall, making it a lively hub for walkers, cyclists and runners. You leave the Dales Way to climb through grassy sheep pastures towards Grassington via the lead mining village of Hebden. Grassington is an attractive market town, with plenty of tearooms and pubs, and a lively calendar of weekend events in its cobbled main square.

Lady Anne's Way once again takes a high route, over the mine-strewn Grassington and Conistone moors. You follow the Conistone turf road down to Kettlewell, with its hostel which also serves as the village's post office and second-hand bookshop. At Starbotton, you briefly rejoin the Dales Way before leaving the River Wharfe and Dales Way to take a lofty moorland route. You are in the heart of literary vet James Herriot country; Grassington and Askrigg have both represented Darrowby in television adaptations. The route into Askrigg takes you over the flanks of Addlebrough, and past the granite Devil's Stone, said to bear the indents of the Devil's fingers.

You are now in Wensleydale, home to the eponymous cheese. Following a wooded trail above the valley floor you reach the market town of Hawes, where the cheese is made. You might find time to visit the Dales Countryside Museum, the legacy of three remarkable women – Marie Hartley, Ella Pontefract and Joan Ingilby – who devoted their lives to recording the everyday lives of Dales folk, and collecting rural artefacts.

◄ THE VIEW EAST DOWN WENSLEYDALE FROM HAWES.
© JOHN COEFIELD

The Way leads you through the town, passing the youth hostel at the western end of Hawes, and through Wensleydale's verdant pastures. After the overgrown Appersett viaduct, once part of the Wensleydale Railway, you climb to join Lady Anne's Highway, an ancient green road with fine views forward towards the Cumbrian fells. At Hell Gill Bridge, where you cross from Yorkshire to Cumbria, you may choose to make a small diversion to enjoy the pretty Hellgill Force. High on the Way, the Watercut stone sculpture makes a river of the blue sky in tribute to the River Eden in the valley below.

Pendragon Castle, purportedly built by Uther, father of King Arthur, was another of Anne's restoration projects and one of her favourites. The now ruined castle stands on a bend in the river, under the shadow of Wild Boar Fell. You follow the Eden on a low, easy route into Kirkby Stephen, a market town that is popular with walkers and is the base for a Mountain Rescue team.

The Eden valley is lush farming country, and you take dew-strewn grassy tracks through fields of sheep and cows. You may be glad to see the crumbling walls of Brough Castle in front of you, as there is an ice cream parlour and tearoom next to the ruins. This Norman castle, built on the site of the Roman fort of Verteris, is one of the oldest on the Way; the Cliffords celebrated Christmas at the castle in 1521 with a great feast, but unfortunately the festive season culminated in a great fire that left nothing but the castle walls intact.

You enter Appleby by the town's castle, having followed nettle-lined paths along the River Eden's banks. The castle is now a privately owned hotel, although you can enjoy afternoon tea or meal in the fifteenth-century dining room should you want to enjoy a little of Lady Anne's lifestyle. Appleby is the one of the best preserved of Lady Anne's castles and you can also book a tour of the castle and grounds.

THE RIVER WHARFE NEAR BARDEN. © JAK RADICE

From Appleby to Penrith, you follow more muddy footpaths through fields, occasionally rejoining the River Eden before finally parting from it as you cross the red sandstone Ousenstand Bridge. The medieval Brougham Hall, once host to Victorian aristocracy and King Edward VII – who, in 1905, visited in a plum-coloured Mercedes – was almost demolished to make way for housing. Winston Churchill commandeered the Hall during World War II to develop a top-secret tank; now, in more peaceful times, it is home to artist studios and a tearoom. You pass another of Anne's castles, Brougham Castle, although you will have to make a small diversion from the route to see the Countess Pillar, a monument constructed by Anne to commemorate her last meeting with her mother. A road-heavy route leads you to the Market Square in Penrith where the Way ends.

Lady Anne travelled frequently between these castles, with a large retinue to carry her luggage; you might choose to use one of the many baggage courier services in the area instead. Lady Anne's Way meanders along riverside paths and farm fields, and contours around the highest fells rather than crossing them. It is a trail that links small villages, seemingly untouched by modernity, and dramatic ruins. There is perhaps no other trail in Britain that packs so much historical punch in such a short distance.

SEDBUSK HIGH PASTURE ABOVE SEDBUSK IN WENSLEYDALE. © JOHN COEFIELD

12 LADY ANNE'S WAY: ESSENTIAL INFORMATION

TRAIL ESSENTIALS

Start:	**Skipton, West Yorkshire, England**
End:	**Penrith, Cumbria, England**
Distance:	**154km**
Ascent/descent:	**2,020m/2,010m**

HOW TO GET THERE

Skipton offers rail connections to Leeds and Bradford, where mainline connections can be made. The closest international airports are Leeds Bradford and Manchester.

Penrith is on the West Coast Main Line, offering direct rail connections to Manchester, with its international airport.

TIME TO COMPLETE

Walking:	**7 days/40 hours**
Trekking:	**5 days/33 hours**
Fastpacking:	**4 days/25 hours**
Trail running:	**3 days/19 hours**

PROS

- **Castles** – the route passes Skipton, Brough, Brougham, Pendragon and Appleby castles, and Penrith Castle, opposite the railway station, is an easy detour.

- **Red squirrels** – Cumbria is one of the last refuges of the native red squirrel, and you may be lucky enough to glimpse one.

- **James Herriot** – the Way leads you through the heart of Herriot country, the landscape and farms so affectionately described in James Herriot's amusing books about being a vet in the Yorkshire Dales.

CONS

- **Cumbria** – some will tell you that this is a trail of two halves – a pleasant meander through the Yorkshire Dales, and a tedious trudge through Cumbria's muddy fields and along oft-flooded riverbanks from Kirkby Stephen onwards. To forego the Cumbrian section, however, is to miss some of the finest ruins and pleasant market towns.

- **Cows** – the trail rarely leaves farmland, and you are likely to encounter a lot of cattle on the route.

- **Flooding** – both the Eden and Eamont rivers have experienced serious flooding in recent years. Even if the rivers are not currently in spate, footpaths in the Cumbrian section may still be difficult to navigate due to flood damage.

GOOD TO KNOW

Lady Anne Clifford, born in 1590, is best remembered for her restoration of castles at Skipton, Pendragon, Brough, Appleby and Brougham as well as churches and the establishing of hospitals and almshouses. However, she did not begin on her career as landholder until she was nearly sixty. For forty years, she pursued legal cases against her uncle and cousin, believing that her father had disinherited her in their favour against entail law, proceedings that she refused to abandon despite the opposition of her husbands and King James I. She eventually inherited the estates when her cousin died childless, and began her programme of restoration. When she died, aged eighty-six, she was probably the wealthiest noblewoman in England and she left behind extensive diaries as well as her *Great Books*, recording Clifford family history.

FURTHER INFORMATION

www.ladyannesway.co.uk; *Lady Anne's Way* (Skyware Press, 2019).

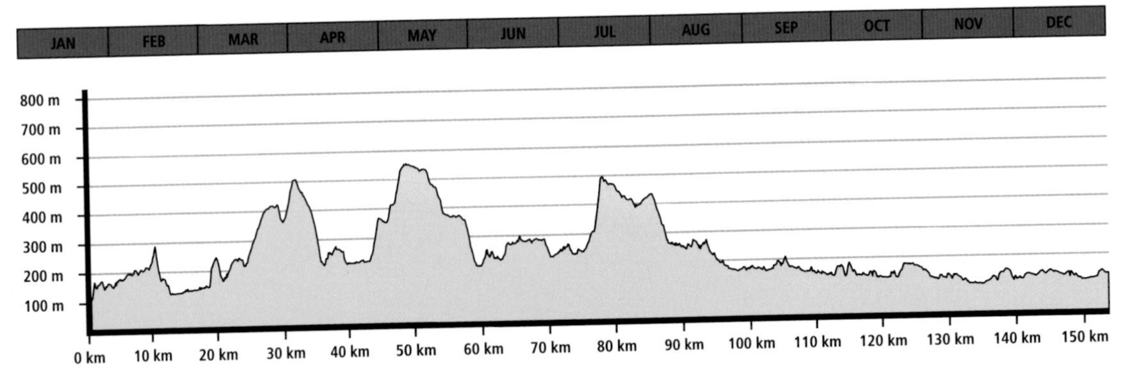

Penrith
Brougham Castle
Brougham Hall
Ousenstand Bridge
Kirkby Thore
Cliburn
Long Marton
Cross Fell
Great Dun Fell
Knock Fell
Herdship Fell
Cow Green Reservoir
Dora's Seat
Dufton Fell
Mickle Fell
Appleby-in-Westmorland
Appleby Castle
Great Ormside
Warcop
Brough
Church Brough
Brough Castle
Kaber
Eden
Barnard Castle
The Pennines
ENGLAND
Lake District National Park
Kirkby Stephen
Nine Standards Rigg
Nateby
Newbiggin-on-Lune
Pendragon Castle
Shoregill
Yorkshire Dales National Park
Howgill Fells
The Calf
Wild Boar Fell
Hugh Seat
Great Shunner Fell
Swale
Kendal
Sedbergh
Knoutberry Haw
Wensleydale
Sedbusk
Askrigg
Nappa Hall
Redmire
Leyburn
Appersett
Hawes
Bainbridge
Ure
Aysgarth
Middleham
Lune
Dodd Fell Hill
Middle Tongue
Whernside
Kirkby Lonsdale
Cray
Buckden Pike
Buckden
Ribble
Starbotton
Great Whernside
Pen-y-ghent
Ingleton
Ingleborough
Kettlewell
Horton in Ribblesdale
Fountains Fell
Wharfedale
Wharfe
recambe
Lancaster
Settle
Grassington
Threshfield
Hebden
Burnsall
Forest of Bowland
Barden Tower
Hellifield
Eastby
Halton East
Embsay
Skipton Castle
Skipton
Ilkley
Barnoldswick
N
0
10 Kilometres
M6
A686
A66
B6276
B6260
A685
A6
A683
B6270
A591
A684
B6255
B6160
A65
B6265
A59

13 LLŶN COASTAL PATH – 158km

The Llŷn peninsula is a finger on the North Wales Coast, pointing out towards Ireland, and the 158-kilometre Coastal Path winds around the fingertip. Sometimes on clifftop paths, sometimes on roads, often on beaches, you will discover some of Wales's quietest, most remote coastal scenery and enjoy views over the Snowdonia mountains and along the Welsh coast. You will pass castles and churches, places of pilgrimage and poets' houses, and discover small, traditional villages.

The Llŷn Coastal Path starts in Caernarfon, across the Menai Strait from Anglesey. Caernarfon was the site of a Roman fort, but the current castle dates from Edward I's conquest of Llywelyn's Gwynedd. You can start the trail at the harbour swing bridge or Caernarfon Castle, where Charles was invested as the Prince of Wales in 1969.

You leave Caernarfon on a quiet road, passing above shingle beaches. Near Llanfaglan, you pass the thirteenth-century church of St Baglan's, stood alone in a cornfield. The salt marshes at the Y Foryd sea inlet attract waders and wildfowl. You follow the sea wall into and through Dinas Dinlle. The Path continues along the road and, on one of the weakest links of the Wales Coast Path, follows the busy A499 main road for several kilometres. There is the backdrop of the mountains of Bwlch Mawr, Gyrn Goch, Gyrn Ddu and Moel-Pen-llechog to distract from the tarmac.

Trefor owes its existence to its quarry, which is rarely operational now, although only granite from here and Ailsa Craig in Scotland is used to produce curling stones for the Winter Olympics and other international competitions.

You leave the village on the quarry road and climb, on a track, to a saddle under the pine-green mountain of Yr Eifl. With the busy road far behind, you are now rewarded with stunning views of the stern mountains, tall cliffs and sparkling sea as you follow a brackened track along the coast.

You descend into Nant Gwrtheyrn. Once a bustling quarry village, it was abandoned in the 1950s as the quarries ceased production. The vision of one man, local GP Dr Carl Clowes, saw it transformed from dereliction into the National Welsh Language and Heritage Centre. It is also now host to a cafe that overlooks the sea.

A grassy, bouldered track leads you up the slopes of Porth y Nant. You contour around the mountains to reach the tiny village of Pistyll with its white chapel. Good tracks carved into the site of the mountains by quarrymen lead to Nefyn, a popular tourist destination because of its long, sandy beach. The Path joins the gorse-lined road out of the village, but many choose instead to walk on the golden beach to reach the tiny fishing village of Porth Dinllaen, now managed by the National Trust. With glorious sea views, there is a traditional pub, the Ty Coch Inn, at the top of the beach here.

A stony track leads you along the shoreline before, by the lifeboat station, you climb to follow the path through the golf course that occupies the Porth Dinllaen peninsula. When you finally leave the manicured greens, you take a grassy path that gently undulates over the clifftops.

◀ THE VIEW EAST FROM MYNYDD RHIW, ACROSS PORTH NEIGWL TO DISTANT SNOWDONIA. © ADAM LONG

SAND DUNES AT PORTH TOCYN JUST SOUTH OF ABERSOCH. © ADAM LONG

Near Tudweiliog caravans and campsites are encountered and the Path, now a narrow, muddy track on the edge of crumbling cliffs, becomes more challenging. This is an isolated stretch of coast, with only the occasional cottage.

At Porthor, the sands whistle; the unique shape of the sand granules mean that they squeak if you stamp or slide on dry sand. You follow a good track across gorsey moorland, with great views of the bumpy coast – be sure to look backwards too. The Path becomes more rugged as you reach the tip of the peninsula. Across the tidal races, you can see the peaks of Ynys Enlli, or Bardsey Island. This was a place of refuge, and burial, for early Christians; the island now has a population of eleven, only four of whom live there all year around. The path takes you down steep steps to the little harbour of Porth Meudwy where you can catch a boat to the island. Otherwise you must climb to the clifftop again to reach the fishing village of Aberdaron, the Land's End of North Wales – boats also sail to Bardsey from here. Welsh poet R.S. Thomas was vicar here, at St Hywyn's Church, from 1967 to 1978.

After Aberdaron, new routes have been negotiated with landowners so that the paths now hug the coast. Just past Rhiw, you pass Sarn-y-Plas, the tiny cottage overlooking the long beach of Porth Neigwl, where R.S. Thomas retired to with his wife. The path no longer traverses Porth Neigwl, or Hell's Mouth, as landslides have damaged the route down the cliff (this popular surfing spot can now only be reached via the dune path). Instead you take the trail on an inland detour through farmland. You will, however, prefer the new route to Abersoch which returns to follow the coast; previously the route followed the roads. However, the cliff path is narrow and, particularly in bad weather, exposed.

You climb out of the popular tourist resort of Abersoch via the heathered headland of Mynydd Tir-y-cwmwd. A solitary figure looks down over the sand and shingle of Llanbedrog beach; the Tin Man sculpture was preceded by another metal, and before that a wooden figurehead from a ship, placed there by Solomon Andrews. A Cardiff entrepreneur, Solomon Andrews was responsible for developing the area as a tourist region in the late nineteenth century. He opened Wales's first art gallery

VIEW NORTH FROM PORTH TOCYN ACROSS THE OLD COURSE TO ABERSOCH. © ADAM LONG

in the Oriel Plas Glyn y Weddw mansion, which the route passes – the gallery closed after World War II, but has now reopened and is run by a charitable trust.

The ancient market town of Pwllheli is the terminus of the Cambrian Coast Line and now home to the National Sailing Academy. You leave the town by the sandy beach, following it for approximately five kilometres, past the site of the old Butlin's holiday camp. You must endure another section of the busy main road; after three kilometres or so, you turn off to take a side road back to the coast. The path takes a low path along the shore into Criccieth, passing the ruins of the thirteenth-century castle.

You follow the railway line out of Criccieth to reach Black Rock Sands where the Path again takes you along the beach. The route climbs to reach Pen-y-banc nature reserve, where a wooded path leads you to the trail's end at Porthmadog, although the Welsh Coastal Path continues on.

A quarter of the Llŷn peninsula is an Area of Outstanding Natural Beauty, and this undiscovered coast, with its sandy beaches, gorsey cliffs and tiny bays is one of Wales's hidden treasures. The small towns and villages, built on fishing and quarrying, have retained a strong sense of Welshness and though you can enjoy views of Snowdonia, the Llŷn peninsula feels remote from the tourist hotspots of the national park and North Wales's seaside resorts.

13 LLŶN COASTAL PATH: ESSENTIAL INFORMATION

TRAIL ESSENTIALS

Start:	**Caernarfon, Gwynedd, Wales**
End:	**Porthmadog, Gwynedd, Wales**
Distance:	**158km**
Ascent/descent:	**2,120m/2,130m**
Also known as:	**Part of the Wales Coast Path**

HOW TO GET THERE

Caernarfon offers frequent bus services to Bangor, which has a railway station. Caernarfon is on the heritage Welsh Highland Railway which connects with the national rail network at the trail's end in Porthmadog. The closest international airports are Liverpool and Manchester; nearby Holyhead also offers a ferry connection to Ireland.

Porthmadog is on the Cambrian Coast Line with connections to Shrewsbury and Birmingham. While Liverpool and Manchester airports are closest geographically, Birmingham's International Airport is easier to reach on public transport.

TIME TO COMPLETE

Walking:	**7 days/42 hours**
Trekking:	**5 days/34 hours**
Fastpacking:	**4 days/26 hours**
Trail running:	**3 days/19 hours**

PROS

- **Part of Wales Coast Path** – since the inauguration of the national path, the Llŷn Coastal Path has been much improved, and is likely to remain well-supported, maintained and waymarked.

- **Isolated** – there are few towns and villages on the Llŷn peninsula and you will often find yourself alone, walking on clifftops with little sign of human habitation and nothing but sea views to admire.

- **Beaches** – from the whistling sands of Porthor beach and the pub on the beach at Porth Dinllaen to the seven-kilometre-long beach at Porth Neigwl, there are plenty of opportunities to enjoy a paddle, eat lunch on the beach and surf or sail.

CONS

- **Roads** – although many road sections have been removed, some still remain and erosion occasionally forces diversions on to the roads. The long stretch near Dinas Dinlle along the busy A499 is a particularly unpleasant road segment.

- **Sheep** – the peninsula is home to its own breed of sheep, the Lleyn, and there are a lot of sheep on the route. You will find yourself fenced on narrow, crumbling paths next to pastures, and may encounter sections deep in sheep muck.

- **Logistics** – there is limited accommodation on the Llŷn peninsula, and the route sections suggested on the Wales Coast Path do not always stop where there is good provision. Public transport around the peninsula is extremely limited, especially in the winter.

GOOD TO KNOW

Plaid Cymru was founded at the 1925 Pwllheli conference on the Llŷn peninsula; originally it was a social and educational movement concerned with the preservation of a Welsh-speaking Wales. R.S. Thomas, the Welsh nationalist poet, made his home on the peninsula as a vicar at Aberdaron; he learnt Welsh too late in life to use it in his poetry, although he did write prose, including his autobiography, in it. The peninsula's Welsh language tradition continues with Carl Clowes's National Welsh Language and Heritage Centre at Nant Gwrtheyrn.

FURTHER INFORMATION

walescoastpath.gov.uk/places-to-go/llŷn-peninsula

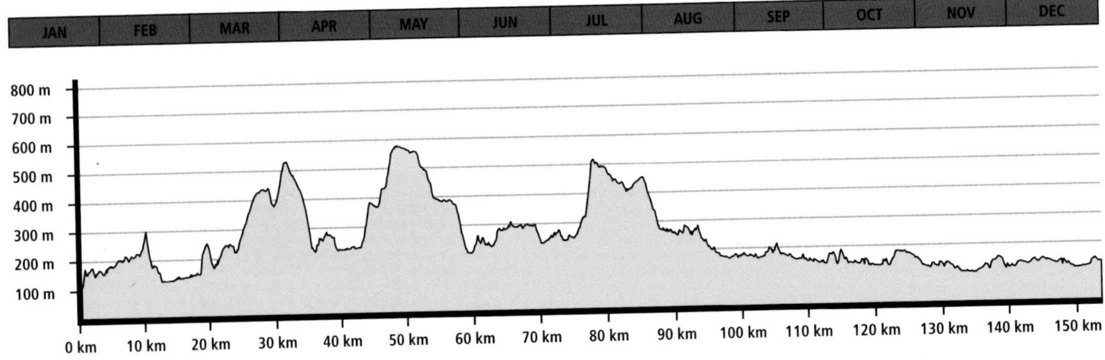

Llangefni
Anglesey/
Ynys Môn
Menai Bridge/
Porthaethwy
Bangor
Rhosneigr
Llangadwaladr
Brynsiencyn
A55
Menai Strait
A487
A4244
A4086
Llanddwyn Island
Llanddwyn Bay
Caernarfon
Y Foryd
A4085
Llanberis
Saron
Moel Eilio
Dinas Dinlle
A499
Caernarfon
Bay
WALES
Pontllyfni
Aberdesach
A487
Clynnog-Fawr
Snowdonia
National Park
Garnedd-goch
Bwlch Mawr
Gyrn Goch
Gyrn Ddu
Pant Glâs
Moel Hebog
Trefor
Nant Gwrtheyrn
Garn Ganol
Llanaelhaearn
Porth Dinllaen
A499
Dolbenmaen
Llithfaen
Pistyll
Nefyn
B4354
Llŷn peninsula
Llanarmon
Llanystumdwy
Criccieth
Porthmadog
A487
Borth-y-Gest
Towyn
A497
Porth Colmon
B4417
Pwllheli
A499
B4415
Sarn Mellteyrn
Llanbedrog
Tremadog Bay
Mynytho
A499
Harlech
B4413
Mynydd Rhiw
Aberdaron
Rhiw
Abersoch
Llanengan
Hell's Mouth/
Porth Neigwl
Cilan
St Tudwal's
Islands
Bardsey Sound
Ynys Gwylan-fawr
A496
Bardsey Island/
Ynys Enlli
N
Cardigan
Bay
Barmouth
0
10 Kilometres
Barmouth Bay

14

14 MORAY WAY – 155km

The 155-kilometre Moray Way is a combination of three trails; the Moray Coast Trail, the Dava Way and the Speyside Way. It is a pleasant, easy loop that leads you through pine woods, contours around gentle hills and across farmland and even offers you the opportunity to spot dolphins on Moray's sandy coastline. This well-waymarked trail follows forestry tracks, quiet country lanes, disused railway lines and good paths, and is a great route to attempt if you have never walked a long-distance trail before.

The trail starts in Grantown-on-Spey – the town was built as a planned settlement in 1765 and established by 'the good' Sir James Grant. Although the town is within the Cairngorms National Park, the peaks are a distant ridge on the horizon. You start on the High Street, just metres from the gold postbox next to Mortimers, painted for local cyclist Craig MacLean, who piloted Neil Fachie to a gold medal in the 2012 Paralympics. You leave town along Seafield Avenue, joining the Dava Way near the caravan park.

From Grantown to Forres, the route follows the old track of the Highland Railway and there is little between the two towns, meaning that those attempting the trail face a long day (of nearly forty kilometres) or will need to negotiate a pickup from one of the roads that occasionally intersect the track. Your first reminder of the railway is when you pass the impressive Castle Grant East Lodge; this once incorporated Lady Catherine's Halt, a private stop built to service the nearby Castle Grant. The lodge and railway halt were built by the Inverness and Perth Junction Railway Company in 1863 as part of the Earl of Seafield's conditions imposed to let the railway pass through his estate.

The railway now leads you through a narrow, wooded gorge. Keen climbers may want to make a detour to Huntly's Cave. The track steadily climbs to reach the exposed, high Dava Moor which shines golden with broom in the summer months. A wooden dragoon stands guard on the moorland, a tribute to the Jacobite Battle of Cromdale in 1690. You descend towards the small hamlet of Dava, where the trail crosses the road. The path is then through woods and farmland, land very much managed for grouse shooting – the sheep that graze are used not for meat or wool, but to control the tick population in the grouse areas.

At Bogeney, a collie stands poised with a parcel at the edge of the track. This wooden sculpture is of Jess, the sheepdog that would race to collect parcels dropped from the passing train. Another reminder of the railway, the Signalman's hut, has now been transformed into a walkers' shelter and information centre.

You get a bird's-eye view of the impressive Divie viaduct before reaching Forres, passing under the Scurrypool and Squirrel Neuk stone bridges. As you enter the town, you pass Dallas Dhu, once a working distillery and now operated by Historic Scotland as a museum. The Moray Way joins the Moray Coast Trail at Forres, to follow a good cycle track to the seaside town of Findhorn.

You can enjoy the view down Moray's beautiful coast as you follow the trail along the beach and through dunes. Passing around RAF Kinloss, you join a clifftop path and then a forestry track. At low tide you rejoin the beach near

◀ THE MORAY FIRTH AT FINDHORN.
© *WALKHIGHLANDS.CO.UK*

Burghead but at high tide must continue through the woods on the Burma Road, nicknamed because it was built during World War II by prisoners of war.

The building of the new town at Burghead in the early nineteenth century destroyed much of the Pictish fort that stood on the promontory, but you can still see two of the elaborately carved bullstones in the visitor centre.

More Pictish carvings can be seen in the Sculptor's Cave at the bottom of the cliffs, but it is difficult to reach and requires a scramble across slippery rocks that are submerged at high tide. The Moray Way instead takes a clifftop path around the Clashach quarry, offering good views of the stunning sea stacks. Near the tall, white Covesea Lighthouse, you return to the sandy beach (a higher path leads through the dunes if the tide is in) to reach the bustling town of Lossiemouth. A second gold postbox can be visited here, painted for Heather Stanning, who with her partner Helen Glover won the first British gold medals of the 2012 Olympics, the first ever British golds in women's rowing.

The Moray Way crosses to East Beach at Seatown, on the outskirts of Lossiemouth, but the bridge to the beach has fallen into disrepair, meaning that you have may have to follow the road to regain the trail near Caysbriggs quarry. However, you may find your route along the coastline further impeded if the firing range near Binn Hill is in use (look for the red flag) – there is a signed diversion. The Way makes use of the old railway bridge over the Spey to reach Fochabers. You may wish to follow the Speyside Way north to visit the Scottish Dolphin Centre if you have not spotted the aquatic locals on your way along the coast.

You join the Speyside Way to follow the path of the river south, past numerous whisky distilleries. The Way is

COVESEA LIGHTHOUSE NEAR LOSSIEMOUTH. © *WALKHIGHLANDS.CO.UK*

generally a well-maintained trail through woods and farmland, although south of Fochabers you do take a country lane that contours high above the river. The road descends to Boat o' Brig where you rejoin farm tracks and green lanes that contour on the wooded hillside under Scots pines. Craigellachie is famous for its cast iron bridge, constructed by Thomas Telford in 1812. It is perhaps even more famous for The Quaich at the Craigellachie Hotel. This whisky bar, founded in 1893, offers a choice of more than 900 single malts from around the world.

Many more whisky distilleries are passed as the Speyside Way criss-crosses across the pure waters of the river. The water is not only vital for the production of the whisky; the Spey is one of Scotland's most important rivers for Atlantic salmon and sea trout, although rod fishing on the best spots on the banks can be an expensive hobby and the river is frequently patrolled to discourage poaching. As you return to Grantown, you also return to the railway track. The trail passes through the Scots pines of Anagach woods, a wildlife haven owned by the local community.

The Moray Way is one of the easiest of the Highlands' long-distance trails. Although often offering fine views of the distant hills, it offers no challenging ascents or descents and no technical sections of path. Between Findhorn and Grantown you frequently pass small villages and towns, with bed and breakfasts or pubs and cafes. It can be attempted at any time of year although you may discover many local hospitality businesses are shut in the quietest winter months, and some sections of the route have been liable to bad flooding. This is a route that offers a little farmland, some long-established Scots pine woods, beautiful sandy beaches and clifftop walks. It is the perfect excuse to reward yourself with a dram or two of Speyside whisky and some locally smoked salmon.

BEACH HUTS AT HOPEMAN. © *WALKHIGHLANDS.CO.UK*

14 MORAY WAY: ESSENTIAL INFORMATION

TRAIL ESSENTIALS

Start: **Grantown-on-Spey, Scotland**
End: **Grantown-on-Spey, Scotland**
Distance: **155km**
Ascent/descent: **1,150m/1,150m**
Also known as: **The Moray Way combines sections of the Moray Coast Trail, the Dava Way and the Speyside Way**

HOW TO GET THERE

Grantown-on-Spey has regular bus services to Aviemore, which has a mainline Scottish rail service, offering connections to Scottish cities (and on to England and Wales). Inverness is the closest international airport, although you will have a wider choice of flights, and destinations, from Glasgow or Edinburgh airports.

TIME TO COMPLETE

Walking: **6 days/36 hours**
Trekking: **4 days/30 hours**
Fastpacking: **3 days/23 hours**
Trail running: **3 days/18 hours**

PROS

- **Whisky** – there are fifty distilleries in the Speyside area, famous for their light, sweet single malts, with a hint of peat and smoke. The Moray Way passes the doors of several distilleries, including Aberlour Cragganmore and Dalmunach, and close to many more. Whisky enthusiasts may want to make a pit stop at the Quaich bar at the Craigellachie Hotel, which has a selection of more than 900 single malts to choose from.
- **Dolphins** – the Moray coast is famous for bottlenose dolphins, and you can take advantage of a boat trip for a closer view. You may also see porpoises, seals and minke whales. You can learn more about the dolphins, and the other local wildlife, at the Scottish Dolphin Centre, which is a short diversion off-route at Spey Bay.

CONS

- **Tarmac** – the trail occasionally follows roads, and also follows tarmacked paths along old railbeds, as well as hard-packed forestry trails.
- **Flooding** – the Moray Way is particularly prone to flooding, which is generally at its worse in winter and early spring. Floods not only prevent access to sections of the trail, but can wash away sections of the path, resulting in diversions while repairs are carried out.

GOOD TO KNOW

The Way from Grantown-on-Spey to Forres follows the disused Inverness and Perth Junction Railway. Tales are still told about this high, haunted railway, particularly of ghost trains on the track. When considering when to tackle the trail, it is worth remembering that two trains were snowbound on the line on 17 December 1880. While all the passengers safely escaped and found shelter, they had to wait several days for rescue as the relief train also got stuck. When the locomotives were finally dug out, they were under around twenty metres of snow. Trains were frequently stranded by the weather on this high, exposed line.

FURTHER INFORMATION

www.morayways.org.uk/routes/the-moray-way

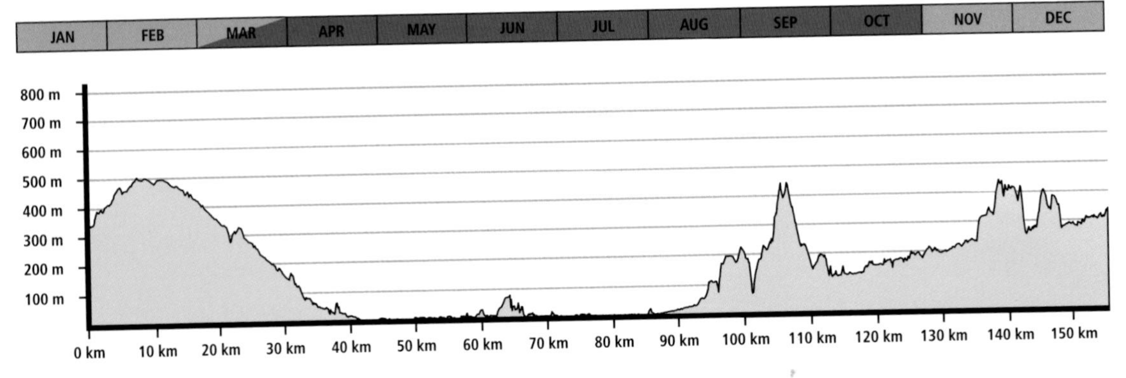

Moray Firth
Lossiemouth
Hopeman
Burghead
Duffus
Burghead Bay
A941
Lossie
B9013
Kingston on Spey
Spey Bay
Garmouth
Findhorn
B9089
Findhorn Bay
Kinloss
A96
Elgin
A96
Mosstodloch
A98
A941
Benromach Distillery
Fochabers
Forres
Fogwatt
A96
Dallas Dhu Distillery
B9103
A96
Spey
A940
Lossie
Dallas
A941
Auchroisk Distillery
Logie
A95
Rothes
Ben Aigan
Carn na Cailliche
A95
Craigellachie
Archiestown
Macallan Distillery
Craigellachie Distillery
B9102
Tamdhu Distillery
Aberlour
A941
Knockando
Carron
Aberlour Distillery
A940
Knock of Braemoray
Dalmunach Distillery
Dailuaine Distillery
Dufftown
Larig Hill
Roy's Hill
A95
Little Conval
A939
Dava
Cragganmore Distillery
Marypark
Carn Ruigh an Uain
Cragganmore
Meikle Conval
Carn na Loine
B9102
Ballindalloch
Ben Rinnes
Advie
Tormore Distillery
Cairngorms National Park
A95
Spey
A941
SCOTLAND
Avon
Glenlivet
B9102
Carn a' Ghille Chearr
Cromdale
N
Grantown-on-Spey
A95
Strath Avon
Strathspey
Dulnain Bridge
A939
Creagan a' Chaise
0
5 Kilometres

15

LONDON
Farnham
Dover

15 NORTH DOWNS WAY – 213km

The 213-kilometre North Downs Way follows in the footsteps of pilgrims, through the wooded lanes and green fields of Surrey and the old orchards of Kent, to the iconic white cliffs of Dover. Never far from the busy roads and bustling towns of South East England, this gentle, pleasant trail is an ideal route for the novice long-distancer seeking a leafy respite from London.

The North Downs Way starts at a busy road junction on the A31 dual carriageway, close to Farnham's rail station. Although the trail soon leaves the road for wooded lanes and a path along the River Wey, the hum of traffic is the soundscape for the first few kilometres of the Way as you follow it towards the Saxon town of Guildford. Weary walkers might want to visit the beautiful lido on the edge of Stoke Park – the fifty-metre pool, opened in 1933, has a grassed picnic area, cafe and, for the adventurous, three flume slides.

As the North Downs Way leaves Guildford, it climbs St Martha's Hill – a church has stood here since Saxon times, but the old church was near destroyed by explosions from the nearby Chilworth gunpowder works in the 1700s. The current church, built in the Arts and Craft style, dates from 1850. The mild weather and chalk ridges of the North Downs are perfect for fruit growing, and the path passes through Denbies, England's largest vineyard, whose Chalk Ridge Rosé won an International Wine Challenge gold medal in 2010.

At the foot of Box Hill, you cross the River Mole on stepping stones, although there is a footbridge further upstream should you want to guarantee dry boots. The trail takes a more direct route to (near) the summit than the famous Zig Zag Road, used as a cycling challenge in the 2012 Olympics. You descend, past the old lime quarry, to the pretty cottages of Betchworth village. This south-eastern corner of the country has always been crucial to England's defence, and the North Downs Way frequently passes nineteenth-century defences and crumbling World War II bunkers. Reigate Fort was built as part of the London Defence Positions scheme of the 1890s and probably formed part of Montgomery's South-Eastern Command during World War II.

Between Merstham and Rochester, the route runs parallel with the M25 and M26 motorways, and also encounters the M23 and M20. Although the undulating paths through pastures and bluebell woods are often pretty, you rarely escape the hum of traffic. Now in Kent, you pass Chevening, the seventeenth-century house that is usually the Foreign Secretary's official country residence. On the hills above Cuxton you glimpse the broad Medway river for the first time.

Next to the Diggerland theme park and in the company of the M2 and the Eurostar, you cross the Medway. You leave the motorway near Borstal; HMP Rochester still stands on the site of the original Borstal that gave its name to youth offender institutes. A quiet country lane leads you at last away from the motorway to Kit's Coty House, a megalithic dolmen burial chamber. You climb through bluebell-rich woods to reach the grassy hilltops of the Downs, with panoramic views.

◀ THE DEVIL'S KNEADING TROUGH IN THE WYE DOWNS, KENT.
© MARK RAINSLEY

At Detling, you cross the busy dual carriageway road on Jade's Crossing, named for Jade Hobbs, an eight-year-old who died crossing the road with her grandmother. Between Hollingbourne and Lenham, on an undulating track through flower-dotted verges and dipping under tree arches, you pass a contemplative pilgrim sitting on a bench; the wooden Brother Percival was installed in 2007. A large, white cross is carved into the hillside above Lenham, a war memorial first dug out in 1922.

You take a flat route through farmer's fields, often golden with rapeseed. After Boughton Lees, you have to make a decision between a northern and southern route, both ending in Dover. Kent is the garden of England, and both variations take you past fruit farms and through orchards. If you want to be a pilgrim, you should take the northern route to Canterbury. This northern route takes you through King's Wood, an old royal hunting ground of beech, fir, pine and sweet chestnut. You reach the medieval village of Chilham with its castle; the house, built in 1616 and still a private home, stands next to the original twelfth-century octagonal keep.

No Man's Orchard is one of few remaining traditional orchards in Stour; first planted in the 1940s, it was bought by local councils in 1996 in order to preserve it. Canterbury, a UNESCO World Heritage Site, is one of England's earliest and most important Christian sites. The eleventh-century cathedral became a popular pilgrimage destination after the murder of Thomas Becket. Becket was not the first archbishop to be martyred there; Cnut's Vikings had murdered Ælfheah there in 1012. The cathedral is now the mother church of the worldwide Anglican Communion. In addition to the cathedral, you may choose to explore the Norman castle ruins, the fourteenth-century city gate, a Saxon church and the ruins of an abbey founded by

LOOKING DOWN FROM CASTLE HILL, FOLKESTONE. © SARAH ROSS

St Augustine. When you leave the city, you cross farmers' fields and woodland tracks to reach a Roman road that will deliver you to Dover, where the North Downs Way ends on the Esplanade.

If you head south, you will find a crown carved into the Downs near Wye; it was created by agricultural students to celebrate Edward VII's coronation in 1902. The high vantage point of Farthing Common offers views across the Downs and the Romney marshes. Another chalk figure, a white horse carved in 2002 as a millennial celebration, greets you as you arrive in Folkestone, by the Eurotunnel terminal. Your clifftop route into Dover offers views of the white cliffs, and takes you past the Battle of Britain memorial. This coast is dotted with the remains of World War II, and you will pass several bunkers as well as the Abbot's Cliff sound mirror, built to amplify the sound of incoming aircraft, and featured in Eric Ravilious's painting *Bombing the Channel Ports*. You descend into Dover via Shakespeare Cliff, named for a scene from *King Lear*, and the nineteenth-century fortifications of the Western Heights.

If you enjoy wild garlic and bluebells, grassy paths over undulating ridges, fields of crops and tree-arched woodland tracks, the North Downs Way is for you. Although it is too often in the company of busy roads, particularly motorways, you will forgive this as you travel southwards over the green, wide-horizoned ridges of the Downs and reach the Kent coast near the white cliffs of Dover.

COLLEY HILL NEAR REIGATE, SURREY. © MARK RAINSLEY

15 NORTH DOWNS WAY: ESSENTIAL INFORMATION

TRAIL ESSENTIALS

Start:	**Farnham, Surrey, England**
End:	**Dover, Kent, Scotland**
Distance:	**213km**
Ascent/descent:	**2,870m/2,930m**

HOW TO GET THERE

Farnham is served by direct rail services to London, where connections to Eurostar or international airports can be made. London Heathrow Airport can be reached via Woking – there is a direct train service between Farnham and Woking, and a National Express coach link from Woking to Heathrow.

Dover is an international ferry port, with services to France. Dover Priory train station offers direct trains to London, where connections to Eurostar or international airports can be made (or change at Tonbridge to reach London Gatwick).

TIME TO COMPLETE

Walking:	**9 days/56 hours**
Trekking:	**6 days/46 hours**
Fastpacking:	**5 days/35 hours**
Trail running:	**4 days/26 hours**

PROS

- **Day hikes from London** – if you can't afford to take days or weeks off work to complete a long-distance trail, the North Downs Way – with Kent's high-speed train connections – is easy to do in parts as day or weekend trips from London.

- **Churches** – as well as Canterbury Cathedral and St Augustine's Abbey, there are plenty of historical churches to visit on the route. Highlights include St Martha's Church high on the hill, the twelfth-century St Nicholas's Church in Barfrestone and Merstham's medieval St Katharine's.

- **Trees** – you often walk on wooded paths and sometimes sunken lanes through native woodland. The trees often muffle the worst of the traffic noise and the woodland is strewn with wild garlic, bluebells and snowdrops. You pass through an old royal hunting forest and a rare heritage orchard.

CONS

- **Motorways** – the North Downs Way not only crosses several motorways, it also runs parallel (and close) to the route of the M25 and M26 for many kilometres. You cross the Medway on a fenced footpath directly next to the M2 motorway.

- **Dover** – is primarily a ferry port and not a holiday destination. As a working town, it has less to offer tourists than other seaside resorts and is not the finest example of the Kentish coast.

GOOD TO KNOW

The most famous group of pilgrims to make the journey to Canterbury are those of Chaucer's *The Canterbury Tales*. Chaucer, a Customs Controller and Justice of the Peace, wrote his rhyming, and often raucous, tale of the motley band travelling from London to Canterbury in the 1380s, in Middle English. You will discover more about, and encounter numerous references to, Chaucer's pilgrims on the way. The North Down's Way ostensibly follows the pilgrimage route to Canterbury although there is scant historical evidence for a single route, let alone that the Way is it.

FURTHER INFORMATION

www.nationaltrail.co.uk/en_GB/trails/north-downs-way

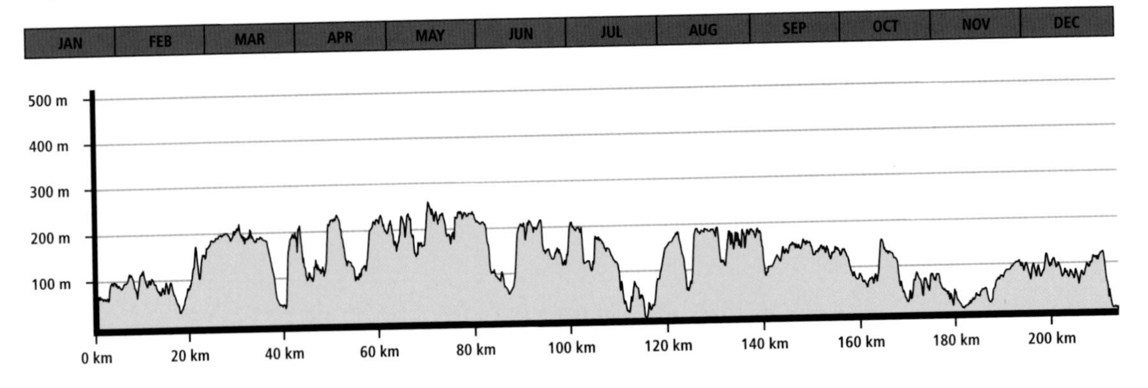

ENGLAND
North Sea
English Channel
Strait of Dover
Chiltern Hills
North Downs
South Downs
South Downs National Park
Surrey Hills
London
St Albans
Chelmsford
High Wycombe
Basildon
Southend-on-Sea
Maidenhead
Reading
Bracknell
Wokingham
Camberley
Woking
Leatherhead
Caterham
Orpington
Bexleyheath
Gravesend
Rochester
Gillingham
Isle of Sheppey
Whitstable
Herne Bay
Margate
Ramsgate
Canterbury
Patrixbourne
Deal
Dover
Shepherdswell
Capel-le-Ferne
Folkestone
Etchinghill
Stowting
Chilham
Boughton Lees
Ashford
Charing
Lenham
Detling
Blue Bell Hill
Upper Halling
Vigo Village
Otford
Knockholt
Sevenoaks
Westerham
Maidstone
Tonbridge
Royal Tunbridge Wells
Merstham
Redhill
Reigate
Westhumble
Dorking
Guildford
Compton
Seale
Aldershot
Farnham
Crawley
Horsham
Haywards Heath
Burgess Hill
Brighton
Chichester
Littlehampton
Worthing
Eastbourne
Bexhill
Hastings
Dungeness
Thames
Medway
Great Stour
Wey
M1
A1(M)
M11
M25
M40
A413
M4
A322
M3
A33
A31
A3
A281
A24
M23
A22
M26
M20
A228
A21
A229
A28
A2070
M2
A299
A256
N
0
20 Kilometres

16

16 PEAK DISTRICT BOUNDARY WALK – 303km

The 303-kilometre Peak District Boundary Walk encircles the Peak District National Park. The new trail, launched in 2017, takes advantage of bridleways, cycle trails, footpaths and the occasional road to trace the outskirts of the Peak, tending to stay just inside the national park. On your journey you will see rolling farmland, the remains of the park's industrial past, the northern giants of Kinder Scout and Bleaklow, rivers, moorland and perhaps even a glimpse of the stately home Chatsworth.

The Peak District Boundary Walk begins in the spa town of Buxton, the highest market town in England. You take a grassy, muddy path up and down gentle hills until you reach the steep and rocky descent into Deep Dale. The official route follows the river through the steeply sided gorge, but a diversion is in place through farmers' fields until at least 2026. You cross the busy A6 road near Topley Pike quarry to join the Pennine Bridleway along the River Wye.

You climb through Wormhill on a country road, and then drop to follow the Limestone Way briefly, before taking an indirect route into Peak Forest, named for the (long disappeared) royal forest. The Walk offers grassy, sometimes muddy and unclear, paths through farmers' fields past disused open cast mines. You skirt Chapel-en-le-Frith to join the Pennine Bridleway again as it contours round Mount Famine in the shadow of Kinder Scout.

After Hayfield, from where the Mass Trespass set off, you continue on the Pennine Bridleway towards Lantern Pike. You leave the bridleway to follow a track to Rowarth and then climb to Cown Edge, a ridge walk that offers views across the Peak District. After dipping in and out of Old Glossop, you reach Swineshaw Reservoir and then continue to Padfield and Bottoms Reservoir. The main route here follows the Pennine Bridleway to contour beneath high gritstone edges to reach Greenfield, but you may choose a higher, more challenging alternative that takes you on a boggy, sometimes unmarked, route following Ogden Brook up to Chew Hurdles. The routes rejoin just before Dove Stone Reservoir.

The grassy footpath of the Oldham Way climbs to an obelisk war memorial. The boulders that strew these slopes, the Pots and Pans stones and the Shaw rocks, are said to have been thrown by the two giants of Saddleworth Moor, Alphin and Alder, as they battled for the affection of a water nymph. The route here follows well-established footpaths and tracks towards Diggle where you join the Pennine Bridleway and then the Pennine Way as it follows a flagged path across tussocky, boggy moorland.

The Walk leaves the Pennine Way at Wessenden Reservoir to head in the direction of Marsden. You are now at the northernmost tip of the Walk. On well-made tracks, you pass Deer Hill, Bilberry and Digley reservoirs. After the small village of Holme you follow the Kirklees Way and then the Holme Valley Circular, across heathered moorland and conifer plantations, to pass more reservoirs. After Dunford Bridge, you take the gravel and tarmac Trans Pennine Trail which runs next to the River Don before heading for Langsett.

◀ DOVE STONE RESERVOIR IN THE CHEW VALLEY.
© ADAM LONG

WINTER VIEW OF SHEFFIELD FROM BROWN EDGE ABOVE RINGINGLOW. © DAVE PARRY

You follow the shores of Langsett Reservoir and then cross the dam, one of the largest earth embankments in Britain, and continue on past Midhope Reservoir. A path through woods that joins roads leads into Bolsterstone, a hilltop village and home to the award-winning Bolsterstone Male Voice Choir. You drop down past Broomhead and More Hall reservoirs, and then climb again up the wooded reservoir slopes.

Muddy paths through high, green farmers' fields take you to another lofty village, High Bradfield, home to Bradfield Brewery. You descend to the neighbouring Low Bradfield and then face a steep climb out of the valley on singletrack country lanes. A good farm track takes you across the edge of Ughill Moors and then a grassy path down to the traffic-heavy A57, the main road between Sheffield and Manchester. The path down to cross Hollow Meadows Brook is usually boggy, and often deep in sheep muck.

Access roads and well-trodden footpaths pass Rivelin Dams and Redmires Reservoirs, until you eventually reach popular mountain biking spot Lady Canning's Plantation. You follow the road, which has poor visibility and fast traffic, passing a Peak District boundary marker, into Ringinglow, with its panoramic views of Sheffield.

You take the stony Houndkirk Road along the edge of Burbage Moor before dropping down to cross, on a good bridleway, the wooded Blacka Plantation. You pass over the grassy top of the Totley tunnel, the second longest railway tunnel in the country when it was completed in 1893; it is still the fourth longest mainline railway tunnel in Britain. Clear, undulating tracks lead you across moorland to a road. You can omit the detour into Milthorpe if you prefer to head straight for Shillito Woods.

The Walk goes along the top of Birchen Edge, passing Nelson's Monument and the nearby rock outcrops, his 'three ships'. A good path across heathered moorland takes you to Hob Hurst's House, an Iron Age barrow. You descend through woods to Beeley and then on to Rowsley, where you cross the busy A6 road. A grassy path high above the River Derwent leads you to the Bronze Age stone circle, Nine Ladies, turned to stone for dancing on a Sunday. After descending, you then reascend on grassy paths to Winster, and follow the Limestone Way, with a small detour to the

ABOVE: EIGHTEENTH-CENTURY MILEPOST ON THE HOUNDKIRK ROAD. © DAVE PARRY
BELOW: FOLLOWING THE RIVER WYE ON THE MONSAL TRAIL IN CHEE DALE. © KATHY ROGERS

lead-mining village of Bonsall. Near Longcliffe, you join the popular High Peak Trail as it follows a disused railway line.

The route passes the limestone Ballidon Quarry to reach Parwich, and it then takes a path by a stream, past the site of Woodeaves Cotton Mill, to reach Fenny Bentley. After Thorpe, the southern tip of the Walk, you follow the River Dove to Ilam, with its Hall which is now a youth hostel. You continue through farmland to the Manifold Valley track, another disused railway, with views of Axe Edge in the distance.

From the hamlet of Waterfall, you follow country lanes and good tracks to reach Tittesworth reservoir. Through farmers' fields, you arrive at Wildboarclough village, reputedly where the last boar in England was killed. From the summit of Shutlingsloe, Cheshire's Matterhorn, you can enjoy wide views across the Peak. In Macclesfield Forest, you encounter more reservoirs. Near Tegg's Nose you join the Gritstone Trail which will take you along the ridge of Kerridge Hill to White Nancy, a bell-shaped folly built to commemorate the Battle of Waterloo.

You leave the Gritstone Trail after Bollington follow the North Cheshire Way, on lanes and farm tracks, down to Lyme View Marina on the Macclesfield canal. The route enters the National Trust's Lyme Park, an estate that belonged to the Legh family from 1388 to 1946. You cross the park to reach Whaley Bridge, where you pass the Toddbrook Reservoir dam that threatened to collapse in 2019, leading to the town's emergency evacuation. Grassy paths lead to more reservoirs, Fernilee and Errwood. You cross Wild Moor on the disused Cromford and High Peak Railway to return to your starting point in Buxton.

The Peak District Boundary Walk reveals the national park in all its diversity – the rivers that dissect it, the high edges and heathered moorland, tall rocks and deep gorges but also the rolling farmland, mines and quarries and ancient routes that run through it.

16 PEAK DISTRICT BOUNDARY WALK: ESSENTIAL INFORMATION

TRAIL ESSENTIALS

Start:	**Buxton, Derbyshire, England**
End:	**Buxton, Derbyshire, England**
Distance:	**303km**
Ascent/descent:	**7,610m/7,610m**

HOW TO GET THERE

Buxton has rail (and bus) services to Manchester, with connections to the mainline rail services and Manchester International Airport. Buxton also has bus services to Matlock, Sheffield and Derby.

TIME TO COMPLETE

Walking:	**16 days/95 hours**
Trekking:	**10 days/78 hours**
Fastpacking:	**8 days/58 hours**
Trail running:	**6 days/42 hours**

PROS

- **Landscapes** – the Walk takes you along gritstone edges, over limestone hills, along the rivers Don, Derwent, Dove and Manifold, through moors, woods and farms, and under the shadow of Bleaklow and Kinder Scout.

- **Getting there** – the Peak District is close to Sheffield, Manchester, Leeds, Nottingham and Derby and there are good public transport links from these cities.

- **Hinterlands** – the Walk does not explore the tourist honeypots of the Peak, but explores the space between the central park and the urban areas that fringe it. You will discover quiet, under-explored beauty spots, working villages and deserted moors that stretch beyond the park's boundaries.

CONS

- **Reservoirs** – the outskirts of the Peak District are fringed with reservoirs, supplying water to Sheffield, Manchester, Leeds and other nearby urban areas. The Walk often takes you along the shores, over the dams or through the wooded slopes of reservoirs.

- **Cycle routes** – the route makes use of several popular Peak District cycle routes, including the Pennine Bridleway, Trans Pennine Trail and High Peak Trail. You will often, particularly at weekends, be sharing the path with bikes.

GOOD TO KNOW

The Peak District was the UK's first national park, created in 1951. Although its formation has been attributed to the 1932 Mass Trespass – when ramblers from Manchester and Sheffield were arrested after trespassing on Kinder Scout – the park was as much the result of seventy years of campaigning by organisations such as the Ramblers, the Campaign to Protect Rural England and the Youth Hostel Association. The world's first national park was Yellowstone, established in the USA in 1872.

FURTHER INFORMATION

www.friendsofthepeak.org.uk/boundary-walk; Peak District Boundary Walk (Friends of the Peak District, 2017).

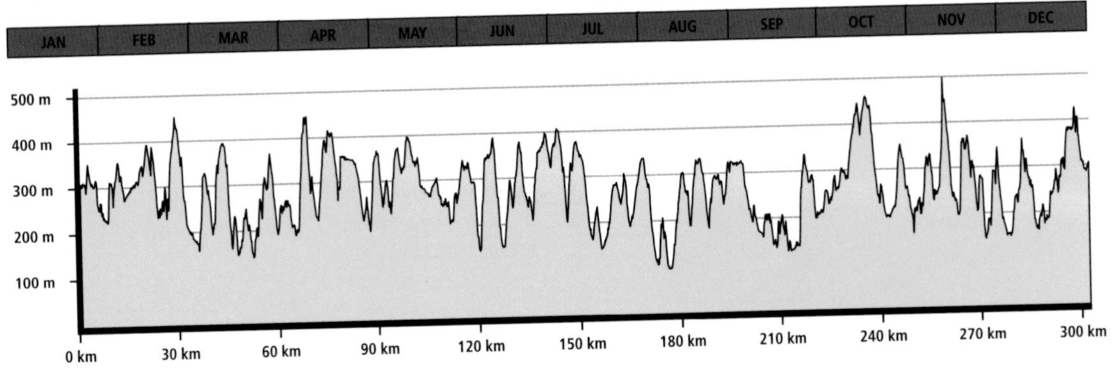

ENGLAND
Rochdale
M62
A640
Marsden
Meltham
Diggle
Holmfirth
Oldham
A635
Holme
Black Hill
A629
Barnsley
A669
Peak District National Park Boundary
Failsworth
Winscar Reservoir
Penistone
M1
Mossley
Hoyland
Langsett
A628(T)
Midhopestones
Woodhead Reservoir
Langsett Reservoir
Stocksbridge
anchester
Stalybridge
Torside Reservoir
Bolsterstone
A629
Hadfield
Margery Hill
Broomhead Reservoir
More Hall Reservoir
Hyde
M67
Bleaklow Head
Glossop
A6102
M60
Howden Reservoir
Agden Reservoir
High Bradfield
Low Bradfield
A626
Stockport
Derwent Reservoir
Damflask Reservoir
Marple
A57
Sheffield
Hayfield
Ladybower Reservoir
Kinder Scout
A57
Rivelin Dams
New Mills
Edale
A6
Poynton
Hope
Bamford
Redmires Reservoirs
Ringinglow
Castleton
A6187
A625
Wood Lanes
Whaley Bridge
Hathersage
Peak District
Chapel-en-le-Frith
Peak Forest
Kettleshulme
Derwent
Dronfield
Bollington
A5004
National Park
A625
Holmesfield
A623
A6
A61
Macclesfield
Wormhill
Tideswell
Buxton
Shining Tor
Calver
A537
Burbage
Wye
Langley
A6
Chesterfield
A54
Chelmorton
A619
Bakewell
Wildboarclough
Beeley
A632
Flash
A54
Dane
Monyash
Rowsley
A515
A53
Longnor
Tinkersley
Peak District National Park Boundary
Wincle
Dove
ton
Clay Cross
A523
Manifold
Birchover
Meerbrook
Upper Hulme
Matlock
Winster
Bonsall
Biddulph
A615
A5012
A515
Leek
A6
Onecote
Wirksworth
A53
Parwich
N
A523
B5056
Stoke-on-Trent
Carsington Water
A520
Ilam
Thorpe
Ripley
Waterhouses
Fenny Bentley
A52
Belper
Ashbourne
A517
0
10 Kilometres
A52

17

St Dogmaels
St Davids
Amroth
CARDIFF

17 PEMBROKESHIRE COAST PATH – 285km

The rugged coast of Pembrokeshire lies at Wales's most south-westerly tip. The 285-kilometre Pembrokeshire Coast Path meanders around the beautiful shoreline, from Amroth in the south to St Dogmaels in the north. It takes vertiginous paths carved into the blustery cliff edges, grassy tracks and trails through farmland and woods, but it always returns to the shore, dropping to sandy beaches, often via steep steps. Although occasionally forced inland, it quickly returns to the sea, and offers some of Britain's best coastal views, charming harbours and seaside towns.

The Path begins at Amroth's spray-whipped, sandy beach which gives way to shingle as you travel west. A bluebelled woodland path takes you to the pretty white houses at Wiseman's Bridge, and you follow the old railway track towards Saundersfoot. You first encounter the coast's undulations here, and though the climbs up and down rarely exceed forty metres the repetition is challenging. The pastel-toned town of Tenby, with its thirteenth-century walls, tempts you on. From sandy South Beach, you can see the rocky, tidal St Catherine's Island, with its nineteenth-century Palmerston fort – this was the filming location for the dramatic conclusion of the *Sherlock* television series.

On Giltar Point, you encounter the first of many military installations on the Path – you may be forced to detour if the rifle range is active. At Lydstep the route drops from the grassy cliffs to the dunes, passing a large caravan park. A wild, gorsey path leads you through Manorbier, with its Norman castle. On this section of coast, the sea has eroded deep dashes into the red sandstone cliffs and carved out, quiet coves.

After crossing the crescent, sandy beach of Freshwater East, you climb up and down over stunning cliffs. Nestled under limestone cliffs, with sea arches and caves to explore, Barafundle Bay has strong claims to be the best beach in Pembrokeshire. The Path now takes you above these dramatic rock faces, which are popular with climbers who come here to scale the Cauldron, Huntsman's Leap and the Elegug Stacks. Built in a fissure in these cliffs, the thirteenth- or fourteenth-century St Govan's Chapel is reputed to be where Govan sought refuge from pirates.

More rifle ranges force you inland on a country road through farmers' fields, but you rejoin the coast at the long, sandy, marram-grass-fringed Freshwater West. Steep climbs over rugged cliffs lead you into the estuary of Milford Haven. The natural harbour of Milford Haven was a safe port, and is still one of the largest docks in Britain in terms of tonnage. In the midst of the oil refineries, the power station and port areas, you pass the spectacular, twelfth-century Pembroke Castle, birthplace of Henry VII.

You can cross the tidal estuary at Sandy Haven on stepping stones at low tide, but will have to make a lengthy inland detour at high tide. On clifftop paths with views to the islands of Skomer and Skokholm, you leave the busy Haven behind you. You face another tidal crossing at The Gann to reach the colourful houses of Dale, a village with shingle beaches and the ruins of a thirteenth-century castle. At the limits of Milford Haven estuary, you pass white St Ann's Head Lighthouse. Marloes Sands is a hidden treasure; a quiet, sandy beach, backed with jagged cliffs, facing impossibly blue sea.

◀ COAST PATH ABOVE MUSSELWICK SANDS, LOOKING NORTH TOWARDS TOWER POINT. © ADAM LONG

A greeny, gorsey trail leads you high over St Brides Bay, but you can choose to cross the beach at Newgale if the tide is low. The trail hugs the coastline past the wild St Non's Bay, birthplace of patron saint David, although you might choose to divert into the eponymous St Davids, Wales's smallest city, which owes its city status to its Norman cathedral. Between Ramsey Island, an RSPB Nature Reserve, and Pembrokeshire's western tip, the dangerous tidal race of the Bitches surges.

While the southern Pembrokeshire coast is pretty, the northern coast is some of the most breathtaking scenery in Britain, and the cliffs are wilder and more rugged. The steep edges of the Blue Lagoon, an old slate quarry, are a popular watersports spot, particularly for cliff diving. The scenery comes at a price – the rocky cliffs force you up and down around jutting headlands. In an inlet you reach Porthgain, framed by the tall buildings which were storage for the bricks and quarried stones that were exported out of the once-busy harbour. It is now popular with tourists and local fisherman. You are reminded of the dangers of this stretch of coast as you follow the Path to the prominent Strumble Head, where an island lighthouse has been built.

In a dark, wooded horseshoe of a cove, you reach the port of Fishguard, which was the site of the last invasion of mainland Britain when revolutionary French forces landed here in 1797. A grassy path around the high cliffs of Dinas Head offers fine views of the northern Welsh coast. The rocky coastline here is dotted with shipwrecks, many from the Great Storm of 1859 which wrecked around 150 ships but also wreaked havoc on the Welsh coast. At Cwm-yr-Eglwys, you pass the ruins of a St Brynach's Church, a victim of this storm, its roof ripped off and parts of the graveyard washed into the sea. Although sea defences have since been built, you can appreciate the power of the sea on the trail to Newport as you watch white-foamed waves surge in.

The Preseli hills, with the jagged peak of Mynydd Carningli, make for a picturesque backdrop to the tough end to the Path. You have little choice but to tackle the up-and-down trail from Newport to St Dogmaels in one day, as there is

ABOVE: A RESIDENT OF SKOMER ISLAND, PEMBROKESHIRE. © MARK RAINSLEY
BELOW: NAVIGATION MARKER AT THE ENTRANCE TO PORTHGAIN, NORTH PEMBROKESHIRE. © ADAM LONG

scant opportunity to leave the trail and there are no facilities. The narrow path, which clings to the edges of the cliff, may be dangerous in wet or windy weather. At Pen yr Afr, on Cemaes Head, you climb to the highest point of the Coast Path (175 metres). You descend through farmland and woods to Poppit Sands, where the route once ended, although now you must continue on to St Dogmaels, with its ruined twelfth-century abbey. The trail into St Dogmaels is on a busy road – although the village is served by a bus, you may choose to carry on another couple of kilometres to the better-connected Cardigan.

The Pembrokeshire coast is the seaside of childhood memories – of green and gorsey high cliffs, of improbable sea stacks and impossibly golden beaches, of emerald wooded coves and turquoise seas. Although you may follow the route in either direction, starting in the south gives you a gentler introduction and time to acclimatise before the challenging northern sections. Pembrokeshire bears the nickname *Gwlad Hud a Lledrith*, the land of mystery and enchantment, and there is perhaps no other section of the Wales Coast Path quite so magical on a summer's day when the grassy clifftops are bejewelled with flowers and the sea sparkles below.

A PATH THROUGH BLUEBELLS AND RED GRAMPION ON SKOMER ISLAND. © ZANA BENSON

17 PEMBROKESHIRE COAST PATH: ESSENTIAL INFORMATION

TRAIL ESSENTIALS

Start:	**Amroth, Pembrokeshire, Wales**
End:	**St Dogmaels, Pembrokeshire, Wales**
Distance:	**285km**
Ascent/descent:	**5,040m/5,050m**

HOW TO GET THERE

Amroth is on the coastal bus route that serves the whole Coast Path, and provides a link to train stations at Kilgetty and Tenby, which provide rail connections to Cardiff via Carmarthen. The closest international airport is at Cardiff. There is an international ferry service from Fishguard to Rosslare in Ireland.

St Dogmaels is on the coastal bus route, but more frequent services depart from Cardigan a little over a kilometre further down the Coast Path. Buses connect with the rail network at Carmarthen and Haverfordwest, and the nearest international airport is Cardiff.

TIME TO COMPLETE

Walking:	**13 days/80 hours**
Trekking:	**8 days/65 hours**
Fastpacking:	**6 days/49 hours**
Trail running:	**5 days/36 hours**

PROS

- **Beaches** – the beaches of Pembrokeshire are some of the best in Britain. They are usually sandy; the sand turns darker on the northern coast and occasionally gives way to shingle. The high cliffs prevent access to some coves. While many are suitable for swimming, some experience strong currents and inexperienced sea swimmers would be well advised to visit in the summer, when many beaches have lifeguards.

- **Watersports** – Milford Haven is a popular sailing and cruising destination, and Pembrokeshire has some of Wales's best surfing beaches, including Freshwater West, Marloes Sands, and Newgale. You can also try coasteering, snorkelling, paddleboarding, cliff diving and kayaking.

- **Seaside towns** – the Path is often on exposed cliffs but, except for the very last stretch, it passes enough towns and villages to provide pleasant lunch spots and overnight accommodation.

CONS

- **Military** – the Ministry of Defence has laid claim to several stretches of the Pembrokeshire coast, and some are closed at all times, while you will only have to detour around others if the rifle range is active.

- **Holidaymakers** – there are several popular holiday spots on the Pembrokeshire coast, and you may find accommodation is booked up in the summer. The Path occasionally passes through large caravan parks, and touristy beaches are fringed by cars, sometimes parked on the sands themselves.

GOOD TO KNOW

The success of the Pembrokeshire Coast Path, which opened in 1970 as Wales's first National Trail, inspired the Wales Coast Path. This 1,400-kilometre trail was the first in the world to follow a country's entire coastline, and can be used to complete a circumnavigation of Wales as it links to the Offa's Dyke Path.

FURTHER INFORMATION

www.visitpembrokeshire.com/explore-pembrokeshire/coast-path; www.walescoastpath.gov.uk

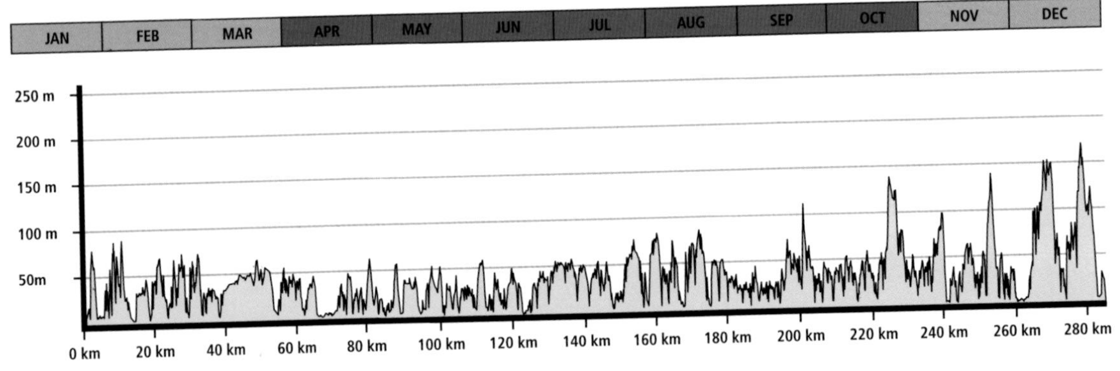

Irish Sea
WALES
Bristol Channel
St Brides Bay
Cemaes Head
Poppit
Cardigan
St Dogmaels
Moylgrove
Strumble Head
Porth Maen
Dinas Head
Newport Bay
Pwllgwaelod
Nevern
Eglwyswrw
Newport / Trefdraeth
Fishguard
Pembrokeshire Coast National Park
Gwaun
Abercastle
Porthgain
Trefin
Mathry
Scleddau
Crymych
Mynydd Preseli
Croes-goch
Letterston
Rosebush
Whitesands/ Porth Mawr
St Davids
Trelerw
Solva
Ramsey Sound
Ramsey Island
St Non's Bay
Hayscastle Cross
Wolf's Castle
Western Cleddau
Eastern Cleddau
Taf
Newgale
Camrose
Nolton Haven
Haverfordwest
Whitland
Narberth
Broad Haven
Little Haven
Skomer Island
Martin's Haven
St Brides
Marloes
Herbrandston
Milford Haven
Tavernspite
Kilgetty
Amroth
Dale
Neyland
Skokholm Island
Saundersfoot
Pembroke Dock
Angle
Rhoscrowther
Pembroke
St Florence
Tenby
Castlemartin
Freshwater East
Manorbier
Lydstep
Shrinkle Haven
Warren
Linney Head
Bosherston
St Govan's Head
Caldey Island
A487
A484
A478
B4582
A40
A4075
A477
B4327
N
0
10 Kilometres

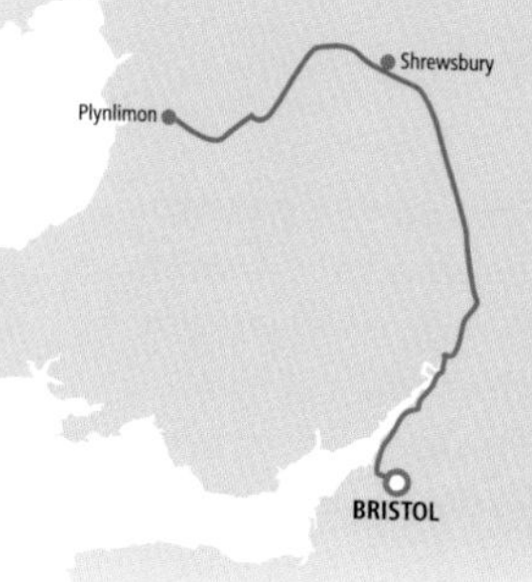

18

18 SEVERN WAY – 360km

At 354 kilometres, the Severn is Britain's longest river and the 360-kilometre Severn Way follows it from its source in the Welsh mountains to the edge of the Bristol Channel, and then goes a little further by following the Avon into Bristol. Although you can follow it in either direction, starting in Bristol and heading north not only saves the wildest scenery for the last day but also puts the prevailing wind at your back. Until it begins its climb up to the source at Plynlimon, the trail is an easy path through pastures and woodland on the banks of the meandering river with plenty of historical towns and cities to pause in.

The Severn Way begins at Bristol's Harbourside area. Now a bustling urban mix of museums, restaurants and bars, this was once one of Britain's economic powerhouses. In the eighteenth century it was Britain's second biggest port, after London, although much of its wealth was founded on approximately half a million slaves that Bristolian ships were responsible for ferrying across the Atlantic. Your journey begins not on the Severn, but on the Avon as you follow this river down the spectacular Avon Gorge, under the iconic Clifton Suspension Bridge.

The muddy waters of the Avon may seem quiet now, but Sea Mills was once a whaling port and before that the Roman Portus Abonae. Near the Avon's meeting with the Severn, you pass the Lamplighters pub built in 1760. It was on this spot that William III landed in 1690 after his victory at the Battle of the Boyne, but Lamplighter's Marsh is now more famous for its bee orchids and birds.

The Way skirts the busy docks at Avonmouth, and you arrive on the banks of the Severn near the concrete Seabank Power Station. On your horizon are the two Severn Bridges, carrying the M4 and M48 motorways from England to Wales. You cross under the newer (1996) Prince of Wales Bridge first, on a scruffy, often overgrown footpath. Between the bridges you pass both New Passage and Old Passage, where ferries once carried people and cars across the Severn, their trade finally disappearing with the opening of the first bridge in 1966. The Severn Way takes you over, but not across, this second bridge before dropping you down to the shore at Aust – it is possible to walk on the beach at low tide.

Little remains of the third iconic Severn Bridge, the railway bridge which was destroyed when two barges, the Wastdale H and Arkendale H, crashed into it in thick fog in 1960. You pass the stone pillars of the bridge just before Sharpness. You follow the Gloucester and Sharpness Canal to skirt around the wildlife haven at Slimbridge Wetland Centre, founded by Sir Peter Scott, founder of the Wildfowl & Wetlands Trust and son of explorer Captain Scott, in 1946.

The Severn has the second largest tidal range in the world, and the section of the river between Frampton and Gloucester is one of the best areas to view the Severn Bore surge wave. You follow grassy paths and occasionally wooded tracks by the sides of the wide river. Gloucester is the first of several historic towns and cities encountered on the banks of the mighty Severn.

◀ THE CLIFTON SUSPENSION BRIDGE IN BRISTOL, NEAR THE START OF THE SEVERN WAY.
© MARK RAINSLEY

You are likely to encounter cattle on the fertile, green banks of the river. At Tewkesbury, you reunite with the Avon and briefly follow it through the town, where it merges with the Severn. Tewkesbury has many medieval and Tudor buildings, but is most famous for its abbey with a Norman tower. While the river path remains flat and easy, you are on the edge of the Cotswolds here and can enjoy views of the distant, rolling hills. As you walk towards the cathedral city of Worcester the Malvern Hills will replace the Cotswolds on the horizon.

Between Stourport – a town that owes its existence entirely to the construction of the Staffordshire and Worcestershire Canal in the 1760s – and Bewdley, you pass the iron-red stone cliff of Blackstone Rock. Bewdley – or Beau Lieu, the beautiful place – is a pleasant waterfront town. You may hear the puffing steam trains on the heritage Severn Valley Railway – it runs parallel you to you as you follow the river north towards Bridgnorth. A second historical railway – the funicular Cliff Railway, which links the riverside Low Town with the High Town – can be enjoyed in Bridgnorth.

As you progress along the trail the Severn, though still wide, narrows and the landscape is changing too as the river meanders through tree-covered slopes. It is these wooded hills that caused Abraham Darby III to build the cast-iron arch of the Iron Bridge across the Severn at Ironbridge. The Way passes the towering ruins of the twelfth-century Buildwas Abbey and on to the quiet village of Wroxeter, which was once the site of Roman Britain's fourth largest city, standing as it does at the end of Watling Street. The Way travels through Shropshire's green countryside, with the Wrekin hill as a backdrop, occasionally meandering away from the river to reach the historic town of Shrewsbury, where it coincides briefly with the Shropshire Way.

BOATHOUSE AND SCHOOL ON THE BANK OF THE RIVER SEVERN AT SHREWSBURY. © ADAM LONG

As you cross the border into Wales, the Way leaves the wiggling Severn and prefers the straight towpath of the Montgomery Canal, built unusually for agriculture rather than industry. The Way makes its path through wilder, lusher countryside now, as the Breidden Hills loom on the horizon. Past Welshpool, the Way rejoins the banks of the Severn, on grassy, sometimes overgrown, paths. The pretty market town of Llanidloes, the first town on the Severn, is the last on the Way – you are likely to meet walkers on the Offa's Dyke Path and Glyndŵr's Way here. Standing tall by the river is a statue of Sabrina, the water nymph associated with the Severn. In the shade of the Hafren Forest, the nascent Severn has gathered enough force to cascade over the Severn-Break-its-Neck waterfall. You climb a mossy path through the forest to where the Way finishes on the high, wild sides of Plynlimon as the Severn gurgles to life.

The fertile green banks of the river make for pleasant fields, bluebell woods and tussocky pastures. They are a haven for butterflies, birds and wildflowers but are also often dotted with cows and sheep. The grassy paths by sparkling waters can be a delight on a spring day, but these are not well-trodden paths and may be overgrown. Sections are very susceptible to flooding, and the trail may be dangerously submerged. It is rarely not muddy. If you want to understand the history of the United Kingdom, there is perhaps no other British trail as revealing. The Severn Way starts at docks built on slavery, crosses over and under marvels of bridge engineering, passes medieval towns and ruined abbeys and visits Ironbridge, the birthplace of the Industrial Revolution.

RHAEADR BLAENHAFREN – BLAENHAFREN FALLS. © ALAN WARD – INTERNATIONAL MOUNTAIN LEADER

18 SEVERN WAY: ESSENTIAL INFORMATION

TRAIL ESSENTIALS

Start:	**Bristol, England**
End:	**Plynlimon, Ceredigion, Wales**
Distance:	**360km**
Ascent/descent:	**1,550m/950m**

HOW TO GET THERE

Bristol has good national rail (and coach) connections. It also has an international airport.

Plynlimon is not easy to reach – you must retrace your steps to the Rhyd-y-benwch car park in Hafren Forest, which is approximately twelve kilometres from Llanidloes. A bus service connects Llanidloes to Caersws, the closest rail station. The nearest international airports are at Birmingham and Cardiff.

TIME TO COMPLETE

Walking:	**13 days/78 hours**
Trekking:	**8 days/65 hours**
Fastpacking:	**6 days/49 hours**
Trail running:	**5 days/38 hours**

PROS

- **History** – from the history-rich city of Bristol to Roman cities, abbey ruins and industrial architecture, the Severn Way is rich in historic sites.

- **Pubs** – on the English stretch of the Severn, there are plenty of riverside pubs to stop at, many having stood for centuries on the riverbanks. Even in the more isolated Welsh sections, there are surprises en route. South of Welshpool, the Way passes the Nag's Head Inn at Garthmyl, winner of the AA's Pub of the Year award for Wales in 2018/2019.

CONS

- **Overgrown** – the fertile banks of the river encourage plants, and on quieter sections of the trail you may have to thrash your way through heavily overgrown paths. The invasive, non-native Himalayan balsam is a particular problem along the Severn.

- **Floods** – the Severn has experienced catastrophic flooding, particularly in Shropshire, Worcestershire and Gloucestershire. It breached its banks in Shrewsbury and Ironbridge in February 2020. Flooding may close pubs, restaurants and accommodation as well as making the Way impassable.

- **Information** – the Severn Way is not a National Trail, and there is little information available about it, other than the Cicerone guidebook. Some counties, through which the Way passes, provide detailed information about the local sections.

GOOD TO KNOW

The Severn has the second highest tidal range, of up to fifteen metres, in the world. This results in the Severn Bore, a surge wave that charges up the river from the Bristol Channel to Gloucester twice daily on approximately 130 days each year. The biggest Bores can attract hundreds of surfers, and in March 2006 local surfer Steve King set a Guinness World Record after surfing the Bore for twelve kilometres.

FURTHER INFORMATION

The Severn Way (Cicerone, 2019).

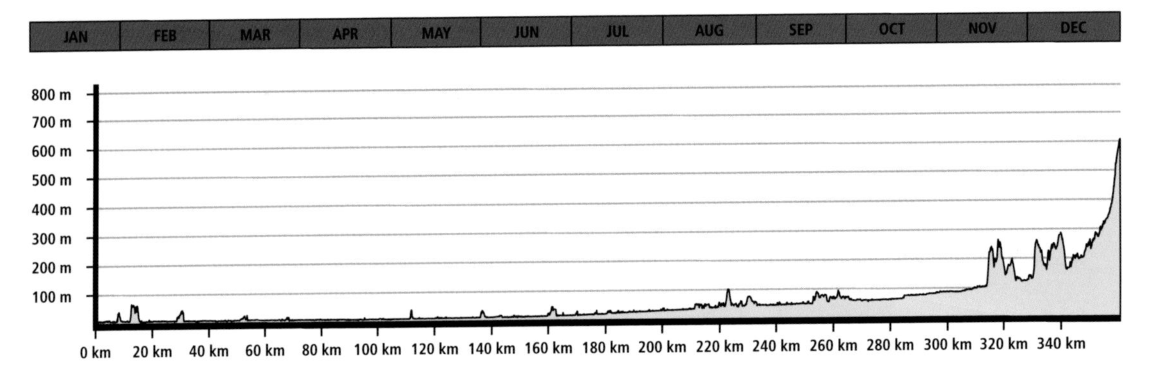

Oswestry
Wem
A53
A49
M6
Stafford
Snowdonia National Park
Newport
Pentre
A41
A458
Shrewsbury
A458
Welshpool
Wroxeter
Telford
Severn/Hafren
M54
Machynlleth
Ironbridge
A49
Cressage
Berriew
Broseley
Wolverhampton
A470
Montgomery
Church Stretton
Abermule
Caersws
Bridgnorth
Birmingham
Newtown
F
A470
Stourbridge
Plynlimon
Severn/Hafren
Llanidloes
Craven Arms
Shropshire Hills AONB
Highley
Clun
Upper Arley
Cambrian Mountains/ Elenydd
Clee Hills
WALES
Kidderminster
Bewdley
Ludlow
A483
Knighton
A456
Rhayader
Stourport-on-Severn
Llandrindod
Holt Heath
Leominster
A44
Severn
Worcester
Builth Wells
ENGLAND
A4112
Kempsey
A49
Great Malvern
A470
A4103
Severn Stoke
Hay-on-Wye
Hereford
M5
Wye
Ledbury
Upton upon Severn
Llandovery
Tewkesbury
A470
A449
M50
Black Mountains
Brecon
A465
Ross-on-Wye
Sandhurst
Black Mountain
Cheltenham
Brecon Beacons National Park
Minsterworth
Wye Valley AONB
Gloucester
Monmouth
Epney
Slimbridge Wetland Centre
Frampton on Severn
Stroud
The Cotswolds AONB
Merthyr Tydfil
A465
A449
Lydney
Cirencester
Sharpness
Cwmbran
Severn
Chepstow
Port Talbot
Oldbury-on-Severn
Pontypridd
Caerphilly
Newport
M4
M5
Yate
N
M4
Avonmouth
M4
Bridgend
Cardiff
Chippenham
M5
Bristol
S
Avon
Bath
0
20 Kilometres

19

19 SHROPSHIRE WAY – 345km

The 345-kilometre Shropshire Way is a walk of two halves. The southern loop is a challenging hilly path over rocky peaks and through the castled landscape of the border Marches country. The northern loop takes you through gentler, greener countryside, along rivers and canal towpaths, past nature reserves and wetlands. The figure-of-eight trail meets in the medieval powerhouse of Shrewsbury, with its handsome Tudor buildings.

From Shrewsbury, the southern route leads you from the private Kingsland toll bridge through the green sliver of the Reabrook valley, and you soon leave the town behind you to gently climb along muddy farmland paths. You are climbing towards the top of Lyth Hill, where you will enjoy a panoramic view of Shropshire and the challenges to come, with the Wrekin, Wenlock Edge and the jagged tors of the Stiperstones on the horizon. Shropshire is one of England's most rural counties, and you will feel far from Shrewsbury's streets with only the deer for company on the remote expanse of Wilderley Hill. From here you follow the prehistoric ridgeway Portway before descending through the bird-rich Golden Valley to reach Bridges.

Legend says that on misty days, the Devil sits on his jagged chair on the top of the Stiperstones. This scree-strewn ridge, with quartzite tors, is the second highest point in the county. The Way descends through the Linley Beeches, a magnificent avenue originally planted by in the eighteenth century, to the hamlet of More, where the path takes you past the sunken remains of a medieval village with motte and bailey castle. You are walking in borderlands of the Welsh Marches, and the Marcher lords built hundreds of small castles here. However, all that remains of the castle built to defend Bishop's Castle from the Welsh is a single ivy-covered wall.

From Churchtown to Clun, the Way briefly follows Offa's Dyke Path, once the frontier between Mercia and Wales, before taking a high, grassy trod over the Cefns ridge. Castled Clun was immortalised in *A Shropshire Lad* although A.E. Housman, a Worcestershire lad, spent little time in Shropshire; he was instead inspired by the county's high ridges on the distant horizon in his childhood.

The southern Shropshire Way is a hilly trail between castles in various states of ruin. After you pass the Iron Age hill fort at Bury Ditches you will reach one of the best preserved medieval fortified manors in England, Stokesay Castle, always intended more to impress than defend. The wooded track of Aldon Gutter leads you past deserted cottages down through Bromfield, and you walk the Teme Valley to reach Ludlow, a pretty market town beloved by Betjeman. You may wish to pause to enjoy the medieval castle and Tudor houses before embarking on the climb over Shropshire's highest hills.

Titterstone Clee is Shropshire's third highest hill, its summit topped by a radar station. Titterstone and your next climb to Shropshire's highest point, Brown Clee (540 metres), were the site of nine World War II aircraft accidents, at a cost of twenty-three lives – you pass a memorial to them on Brown Clee. After a descent through green pastures you reach one of the YHA's more unusual youth hostels at the Elizabethan manor of Wilderhope.

◀ VIEW OF TITTERSTONE CLEE FROM CLEE BURF.
© AUDREY MENHINICK

With the highest hills behind you, an easy quarry railway route leads you to Much Wenlock, a town famed for resurrecting the Olympics in its modern form. After walking along a pleasant wooded path past the Elizabethan Benthall Hall, you face a steep descent into Ironbridge, the town at the heart of the Industrial Revolution that is named for its dramatic red bridge, the first bridge in the world to be made of cast iron. The landscape that you climb through as you leave the Severn's gorge behind you has been shaped by this Industrial Revolution, and mined for coal and iron. The climb up the Wrekin, Shropshire's 'little mountain' that dominates the Black Country landscape, may be something of a scramble.

The southern loop passes through Wellington before meeting the northern loop at Haughmond Hill, although there is also a link route back to your starting point in Shrewsbury. Northern Shropshire is a flatter, more pastoral landscape than the hilly south of the county. Through farmers' fields, with the path sometimes difficult to distinguish, there is only one climb over Grinshill near the start of your circuit.

The market town of Wem is famous for being the birthplace of the modern sweet pea and its legendary treacle mine, although sceptics suggest that the myth grew out of a confectioner who never ran out of sweets despite wartime sugar rationing. The Way follows grassy trods and country tracks through farmland. You now face a choice of whether or not to follow a spur to Whitchurch, believed to be the site of the Roman settlement of Mediolanum – the town has certainly yielded plentiful archaeological finds. The spur takes you through sites of special interest at Brown Moss and Prees Heath, where in June and July you might see the rare silver-studded blue butterfly.

THOMAS TELFORD'S BRIDGE OVER THE SEVERN AT MONTFORD BRIDGE. © AUDREY MENHINICK

If you skip the spur, the trail skirts the edge of the Fenn's, Whixall and Bettisfield Mosses National Nature Reserve, a wetlands habitat dotted with bog cotton, before joining the Shropshire Union Canal. The Way follows the towpath through Ellesmere and on to the border village of Llanymynech – as part of the village is in Wales, it was once only legal to drink in the two English bars of the Lion Hotel (now closed) and not its Welsh bar.

The trail follows the course of the often flooded River Vyrnwy to meet the Severn at Melverley, where you might choose to visit the rare black-and-white, timber-framed church. You join with the Severn Way to return to Shrewsbury, although the Shropshire Way does make a brief diversion from the Severn and its Way to climb Nesscliffe Hill, where you pass an Iron Age hill fort. The ascent to the summit rewards you with views of the Welsh hills. As you return to the Severn Way, you might make a small detour to two-roomed Kynaston's Cave, the lair of the outlawed sixteenth-century highwayman, Wild Humphrey Kynaston. With the Severn Way, you return to Shrewsbury through often muddy river meadows.

The Shropshire Way was first imagined by the Ramblers' Association in the 1970s and came into being in the 1980s, but gradually a plethora of variations were added. The confused route fell into neglect, and paths became overgrown and under-walked. Thanks to the Herculean efforts of the Shropshire Way Association, a new charitable trust, the route was rejuvenated with the new 'Main Route' completed in 2018. The trail now takes you through the best and most rural regions of Shropshire's lush countryside while allowing you to discover little-known historical gems. Take your opportunity to enjoy this quiet trail, before the walkers on Offa's Dyke Path and the Severn Way notice the buzzard waymarks and decide to explore it for themselves.

LOOKING EAST FROM THE CEFNS RIDGE NEAR CLUN. © NORMAN LINES

19 SHROPSHIRE WAY: ESSENTIAL INFORMATION

TRAIL ESSENTIALS

Start:	**Shrewsbury, Shropshire, England**
End:	**Shrewsbury, Shropshire, England**
Distance:	**345km**
Ascent/descent:	**4,350m/4,350m**

HOW TO GET THERE

Shrewsbury has a train station, with good connections to Birmingham and Manchester, both of which have international airports.

TIME TO COMPLETE

Walking:	**15 days/89 hours**
Trekking:	**9 days/73 hours**
Fastpacking:	**7 days/55 hours**
Trail running:	**6 days/41 hours**

PROS

- **Roads** – except where the route passes through towns and villages, the Way tends to keep you away from roads, even the quieter country lanes.

- **Industrial heritage** – the rich resources of Shropshire have been mined and quarried for centuries. Mining began in the Bronze Age near Llanymynech and limestone was quarried nearby. Grinshill sandstone can be found in Haughmond Abbey and the prime-ministerial residence of Chequers. More recently, Ironbridge was nicknamed the birthplace of the Industrial Revolution, and the Shropshire Union Canal turned Shropshire towns into transport hubs.

- **Countryside** – this is the landscape that inspired poets with its quintessential Britishness. It is not rugged mountains or wild moorland but rolling hills, green farmlands, hedgerows and rivers. In rural Shropshire it is as though time has stood still but simultaneously left its mark in the castles, houses and hill forts.

CONS

- **Flooding** – both the Severn and Vrynwy rivers are liable to flooding, and the centre of Shrewsbury has been badly flooded on several occasions.

- **Route change** – the Shropshire Way has undergone a major route revision from 2016 so you should be wary of relying on outdated information sources, such as maps, GPX files and books. You must follow the Main Route waymarkers if you want to follow the new route.

GOOD TO KNOW

Many in the West Midlands enjoy a distant view of the solitary Wrekin, Shropshire's 'little mountain', and it has entered the public imagination. There is a popular local phrase, 'All around the Wrekin', which means going the long way about something, and, in 1981, 17,000 local schoolchildren and adults joined hands around the base of the Wrekin in an attempt to set a Guinness World Record for the longest human chain.

FURTHER INFORMATION

www.shropshireway.org.uk

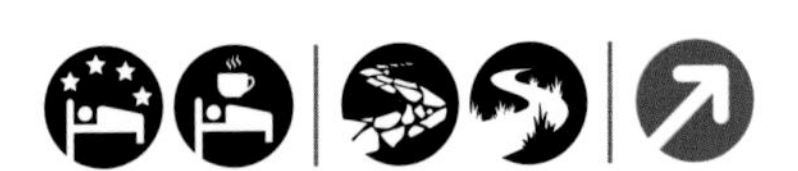

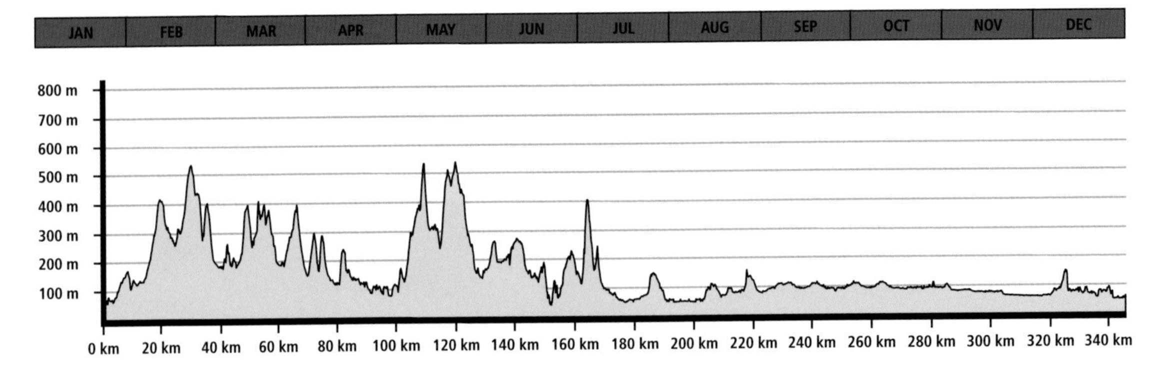

Wrexham
A49
A41
A530
M6
Bangor-on-Dee
Llangollen
A539
A525
Whitchurch
A525
Audlem
A51
A539
Penley
Chirk
Dee
A528
Tilstock
Welsh End
Welshampton
Ellesmere
A41
A53
Whixall
A495
Lyneal
Tetchill
Whittington
Market Drayton
Oswestry
A528
Wem
A41
Tilley
Tern
Burlton
Maesbury Marsh
A5
Grinshill
A53
Llansantffraid-ym-Mechain
Llanymynech
Meese
A41
Nesscliffe
Vyrnwy
Wilcott
Astley
A528
B5062
Newport
WALES
Melverley
Severn
Shrewsbury
Rodington
A518
Shrawardine
Montford
A490
A483
Uffington
A458
A5
Wellington
A458
A5
Telford
Westbury
Hanwood
Welshpool
Bayston Hill
The Wrekin
M54
Little Wenlock
ENGLAND
A458
A458
Severn
B4386
Minsterley
Dorrington
Cressage
Ironbridge
Madeley
Broseley
Harley
Stiperstones
A49
Picklescott
Chirbury
Stiperstones
Leebotwood
Much Wenlock
A442
Montgomery
Bridges
Long Mynd
A458
Longville in the Dale
Easthope
Churchstoke
Church Stretton
Bridgnorth
Wilderhope
Shipton
Lydham
Holdgate
Ape Dale
Bishop's Castle
Wenlock Edge
Churchtown
Corve Dale
Cleobury North
Clun Forest
Brown Clee Hill
Abdon
Rea
Onny
Hopesay
Craven Arms
Corve
Newcastle
Bury Ditches
Kempton
Stokesay Castle
Clun
Clunton
Titterstone Clee
Shropshire Hills AONB
Bromfield
Cleobury Mortimer
N
A4113
Cleehill
A4117
Bewdley
Knighton
Ludlow
Teme
A4113
A456
A4110
A49
0
10 Kilometres
Tenbury Wells

Cockburnspath
Berwick-upon-Tweed
Dumfries
Portpatrick

20

20 SOUTHERN UPLAND WAY – 347km

The 347-kilometre Southern Upland Way, one of Scotland's Great Trails, was Britain's first official (east–west or west–east) coast-to-coast route. It begins in the Rhins of Galloway, on the edge of the Irish Sea, and passes through the Scottish Marches, Scotland's border country. This countryside, once the land of soldiers and bandits, is some of the most sparsely populated in the British Isles. The hilly trail does not summit giants, but does take an up-and-down route over high, heathered moors. The Way ends on the edge of the North Sea at Cockburnspath.

The Southern Upland Way begins not on the high moorlands but on the coast, at the village of Portpatrick on the Rhins of Galloway peninsula. A narrow, sometimes steep-stepped, coast path leads around the cliffs, past Port Mora and Port Kale, where the first telegraph cable was laid between Britain and Ireland. Near the white Killantringan Lighthouse, the trail turns inland on farm tracks to pass Knockquhassen Reservoir and across Broad Moor, where an 'Ultreia' plaque prompts you to search for your first kist. You skirt above Stranraer on the shore of Loch Ryan and follow wooded paths to Castle Kennedy with its castle ruins. By the bird-rich White Loch, you will also have views of Lochinch Castle.

The Way is on good paths across farmlands and moors, forestry trails and occasional roads. In the middle of the forest, you pass one of many bothies en route, the Beehive bothy. Nearby are the Laggangairn Stones, a pair of standing stones that are probably the remains of a full circle. In the middle of the Kilgallioch Forest, there is signed detour to the holy springs of the Wells of the Rees, although they are now dried up. The first proper climb of the Way is over Craig Airie Fell, the highest hill in Wigtownshire.

While the trail offers you views of the rugged Galloway Hills, and of Loch Dee and Clatteringshaws Loch, you will rarely not find yourself under tree cover as you walk through the Galloway Forest Park. The largest forest in Britain, the Park was the first in the UK to be granted Dark Sky Park status. It is not until you reach the quiet village of St John's Town of Dalry, once the centre of the 1666 Pentland Rising in opposition to government imposition of episcopalianism, that the trail changes as you reach the Southern Uplands for which the Way is named. The route begins to climb, first on roads and then grassy trails towards Manquhill Hill, and then the summit of Benbrack (580 metres). On top of Benbrack, you'll find an imposing red sandstone arch, one of Andy Goldsworthy's three Striding Arches artworks.

Grassy, sometimes muddy, paths lead you towards Sanquhar, where you can visit the ruins of a thirteenth-century castle, although nearby ancient hill forts suggest a much longer history of inhabitation. The castle has hosted Robert the Bruce, William Wallace and Mary, Queen of Scots. This is a landscape of heathered moorland, exposed hills and boggy paths. Although you are unlikely to meet other walkers, you will see the scars of lead mining on the exposed hills. In the Lowther Hills, in Scotland's highest village of Wanlockhead (467 metres), you can visit the Museum of Lead Mining where you can also descend into a mine.

◀ HEADING FOR THE SUMMIT OF LOWTHER HILL.
© *WALKHIGHLANDS.CO.UK*

Lowther Hill – with its golf ball radar station – is the highest point of the Southern Upland Way at 725 metres. Although the route begins to descend, it still kicks up and down, eventually passing the shepherd cottage bothy of Brattleburn. Somewhere here, near Beattock, with the thunder of the M74 motorway and main railway line in the background, you pass the halfway point of the Way. Past Moffat, a gravel track leads you through forest.

A recent revision to the route sees it climbing over Croft Head and Cat Shoulder to reach Ettrick Head, although the old, level route along forestry tracks is still an option. Once the Tibbie Shiels Inn was a welcome respite for walkers and runners, but the tavern is now closed, perhaps permanently. However, camping is still available and the Over Phawhope bothy is also on the trail. You follow clear tracks, first gravel then grass, down the green Ettrick valley to reach St Mary's Loch, where you can enjoy a five-kilometre path along the lake's eastern shore. At the foot of the loch, it is worth making a short detour to Dryhope Tower, a rare example of a fortified sixteenth-century peel tower. The Southern Upland Way crosses border country, disputed by Scots and the English and violently raided by the Reivers, and the ruins of these conflicts are occasionally seen along the trail.

The summit of Blake Muir stands between you and Traquair, location of Traquair House, Scotland's oldest inhabited home, and also site of the Traquair House Brewery. The old drovers' Minch Moor Road possibly dates back to the thirteenth century, and as you follow it you reach the Cheese Well, where people still leave small offerings to appease the fairies. After the forest, you reach high, exposed moorland topped by three cairns, known as the Three Brethren, that mark the boundaries of three estates.

COVE HARBOUR. © *WALKHIGHLANDS.CO.UK*

You will have to make a short detour from the trail if you want to visit Abbotsford House, home of Sir Walter Scott, close to Galafoot Bridge where the Way crosses the Tweed to avoid the centre of Galashiels. You follow the river to reach Melrose, famous for its twelfth-century Cistercian abbey, the final resting place of the heart of Robert the Bruce. An early, nineteenth-century suspension bridge takes you over the Tweed again.

Nestled in the green dip of gentle hills, the historic town of Lauder is the last big town on the Way. The trail passes below the red walls of the sixteenth-century Thirlestane Castle. You climb to grassy paths over the high heather moorland of Lammermuir, where you will reach the Twin Law Cairns, reputedly a memorial to brothers who, separated in childhood, fought on opposing sides at the Battle of Twinlaw. On a clear day, you may get your first glimpse of the North Sea from the cairns. A track descends to Watch Water as it joins the bigger Whiteadder Water, which you follow to reach a wooded path into the village of Abbey St Bathans.

Farm roads and tracks lead you through Penmanshiel Wood, but then the trail climbs to offer a view of the sandy bay near the Way's end (and the caravan park on the sandstone cliffs above it). Through the wooded gorge of the Pease Dean nature reserve, you descend to Cove Harbour and on to the war memorial in the village of Cockburnspath, where the Way ends.

Tourists flock to Edinburgh and Glasgow; the wilderness of the Highlands is famous, and the Trossachs are a popular destination. But there is a secret, undiscovered, wild Scotland that few uncover in the Southern Uplands. The Southern Upland Way is not an easy trail, even for the experienced hillwalker or runner, but it is an exceptionally beautiful one.

ABOVE: LOOKING NORTH FROM WARD LAW CAIRN. © RONA DODDS

BELOW: CROSSING THE WATERSHED AT ETTRICK PEN. © *WALKHIGHLANDS.CO.UK*

20 SOUTHERN UPLAND WAY: ESSENTIAL INFORMATION

TRAIL ESSENTIALS

Start:	**Portpatrick, Dumfries and Galloway, Scotland**
End:	**Cockburnspath, Scottish Borders, Scotland**
Distance:	**347km**
Ascent/descent:	**6,930m/6,870m**

HOW TO GET THERE

Portpatrick has bus services to Stranraer, which has a rail station. The nearest international airports are Glasgow and Prestwick, and the ferry port at Cairnryan offers connections to Larne in Northern Ireland.

Cockburnspath has buses to Berwick and Dunbar, which both have rail stations. The nearest international airport is Edinburgh, although Glasgow's airports are also easy to reach.

TIME TO COMPLETE

Walking:	**17 days/101 hours**
Trekking:	**11 days/83 hours**
Fastpacking:	**8 days/62 hours**
Trail running:	**6 days/45 hours**

PROS

- **Bothies** – Beehive, White Laggan, Poleskeoch, Brattleburn and Over Phawhope bothies are all on, or very close to, the Southern Upland Way.

- **Wild camping** – wild camping is legal on unenclosed land in Scotland, and the Southern Upland Way is a great place to experience it. It is easy to find shelter from the worst of the weather in the lee of a hill or amongst the trees. The best way to attempt the Southern Upland Way may be a combination of camping and bothying.

- **Treasure Hunt** – there are several artworks to enjoy along the Way, but also hidden treasure. Along the Way, you may see 'Ultreia', an old pilgrim's cry urging you on. These indicate where you should search for hidden kists, or chests – each contain unique waymarks, small metal 'coins' with a design specific to the Way for you to collect.

CONS

- **Wind turbines** – the high, rolling Southern Uplands are perfect spots to catch the breeze and advantage has been taken of this. If you feel that giant white turbines ruin the vista, the Southern Upland Way is not the route for you – there are large wind farms at Killgallioch and Lammermuir, and many other turbines.

- **Shops** – villages are few and far between on sections of the Southern Upland Way, and many have lost their local shop. If you are backpacking, you need to plan resupplying carefully.

- **Forests** – the Way has extensive forest sections, particularly near the start. You may find your path diverted to avoid logging operations.

GOOD TO KNOW

The Southern Uplands are the landscape of James Hogg, the 'Ettrick Shepherd', and the Way passes his home, Blackhouse. Born on a farm in 1770, this self-educated man became one of the Scotland's most influential poets and novelists. He is an ancestor of Canadian short story writer Alice Munro.

FURTHER INFORMATION

dgtrails.org/southern-upland-way

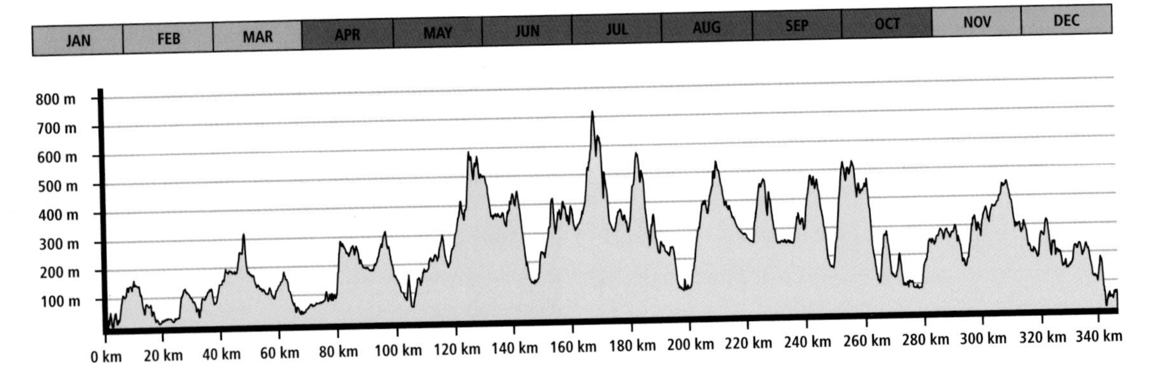

North Sea
The Trossachs National Park
Grangemouth
North Berwick
Dunbar
M80
Cumbernauld
Edinburgh
A1
Cockburnspath
Glasgow
M8
Eyemouth
Abbey St Bathans
A6112
A1
A68
Longformacus
Duns
Isle of Arran
M77
A703
Blackhope Scar
Lauder
A6105
Berwick-upon-Tweed
Strathaven
Lanark
Peebles
Windlestraw Law
Coldstream
Kilmarnock
Biggar
A68
Galashiels
A6089
Irvine
Innerleithen
Melrose
Kelso
A697
Traquair
Tweed
A76
A70
M74
Dun Rig
A708
Selkirk
A698
St Mary's Loch
Ayr
Cumnock
Broad Law
Jedburgh
Great Hill
New Cumnock
Wanlockhead
Hawick
Sanquhar
Lowther Hill
Moffat
Mennock
Daer Reservoir
Wind Fell
A6088
A7
Beattock
Northumberland National Park
Girvan
Benbrack
Cairnsmore of Carsphairn
Thornhill
SCOTLAND
Irish Sea
A702
Galloway Forest Park
Corserine
A76
Lockerbie
St John's Town of Dalry
Bargrennan
Lamachan Hill
Dumfries
ENGLAND
A712
Clatteringshaws Loch
A74(M)
Laggangairn Standing Stones
A75
Loch Ryan
Cairnryan
Newton Stewart
Gretna
Haltwhistle
N
A69
Stranraer
New Luce
A75
Brampton
Castle Kennedy
A75
Wigtown
Portpatrick
Kirkcudbright
Carlisle
Solway Firth
Alston
M6
A689
0
20 Kilometres
Maryport
Penrith

JENNA H.
BK·69
JENNA H.
BK·69

21

21 ST OSWALD'S WAY – 154km

The 154-kilometre St Oswald's Way is a modern pilgrimage path that leads you from Hadrian's Wall across the Northumberland moorland and farmland, to the gorgeous coast and the Holy Island of Lindisfarne. It starts at Heavenfield, where Oswald lay claim to his crown, and ends at his most enduring legacy, the site of the early Christian monastery on Lindisfarne, passing on the way places associated with his life.

St Oswald's Way begins at Heavenfield, on the line of Hadrian's Wall. It is somewhere here that Oswald, exiled to the monastic island of Iona as a child, laid claim to the crown of Northumbria by defeating the Welsh and Mercian armies. On the night before the battle, he set up a wooden cross and prayed. A twentieth-century replica wooden cross still stands here, erected to replace an older stone cross. Nothing remains of the Anglo-Saxon church built to celebrate Oswald's victory. The small red-doored church dates to 1817 although it has carved Roman tablets incorporated into its altar.

The grey stone fortifications of Hadrian's Wall here have long been buried under General George Wade's Military Road, built to move troops to quell the Jacobite risings. However, the grassy ridge and ditch of the Vallum earthworks remain in evidence as you follow the Hadrian's Wall Path eastwards. Just before reaching the hamlet of Wall Houses, you leave the busy, straight Military Road, and Hadrian's Wall Path, to take a grassy trod across pastures towards Great Whittington, passing the grey stone tower of the abandoned eighteenth-century windmill.

North of Great Whittington, you find yourself on a country lane but soon turn off to cross wide, flat, arable fields.

There is little in the villages of Great Bavington or Kirkwhelpington to detain you. A grassy trod through sheep gives way to a long forestry track. Harwood Forest was one of the giant conifer plantations established after World War II to combat timber shortages. It is eleven kilometres north to south, and seven kilometres east to west, and you must pass through most of it from its southern boundary.

You leave the forest behind you at the peak of Coquet Cairn, at 300 metres the highest point on the Way. At Lordenshaws, you pass a rock dotted with Neolithic cup and ring carvings. From the charming town of Rothbury, the course of the River Coquet is followed to the North Sea, taking advantage of the disused trackbed of the Northumberland Central Railway. At a bend in a river you look down on the twelfth-century Brinkburn Priory, but you will have to leave the trail and cross the river if you want to visit. The church of St Michael and All Angels at Felton also dates to the twelfth century, but the original church is now almost entirely enclosed in later alterations.

The concrete mushroom of Morwick Water Tower heralds your arrival at Warkworth, where St Oswald's Way joins the Northumberland Coast Path. A castle has stood at Warkworth since the twelfth century, but the fortified keep that stands now dates from the fourteenth century and successfully repelled Scottish assaults twice. This was the ancestral home of the Percys, and the Dukes of Northumberland. A golden beach links Warkworth to Alnmouth, and the Way takes a sandy path through the dunes.

◀ LINDISFARNE CASTLE AND HARBOUR ON THE HOLY ISLAND OF LINDISFARNE.

The squelchy crossing at the River Aln is tidal; if the tide is too high, you face a lengthy detour inland to the road bridge.

Leaving Alnmouth, once you pass the golf courses the trail continues on pleasant paths along the low coastline with Dunstanburgh Castle on the horizon. You pass the fishing villages of Boulmer and Craster. Only one smokehouse, built in 1856, still operates in Craster, smoking the village's famous kippers. The grassy path skirts Dunstanburgh Castle, which sits on top of the edge of Whin Sill. It is a short detour to visit the ruins of the fourteenth-century fortifications, built to take advantage of the natural defence of the tall sea cliffs. Another golf course is passed before you reach a dune path, although you might choose instead to walk across the soft sands of the beach to Low Newton by-the-Sea, with its fisherman cottages and popular Ship Inn.

A bridge has been constructed to keep your feet dry as you ford Long Nanny burn. Officially the Way follows a grassy path behind the dunes, but at all except the highest of tides you can again walk along the beach if you prefer to Beadnell Bay. The curve of the bay gives Beadnell the only west-facing harbour on the east coast of England. You can take a boat trip from the harbour to see the Tommy Nodders, or puffins, on the Farne Islands.

Most will choose to continue on the sandy beach, with its rock pools, rather than follow the narrow path next to a busy road to reach Seahouses. The charming village is not just a popular tourist destination but also still a working fishing harbour. The Way makes another turn inland to cross farmers' fields on a grassy track. The narrow beach only provides a seaside alternative at lower tides, although it is an easy scramble across the dunes to the Links Road.

VIEW OF ALNMOUTH FROM CHURCH HILL ACROSS THE MOUTH OF THE RIVER ALN. © RUDOLF ABRAHAM – *WWW.RUDOLFABRAHAM.COM*

You pass through the village of Bamburgh, once Oswald's capital, under the shadows of the imposing Norman castle. After Budle Bay, from where you can enjoy views of the distant ridge of the Cheviot Hills, the route heads inland for a final time to reach Belford. There is a pedestrian level crossing at Belford, and you must phone the signalman for permission to cross this dangerous section of the main railway line.

St Oswald's Way now joins St Cuthbert's Way to follow the pilgrim's path to Lindisfarne. You leave the shore near the site of annual Lindisfarne Festival (which takes place every September). Tall wooden poles in the sand mark the safe walking route to the island – you should allow at least one hour to make the tidal crossing, and it is only safe to cross before or at low tide. There is a longer window for crossing on the tarmac causeway, but this is narrow and heavily used by cars. Lindisfarne, or Holy Island, is the end of St Oswald's Way. Aidan came from Iona in Scotland to establish a Christian monastery on Lindisfarne at Oswald's invitation, and the island remains an important point of pilgrimage. In addition to the ruined priory, there is a small sixteenth-century castle, renovated in the Arts and Crafts style by Edwin Lutyens in the early 1900s.

St Oswald's Way is well waymarked, with markers bearing the symbol of a raven – the raven is associated with Oswald because, according to legend, a raven carried his arm into an ash tree after he perished in battle. The trail follows good paths, sometimes flagged in moorland sections, woodland tracks and the occasional road. It offers ample opportunity to walk barefoot on the beach and to dip your toes in the bracing North Sea. You do not have to be a pilgrim to find heaven in the Way's peaceful moorland and Northumberland's golden beaches.

THE SNOOK, HOLY ISLAND OF LINDISFARNE. © RUDOLF ABRAHAM – *WWW.RUDOLFABRAHAM.COM*

21 ST OSWALD'S WAY: ESSENTIAL INFORMATION

TRAIL ESSENTIALS

Start: **Heavenfield, Northumberland, England**
End: **Lindisfarne, Northumberland, England**
Distance: **154km**
Ascent/descent: **1,150m/1,360m**

HOW TO GET THERE

Heavenfield is not on a public transport route so you must continue along the Hadrian's Wall Path for three kilometres to reach Wall, which has bus services to Hexham; this town has frequent bus and train services to Newcastle upon Tyne, and the nearest international airport. Newcastle also offers an international ferry service to the Netherlands.

Lindisfarne is infrequently served by buses, and you have a choice of crossing by foot (which is challenging within the safe crossing window) or travelling by car or taxi. Express buses from Newcastle to Berwick-upon-Tweed (both with mainline rail connections) stop on the main road at Beal.

TIME TO COMPLETE

Walking: **6 days/37 hours**
Trekking: **4 days/30 hours**
Fastpacking: **3 days/23 hours**
Trail running: **3 days/18 hours**

PROS

- **Fishing villages** – there are plenty of opportunities to sample Northumberland's fish along the Way. Only one smokehouse still smokes kippers in Craster; in nearby Seahouses, the aptly named Swallow Fish is one of the oldest smokehouses in England. At journey's end, you might enjoy the Lindisfarne oysters.

- **Inns** – at the Ship Inn in Low Newton, you can enjoy beer from its own microbrewery in front of an open fire or take in the views of the North Sea from the beer garden of the Jolly Fisherman in Craster. The Olde Ship Inn in Seahouses, first licensed in 1812, is famous for crab sandwiches and an excess of sea-faring memorabilia.

- **Churches** – the trail starts at the small stone church on Hadrian's Wall and ends on the Holy Island, with its ruined priory. En route you may want to visit the ruins of Brinkburn Priory and Felton's twelfth-century church within a church.

CONS

- **Dangerous crossings** – there are two hazardous crossings, the first at Belford where you must phone for permission to use the level crossing because trains travel in excess of 160 kilometres per hour. The five-kilometre tidal crossing to Lindisfarne is so dangerous that refuge towers are provided for those who find themselves stranded; it should only be attempted by foot on a receding tide.

- **Rural facilities** – from Heavenfield to Warkworth, many village pubs have pulled down their shutters for the last time, shops have been turned into homes and bed and breakfast owners have retired. You may have to rely on public transport or a taxi to reach Newcastle.

GOOD TO KNOW

In Bambugh, you can visit the Grace Darling Museum to find out more about the twenty-two-year-old daughter of the Longstone lighthouse keeper, who rowed with her father to rescue shipwrecked survivors when the steamship *Forfarshire* foundered on Harcar Rock in a storm in 1838. Terrible weather saw the nine survivors and lifeboat crew stranded at the lighthouse for three days. Plays and poems were written about Grace's heroism and a public subscription raised £700 for her. The attention did little for the health of the shy girl, and she died aged twenty-six of tuberculosis. She is buried with her family in the Bamburgh graveyard.

FURTHER INFORMATION

www.stoswaldsway.com; St Oswald's Way and St Cuthbert's Way (Cicerone, 2019).

JAN FEB MAR APR MAY JUN JUL AUG SEP OCT NOV DEC

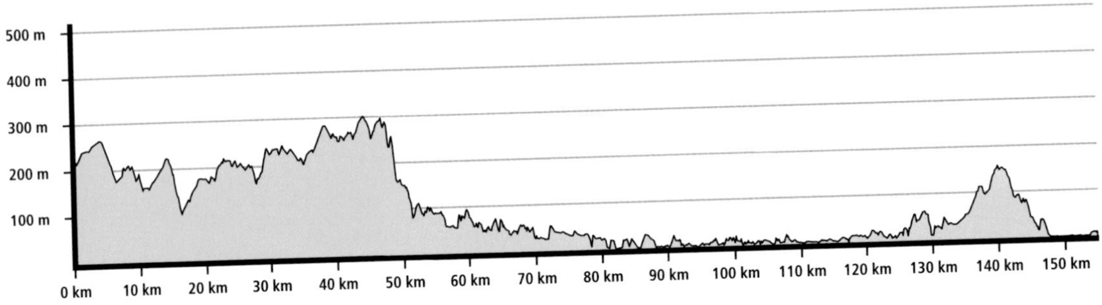

500 m
400 m
300 m
200 m
100 m
0 km 10 km 20 km 30 km 40 km 50 km 60 km 70 km 80 km 90 km 100 km 110 km 120 km 130 km 140 km 150 km

SCOTLAND
Berwick-upon-Tweed
North Sea
A698
Tweed
Causeway
Holy Island of Lindisfarne
Coldstream
Fenwick
A698
Buddle Bay
Farne Islands
Bamburgh
Till
Belford
Seahouses
Lowgos Bay
Beadnell
Wooler
A1
Beadnell Bay
B1340
Low-Newton-by-the-Sea
Embleton Bay
Black Hag
Hills
Embleton
Dunstanburgh Castle
Cheviot
The Cheviot
Craster
Breamish
Aln
Butt Roads
Boulmer
Beefstand Hill
A697
Alnwick
Hipsburn
Alnmouth
ENGLAND
Coquet Head
Warkworth
B6341
Amble
Northumberland
Rothbury
Longframlington
Felton
A68
Lordenshaws
Coquet
National Park
A1068
Druridge Bay
Brinkburn Priory
Coquet Cairn
A697
B6342
Font
A1
A696
Ashington
Newbiggin Bay
West Woodburn
Morpeth
Kirkwhelpington
Bellingham
Wansbeck
Blyth
A696
A68
A1
Cramlington
Great Bavington
North Tyne
N
Whitley Bay
B6320
A6079
Pont
Ponteland
Great Whittington
Chollerford
Heavenfield
Tynemouth
A1
Wall
B6318
Wallsend
Acomb
Bardon Mill
Haydon Bridge
A69
A69
Newcastle upon Tyne
Tyne
Hexham
Corbridge
Prudhoe
Gateshead
0
10 Kilometres
A68
A692
A194(M)
Sunderland
Washington

22

Dufton

South Gare

22 TEESDALE WAY – 154km

The 154-kilometre Teesdale Way begins at the mouth of the River Tees, on the sandy beaches near Redcar, then follows the river through green countryside and over pastured floodplains and wooded banks. This low, gentle riverside route is often muddy as it passes between small towns and villages, and through the historic town of Barnard Castle. It joins the Pennine Way at Middleton-in-Teesdale and leaves the riverside for one spectacular final climb over High Cup Nick to finish in the verdant Eden Valley at Dufton.

The Way begins out on the spur of the long breakwater of South Gare but many choose instead to begin by Redcar Central train station. Although you may choose to trek the tarmac track above the dunes, the better option is to walk along Redcar's expansive sandy beach, past the iconic blast furnace (now threatened with demolition). A path through the golf course leads away from the beach and into Coatham Marsh.

After the nature reserve, the trail into Middlesbrough is a reminder of Teesside's industrial heritage. Hemmed in next to the railway, the route follows the Black Path, the track once used by sailors to reach their ships and later by steelworkers. This section of the route has little to recommend it to any but the most fervent fans of industrial architecture or railways. The Dorman Long tower stands silent now, but steel from here can be found in bridges across the world – Dorman Long built the Sydney Harbour Bridge in 1932. There are hidden delights to be found on route. You can still enjoy the wildlife paintings that Lackenby steelworks shunter, Joe Parkes, painted on walls along the path in his lunchtimes. If you take the short detour off-route at Cargo Fleet Wharf, you will not only get your first proper view of the Tees as it curves through Middlesbrough but also discover a secret gallery on a bridge.

The trail enters Middlesbrough near the Tees Valley Giants sculpture Temenos, and then passes the Transporter Bridge, once the longest working transporter bridge in the world, but since 2020 out of action and awaiting urgent repair. Ironopolis has now been grassed over at Teessaurus Park, where giant metal dinosaurs lurk on the now-green slag heap. As you follow the riverbanks towards Stockton-on-Tees, the scenery becomes more rural. At the Tees barrage, you may glimpse a seal waiting to snaffle a salmon for lunch. There is an International White Water Centre next to the barrage, and this stretch of the Tees is a popular watersports area – Olympic Gold medal rower Kat Copeland and 2016 Paralympic Gold medallist Laurence Whiteley both trained at Tees Rowing Club.

Industrial Teesside is firmly left behind you as you cross the Bowesfield Wetland Nature Reserve. The Way is now shaded tracks beside the river or muddy paths around ploughed fields, with the route only leaving the river to pass through villages pretty enough for biscuit boxes. Between Redcar and Darlington, the river and railway run roughly parallel, offering plenty of opportunities to take advantage of public transport to reach accommodation. The river passes a few kilometres south of the market town of Darlington, home to the world's first passenger railway, the Stockton and Darlington Railway.

◀ THE CLASSIC U-SHAPED VALLEY OF HIGH CUP NICK.
© ANDREW LOCKING – *ANDREWSWALKS.CO.UK*

Near Broken Scar, you occasionally find yourself by busy roads for short sections. You reach the Tees Cottage Pumping Station, a Victorian pumping station that is now a museum with two original pumps still in working order. At Piercebridge, you pass under the shadow of a Roman wall – although this is reconstructed, you can visit the ruins of the large Roman fort that once stood at this strategic river crossing. Gainford is one of three spa towns en route, and a short diversion will take you to the sulphurous riverside fountain. The Way crosses over the historic Whorlton Suspension Bridge, temporarily closed in 2020, so you may find diversions along footpaths on the northern banks. The bridge was always challenging – construction begin in June 1829, but the bridge was washed away in the October of the same year; a new bridge was completed in 1831.

A grassy path passes in front of Mortham Tower, a fortified fourteenth-century manor which is still a private home, just before you reach the furious, tumbling Meeting of the Waters where the River Greta joins the Tees. The trail prefers the edge of Barnard Castle rather than the centre; the wooded riverside path passes directly beneath the castle walls. You can choose which side of the river you prefer here. The riverside paths are shaded by trees, offering shelter from the worst of the weather.

You leave the river's banks at Eggleston, where the narrow, pathless stone bridge, dating back to the fifteenth century, is unpleasant for pedestrians to negotiate if the road is busy. After a high path through farmers' fields, which offers fine views of the Pennines, you return to the riverbank. The long trek into Middleton-in-Teesdale is a stony path, that often makes a rocky climb up and down through the riverbank's wooded sides. Middleton-in-Teesdale is a small market town with plenty to offer in the way of food, drink and accommodation.

WHEYSIKE HOUSE, AN ABANDONED FARM NEXT TO THE RIVER TEES. © ANDY WASLEY

The route joins the Pennine Way to follow a good, flat path along the river, and between the wobbly Wynch Bridge and Low Force Waterfall you pass a sculpture of Herdwick Sheep, carved by local artist, Keith Alexander. You reach the popular beauty spot of the High Force Waterfall, although you may still hear the noise of the nearby quarry over the foaming rush of the waters. The boulder-strewn path to Cauldron Snout can be tricky, particularly when wet. The Tees's source lies on the slopes of Cross Fell, but the Way leaves the river and continues to follow the Pennine Way along Maize Beck. The path across exposed moorland is often boggy and muddy.

A gradual climb through grey-green bogs ends abruptly at the stunning High Cup Nick, where the Way suddenly arrives on the top of a curved cliff high above a long, green valley. At 600 metres, this is the highest point on the Teesdale Way. The trail descends by following the cliff edge around the top of the valley, eventually joining a wide, stony miners' track that leads all the way into Dufton. Although Dufton is the end of the Teesdale Way, you may choose to continue on another five kilometres into the market town of Appleby-in-Westmorland, which has better transport links.

The Teesdale Way is a gentle riverside trail, with a sting in its tail. Although many will not consider the path near Middlesbrough scenic, it does give a unique view of the industrial heritage of the area and the windswept, sandy beach near Redcar is an undiscovered gem on the English coast. As you put the chimneys, pipes and rails behind you, the Teesdale Way becomes a gentle, albeit often muddy, path that is easy to follow along the wide river. Villages and towns on the Way offer ample opportunity for coffee and cake, and you will often find yourself sheltered from the worst of the weather by woods. However, the trail changes dramatically in nature at Middleton-in-Teesdale where you join the Pennine Way walkers. The long, boggy slog along Maize Beck is rewarded by the stunning scenery of High Cup Nick. While you may walk the Way in either direction, following it from coast to country saves the very best until last.

ABOVE: HIGH FORCE WATERFALL ON THE RIVER TEES ALONGSIDE THE PENNINE WAY. © ANDY WASLEY
BELOW: SHEEP NEAR MIDDLETON-IN-TEESDALE. © ANDY WASLEY

22 TEESDALE WAY: ESSENTIAL INFORMATION

TRAIL ESSENTIALS

Start:	**South Gare, North Yorkshire, England**
End:	**Dufton, Cumbria, England**
Distance:	**154km**
Ascent/descent:	**1,170m/1,000m**

HOW TO GET THERE

South Gare is only accessible on foot (although there is a private road). The nearest train station is approximately five kilometres away at Redcar, and the closest international airport is Teesside. You may choose to join the trail at Coatham, approximately two kilometres from Redcar Central train station.

Dufton is poorly served by public transport, and you will have to travel by foot or car to Appleby, which has a train station. Teesside and Leeds are the closest international airports.

TIME TO COMPLETE

Walking:	**6 days/36 hours**
Trekking:	**4 days/30 hours**
Fastpacking:	**3 days/23 hours**
Trail running:	**3 days/18 hours**

PROS

- **Bridges** – from the iconic Middlesbrough Transporter Bridge to the wobbly Wynch Bridge, paid for by lead miners over 200 years ago, the River Tees is defined by the bridges that span it. The Newport Vertical Lift Bridge no longer rises, and the historical Whorlton Suspension Bridge is now closed, but new bridges, such as the curved white arches of Stockton's Infinity Bridge, provide new routes across the river.

- **Birds** – you may see goosanders, grey wagtails, herons and the blue flash of a kingfisher along the river. Wildlife reserves at the Tees barrage and Coatham Marshes are particularly bird-friendly.

- **Easy navigation** – the path rarely leaves the river, although there is sometimes a choice of banks. If you find yourself diverted from the route, it is straightforward to get back on the trail by heading for the river. When the Way finally leaves the River Tees, it follows a well-waymarked section of the Pennine Way.

CONS

- **Not a National Trail** – the Teesdale Way is not a flagship National Trail, and in parts suffers from neglect. Paths on the edge of farmers' fields are occasionally ploughed over and waymarkers vandalised in more urban areas. There is limited information available on the trail and it sometimes lacks the infrastructure of more popular trails.

- **Traffic** – the path often runs parallel to busy roads, and sometimes the railway. You are rarely on the trail without the background hum of traffic, although the roads also provide good public transport links and helpful pickup points.

- **Riverside** – the riverside path is often muddy and sometimes slippery. Sections of the path are prone to flooding, particularly in winter.

GOOD TO KNOW

In the George Hotel in Piercebridge, Henry Clay Work saw the clock that had stopped when the landlords, the Jenkins brothers, died and was inspired to write the popular children's song, *My Grandfather's Clock*, in 1876.

FURTHER INFORMATION

www.enjoyteesvalley.com; *The Teesdale Way* (Cicerone, 2019).

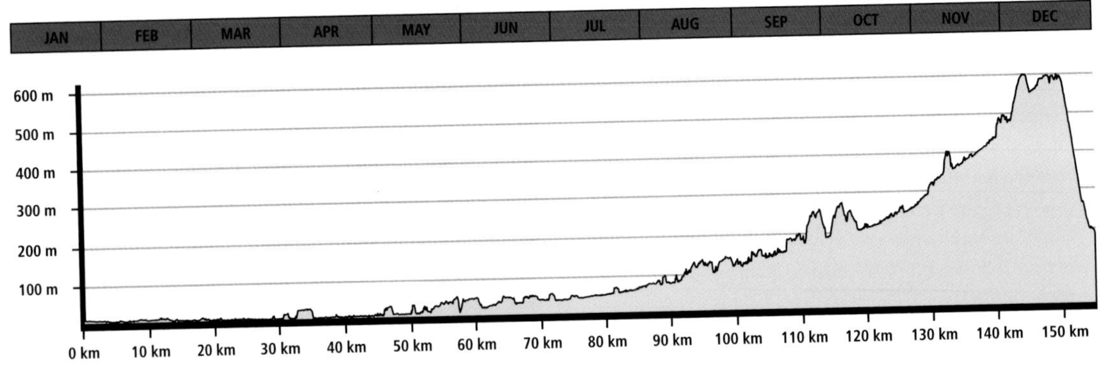

North Sea
Allendale
Consett
Seaham
Alston
Durham
Peterlee
Stanhope
The Pennines
Crook
Spennymoor
Hartlepool
Tees Bay
South Gare
Cross Fell
Great Dun Fell
Knock Fell
Cow Green Reservoir
Fendrith Hill
Bishop Auckland
Newton Aycliffe
Shildon
Newbiggin
Middleton-in-Teedale
High Force
Cauldron Snout
Dufton
High Cup Nick
Mickle Fell
Eggleston
Romaldkirk
Cotherstone
Redcar
Stockton-on-Tees
South Bank
Middlesbrough
Guisborough
Appleby-in-Westmorland
Brough
Barnard Castle
Whorlton
Winston
Gainford
Piercebridge
Darlington
Eaglescliffe
Middleton One Row
Yarm
Low Worsall
Hurworth-on-Tees
Stokesley
Kirkby Stephen
ENGLAND
Richmond
Catterick
Northallerton
Tees
Wear
Eden
Greta
Swale
Ure
Leven
North York Moors National Park
Yorkshire Dales National Park
The Calf
Sedbergh
Hawes
Leyburn
Bedale
Thirsk
A689
A686
A68
A1(M)
A19
B6277
B6278
A66
A688
B6275
A685
A683
B6270
A684
A167
A168
A172
N
0
10 Kilometres

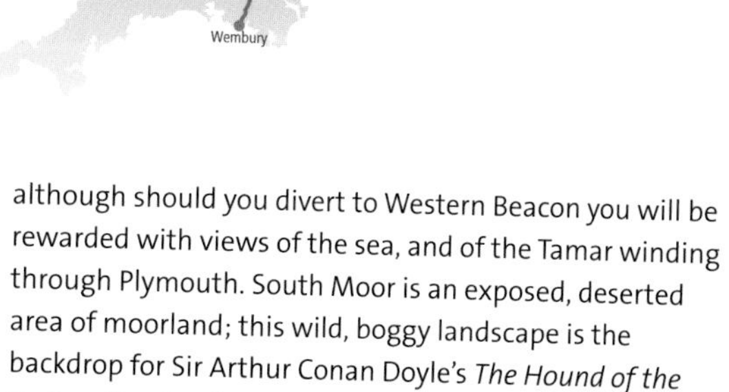

23 TWO MOORS WAY – 172km

Thousands flock to Devon for its sandy beaches, dramatic cliffs and seaside towns, but there is a quieter side of the county to be discovered. The 172-kilometre Two Moors Way starts in the pretty coastal village of Wembury and crosses the beautiful South Hams to reach the wild, isolated Dartmoor and then the green Exmoor. Although you may choose the Two Moors Way for the opportunity to traverse two national parks – Dartmoor and Exmoor – you'll be surprised by the pastoral beauty of the farmland between the moorland, a hidden gem rarely discovered by tourists. The route returns to the coast with a dramatic descent into Lynmouth. The Two Moors Way offers a little of everything: moorland, coast, Iron Age hill forts and pretty villages. It may be Devon's best-kept secret.

Once the Way began in Ivybridge, but most begin now at the seaside town of Wembury. On the pebbly beach at Wembury, you may discover spiny starfish, shrimps, anemones and sea scorpions – it is one of the best beaches in Britain for rock pooling. The route follows the Erme-Plym Trail out of Wembury across the South Hams, an Area of Outstanding Natural Beauty. As you follow shaded lanes and green fields next to the River Erme, you'll see Dartmoor rising in front of you. In spring, the woods of the Flete estate will be carpeted with wild garlic and bluebells.

Ivybridge is the gateway to Dartmoor and the largest town on the trail. You climb towards Western Beacon, Dartmoor's most southerly tor. The route follows the old Redlake Tramway to skirt the summit of the beacon, and of Weatherdon Hill, although should you divert to Western Beacon you will be rewarded with views of the sea, and of the Tamar winding through Plymouth. South Moor is an exposed, deserted area of moorland; this wild, boggy landscape is the backdrop for Sir Arthur Conan Doyle's *The Hound of the Baskervilles*. On the edge of the warren at Huntingdon, where rabbits were bred to feed Dartmoor's tinners, you cross the River Avon on the clapper bridge.

The Way leaves the moors to pass through the villages of Scorriton and Holne. Holne is the birthplace of Charles Kingsley, and the Dart is the river that Tom tumbles into in *The Water Babies*. The Dart is still a popular wild swimming spot and you could choose to have a dip in Holne Pool or at Spitchwick Common near Newbridge, where the Way leaves the river. However, watch out – the stretch of river between Newbridge and Holne, the Dart Loop, is a popular whitewater route for kayakers and canoeists.

The trail returns to the moor via Dr Blackall's Drive, built so that the doctor and his wife could enjoy the best views of Dartmoor from their carriage. You might choose a short detour from the Way to visit the small village of Widecombe in the Moor, where you can sit in old Uncle Tom Cobley's chair. This remote, high moor section passes Grimspound, where the remains of twenty-four Bronze Age hut circles can be explored. The route crosses the old turnpike road that traverses the moor, near the Warren House Inn, the highest pub in Southern England, where the 'eternal fire' has burned in the hearth since 1845.

◀ THE RIVER BARLE IN EXMOOR NATIONAL PARK.
© MARK RAINSLEY

An Iron Age stone row guides you, in the company of Dartmoor's wild ponies, towards Chagford. You follow the River Teign through its spectacular, wooded gorge before facing a steep climb up to Castle Drogo, with its leaky roofs, which was built to Edwin Lutyens's designs for twentieth-century department store magnate, Julius Drewe. You follow a high route across Piddledown Common before reaching the edge of Dartmoor, near Drewsteignton.

The green fields, shady woodland and pretty villages of farm-rich mid-Devon are a pleasant surprise to Two Moors Way trekkers. Morchard Bishop marks the halfway point of the Way. Knowstone lies in the middle of Knowstone moors, host to Devon's magnificently antlered red deer, and here you can enjoy a meal at the Mason's Arms, a Michelin-starred pub.

Views of both Dartmoor and your destination of Exmoor can be viewed from this quiet mid-section. The trail climbs by road to meet the moor at Badlake Moor Cross. Exmoor's wild landscape inspired R.D. Blackmore to write *Lorna Doone*, a tale of outlaws and romance. At Tarr Steps, you cross the River Barle on the seventeen-slabbed clapper bridge. The Devil reputedly built it and likes to sunbathe there, but is not the most reliable maintenance man – the stones have now been numbered as they are occasionally washed away in high waters.

You reach Somerset as a riverside path leads you to Withypool, where Blackmore wrote part of *Lorna Doone* in the bar of the Royal Oak. Withypool was once at the centre of the Royal Forest, a hunting ground where settlement and building were forbidden, and even today this section of moor feels remote and uninhabited. After skirting the Iron Age Cow Castle hill fort and the tiny village of Simonsbath, you climb up over Dure Down, past Exe Head where the River Exe bubbles out of the moor.

The whaleback Cheriton Ridge marks the border between Devon and Somerset, and the Two Moors Way, now back in Devon, saves its best for last. The coast is now in sight, and on a clear day you can enjoy superb views across the Severn Channel to South Wales. You make a dramatic descent

ABOVE: LOOKING OUT OVER THE DART VALLEY FROM DR BLACKALL'S DRIVE. © HOLLY STEVENS
BELOW: DARTMOOR PONY. © JOHN COEFIELD

towards the sea through the deep, wooded gorge of Myrtleberry Cleave. The Way reaches its end in Lynmouth, the pretty seaside village where Percy Bysshe Shelley honeymooned. Once you have explored the harbourfront fishing villages, you might be tempted to catch the cliff railway up through Devon's Little Switzerland to enjoy the Victorian charms of Lynton.

The Two Moors Way is not particularly challenging in terms of terrain or ascent, but you will often be on remote moorland, far from even the smallest of villages. You may struggle to find a pub, shop or bed and breakfast and in a landscape steeped in legend, whispered tales of a bus are amongst the most unbelievable. Completing the Way usually requires meticulous planning, and sometimes long days on the trail.

Two halves of a granite boulder sit facing out towards each other on the edge of Exmoor and Dartmoor, a sculpture created by Peter Randall-Page in memory of Joe Turner, the Exmoor Rambler, who devised the Two Moors Way. Devon's Coast to Coast, short though it is in comparison to its northern namesake, reminds you that Devon's beauty is not only to be found on its shores. The wild moorland country has inspired writers and painters, and as you stand amongst the heather, or bluebells, or marsh orchids, you will enjoy the secret, peaceful Devon that the grockles (or tourists) rush past.

MELISSA MONTAGUE DESCENDS INTO THE TEIGN VALLEY ON HER WAY TO WINNING THE RACE WITH NO NAME ULTRA ACROSS DARTMOOR IN 2020.
© NIK LANGDON-WARD, LENSPULSE PHOTOGRAPHY

23 TWO MOORS WAY: ESSENTIAL INFORMATION

TRAIL ESSENTIALS

Start:	**Wembury, Devon, England**
End:	**Lynmouth, Devon, England**
Distance:	**172km**
Ascent/descent:	**3,710m/3,710m**
Also known as:	**Devon Coast to Coast**

HOW TO GET THERE

Wembury is served by buses from Plymouth, which has a mainline railway station. Plymouth is an international ferry port, with services to France and Spain. Exeter is the closest international airport.

Lynmouth has a bus service to Barnstaple (and a summer service to Minehead). Barnstaple has a local rail service, which connects to the mainline via Exeter. National Express coach services connect Barnstaple to Bristol, Birmingham and London.

TIME TO COMPLETE

Walking:	**9 days/51 hours**
Trekking:	**6 days/42 hours**
Fastpacking:	**4 days/32 hours**
Trail running:	**3 days/23 hours**

PROS

- **Cream teas** – unlike their Cornish neighbours, Devonians prefer their cream teas with clotted cream spread thickly on a scone, and jam on top.

- **Wild camping** – Dartmoor is the only place in England where wild camping is permitted. On other sections of the trail, pubs or farms are often happy to let you pitch a tent outside.

- **Ponies** – both Exmoor and Dartmoor have their own rare breeds of semi-feral moorland ponies. You should not feed the ponies – it encourages them to stray into roads, car parks and villages.

CONS

- **Logistics** – public transport is very limited in Devon's moorland areas. Pubs and shops have closed, and those that remain often offer limited opening hours. There are limited accommodation options. Completing the Two Moors Way may require taxis, lifts from helpful bed and breakfast owners and detours from the trail.

- **Dartmoor mist** – the mists and bogs of Dartmoor famously inspired Conan Doyle to write *The Hound of the Baskervilles* and Dartmoor is often still swathed in atmospheric mist.

GOOD TO KNOW

The Devon Coast to Coast Ultra, an Ultra-Trail du Mont-Blanc qualifying event, is a challenging race run over the Two Moors Way every May. It can be run as a four-day or non-stop challenge; the fastest finishers complete the course in approximately twenty-four hours. Other events, such as the Two Moors Ultra, also make use of the route.

FURTHER INFORMATION

twomoorsway.org

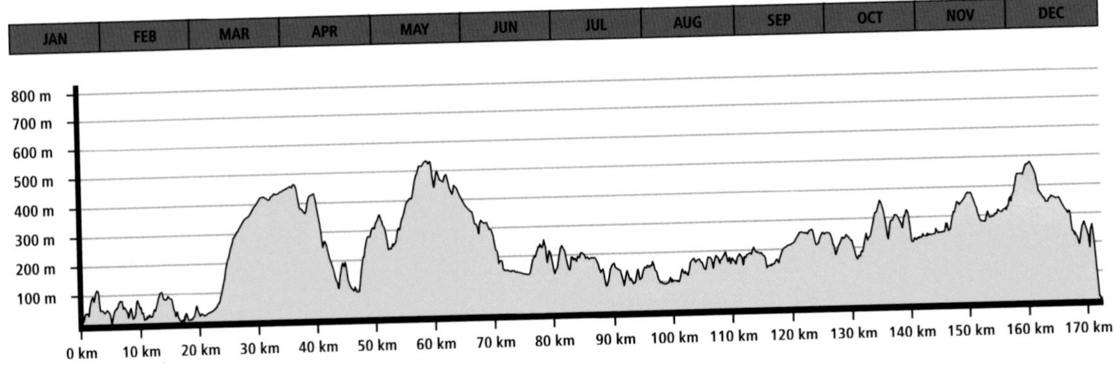

Bristol Channel
Lynmouth
Lynton
Ilfracombe
Combe Martin
A39
Porlock
Minehead
Watchet
A396
Hoaroak Hill
Exe Head
Exmoor National Park
A361
Simonsbath
Barle
Exe
Wheddon Cross
A399
Withypool
Tarr Steps
Bideford Bay
Barnstaple
Hawkridge
Westward Ho!
Bideford
Clovelly
South Molton
Yeo
Taw
Bray
West Anstey
Knowstone
B3227
Great Torrington
B3137
Wellington
A386
Little Dart
Witheridge
Tiverton
Washford Pyne
A3124
Dalch
A377
M5
Torridge
Morchard Bishop
Cullompton
A373
Holsworthy
A3072
Okement
North Tawton
Bow
Clannaborough
Crediton
A3079
ENGLAND
A388
Okehampton
A30
Hittisleigh
Exeter
Castle Drogo
Drewsteignton
B3212
Teigncombe
Chagford
Launceston
Dartmoor National Park
Grimspound
Bovey
A382
Hameldown Tor
Exmouth
Tamar
Bovey Tracey
Widecombe in the Moor
Tavistock
B3357
Ponsworthy
A38
Dawlish
Princetown
Poundsgate
Teignmouth
A390
Holne
Newton Abbot
Scorriton
Buckfastleigh
Liskeard
Ugborough Moor
Torquay
Dart
Weatherdon Hill
Saltash
Paignton
Western Beacon
Ivybridge
Avon
Torpoint
Plymouth
Brixton
Yealmpton
Ermington
A3122
Whitsand Bay
Dartmouth
N
A381
Wembury
Kingsbridge
Wembury Bay
Salcombe
0
10 Kilometres
English Channel

24

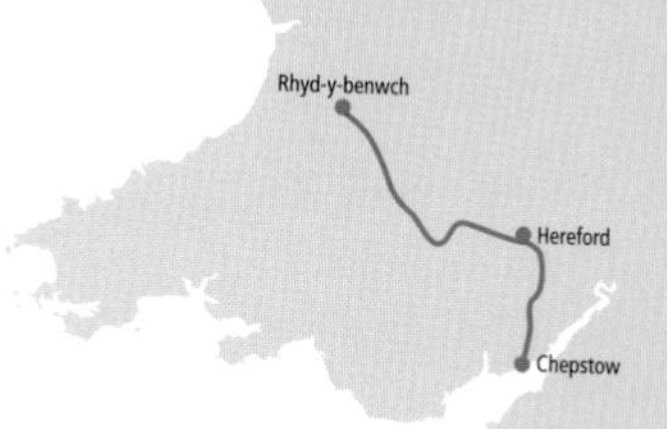

24 WYE VALLEY WALK – 222km

If a Big Trail is a route walked for pleasure rather than trade or work, the 222-kilometre Wye Valley Walk is perhaps one of the earliest of Britain's Big Trails. When the Napoleonic Wars put a temporary stop to the Grand Tour, the Wye Tour became a popular alternative – tourists would take a boat or walk the lofty banks of the Wye from Ross-on-Wye towards Chepstow, enjoying the picturesque sights along the river. Wordsworth wrote *Tintern Abbey* on a walking tour of the Wye. In its lower stretches, the Wye is now an Area of Outstanding Natural Beauty. The Wye Valley Walk follows the River Wye all the way from Chepstow to the Wye's beginnings in the Hafren Forest on the slopes of Plynlimon. The Walk begins and ends with the Wye's meetings with the River Severn, but although the trail is defined by rivers, the path often leaves the riverbanks to climb hills and follow high moorland trods.

You leave Chepstow by passing the walls of Chepstow Castle, a Norman castle that is said to be the oldest stone fortification still standing in Britain – although the best views of the castle are from the opposite riverbank. At the height of the Wye Tour, Valentine Morris landscaped Piercefield Park, with the help of Capability Brown, to provide picturesque landscapes and viewpoints over the Wye, and you face a steep climb up to this park. The grandiose Piercefield House has fallen into disrepair, but you can still enjoy the Giant's Cave as it tunnels through the cliff and climb 365 steps to the Eagle's Nest high viewpoint. The Walk descends steeply through tricky wooded paths to reach Tintern, with its famous ruined Cistercian abbey.

After a meadowed path by the river, you climb again through bluebell-filled woods to reach Cleddon Shoots, where Wordsworth is believed to have composed *Tintern Abbey*. After Whitebrook you take a flat route, following the Wye Valley Railway line, along the riverside to reach Monmouth. The route stays close to the River Wye, which skirts Monmouth, so if you want to see the castle and fortified Monnow Bridge you will have to leave the Wye Valley Walk temporarily – the Offa's Dyke Path, which has also been following the River Wye, will take you into the town centre.

You part company with Offa's Dyke Path at Monmouth, as the Wye Valley Walk follows the river across the border into England, towards Hereford. This stretch of the way between Monmouth and Symonds Yat is particularly popular with canoeists and kayakers. It is a short detour to Symonds Yat Rock, which not only offers spectacular views along the Wye and over the cliffs, but is also a great place to spot peregrine falcons. After a stretch along a disused railway, you have a steep climb over Chase Hill before descending to Ross-on-Wye, the Herefordshire town where Wye Valley tourism began.

While the Walk stays close to the river it remains flat, but as it leaves the river it climbs, passing the Iron Age earthworks at Capler Camp. You descend to the river again to reach Hereford. The site of the first bridge across the Wye, Hereford was a trading hub but is now most famous for its twelfth-century cathedral. Through meadows and cornfields, the Walk takes an undulating path with the dramatic backdrop of the Malvern Hills and Black Mountains.

◀ THE RIVER WYE IN HEREFORDSHIRE, FROM SYMONDS YAT ROCK.
© MARK RAINSLEY

The trail also passes large orchards; local firm Bulmers grows most of its cider apples in Herefordshire. After Monnington House, you walk in the shade of fir trees that line the seventeenth-century Monnington Mile avenue. There is a stern climb up Merbach Hill before you reach Hay-on-Wye, the border town famous for its bookshops and annual literary festival.

After Hay-on-Wye you follow the river's course more closely, although you still face the occasional climb over bracken-thick commons and short road sections. You are close to the edge of the Brecon Beacons National Park and have stunning views of the mountains. You turn north, with the river and a trail on the disused railway track, leaving the Beacons behind you to head for Builth Wells. At Llanstephan, you cross the river on a rare example of a Rowell suspension bridge built for cars, not just walkers – though it seems unlikely, cars are still allowed to drive across the narrow, timber-slatted bridge.

The Wye meets the Irfon at Builth Wells, and the town's location made it an important medieval marketplace. Builth was the site of one of the first four castles that Edward I built in Wales, although all that now remains are the earthworks. It was just west of Builth that Llywelyn ap Gruffydd, last sovereign Prince of Wales, died at the Battle of Orewin Bridge in 1282. After a pretty stretch by the tumbling river, you begin your ascent towards the river's mountain source, climbing to a high ridge near Carngafallt.

Rhayader is now the gateway to the beautiful Elan Valley, but it has always been an important town on drovers' and traders' routes. In 1843, local farmers disguised as women destroyed six of the town's extortionate tollgates in the Rebecca Riots. The Walk now becomes more rugged as it climbs into the foothills. Gilfach Nature Reserve is home to buzzards, red kites and kestrels, otters, badgers and hares.

BROCKWEIR ON THE TIDAL SECTION OF THE RIVER WYE, GLOUCESTERSHIRE. © MARK RAINSLEY

The Walk drops to the small village of Llangurig, before beginning its final climb. Llangurig is tiny, and you may have to arrange accommodation in nearby Llanidloes, although things might have been different if it were not for the railway. Llangurig is famous for having the shortest-lived working line, with only one goods train ever making the journey between Llangurig and Llanidloes in the 1860s – with no viable through-route over Plymlimon, the line was not deemed profitable.

You follow forestry tracks to climb through the Hafren Forest. The route joins the Severn Way in the trees, but the Wye Valley Walk ends at Rhyd-y-benwch on the slopes of Plynlimon. Rhyd-y-benwch was one of the twelve sheep farms that were purchased by the Forestry Commission to plant Hafren Forest in the 1930s, but it is now a car park and picnic area. You can choose to continue on the Severn Way to the source of the Severn near the mountain top, but you would then have to retrace your steps through Hafren Forest.

River trails often follow muddy paths through the flood plains of gently climbing rivers. The Wye Valley Walk is not a typical river path. The Wye has carved a deep course through high cliffs and hilly countryside, and you will find yourself standing on a clifftop viewpoint or following moorland paths with the river far beneath you. The Walk first takes you through medieval market towns and a city, through the farming landscape of Herefordshire, before reaching a wilder, more rugged Welsh countryside. No two days are the same on the Wye Valley Walk and you will find views to delight you, and surprises at every turn.

THE VALLEY OF THE AFON MARTEG IN POWYS. © MARK RAINSLEY

24 WYE VALLEY WALK: ESSENTIAL INFORMATION

TRAIL ESSENTIALS

Start:	**Chepstow, Monmouthshire, Wales**
End:	**Rhyd-y-benwch, Powys, Wales**
Distance:	**222km**
Ascent/descent:	**3,620m/3,300m**

HOW TO GET THERE

Chepstow has rail connections to the nearby city of Bristol, which offers onward connections to other British cities and has an international airport.

Rhyd-y-benwch is not served by public transport. You will either need to arrange a pickup or follow the Severn Way to Llanidloes. A bus service connects Llanidloes to Caersws, the closest rail station. The nearest international airports are at Birmingham and Cardiff.

TIME TO COMPLETE

Walking:	**10 days/60 hours**
Trekking:	**7 days/50 hours**
Fastpacking:	**5 days/38 hours**
Trail running:	**4 days/28 hours**

PROS

- **Villages and towns** – there are plenty of towns and villages on the Walk, making it easy to plan a daily itinerary including lunch stops. Many have good public transport connections.
- **Cider** – the Walk wends through cider apple orchards. Herefordshire is home to large producers, such as Westons and Bulmers, but smaller, local producers include Gwatkin, Oliver's, the Ross & Wye Cider & Perry Company and Celtic Marches. If you want to find out more about the history and production of cider, you can visit the Hereford Cider Museum.
- **Varied** – the Wye Valley Walk is more varied than most river walks, offering riverside sections, high moorland ridges, the occasional hill and a climb into the edge of the Cambrian Mountains. It crosses back and forth between England and Wales, and visits a medieval city, border towns and Welsh villages.

CONS

- **Livestock** – Herefordshire is famous for its cows, but you are also likely to encounter plenty of sheep. Cows can be dangerous to walk through, particularly when mothers with young calves are present. Dog owners should take care around both cows and sheep.
- **End** – the Walk ends in a car park in the large Hafren Forest, a somewhat anti-climactic finish to a scenic route. Once you have taken the obligatory 'after' selfie in the picnic area, you have little choice other than to travel by taxi or car, or walk approximately twelve kilometres along the Severn Way into Llanidloes.

GOOD TO KNOW

Hereford is famous for its much-reconstructed cathedral, a site of worship having existed at the cathedral's location since the eighth century. It was renovated by the Normans, but repeatedly remodelled and extended over the next four centuries before being damaged during the Civil War (which probably was the cause of the fall of the western tower in 1786). Nineteenth-century renovations were carried out by George Gilbert Scott, architect of King's College Chapel and the Midland Grand Hotel in London. It is of interest to navigators because, in addition to one of four extant copies of the Magna Carta, it has the Mappa Mundi, the largest medieval map.

FURTHER INFORMATION

www.wyevalleywalk.org

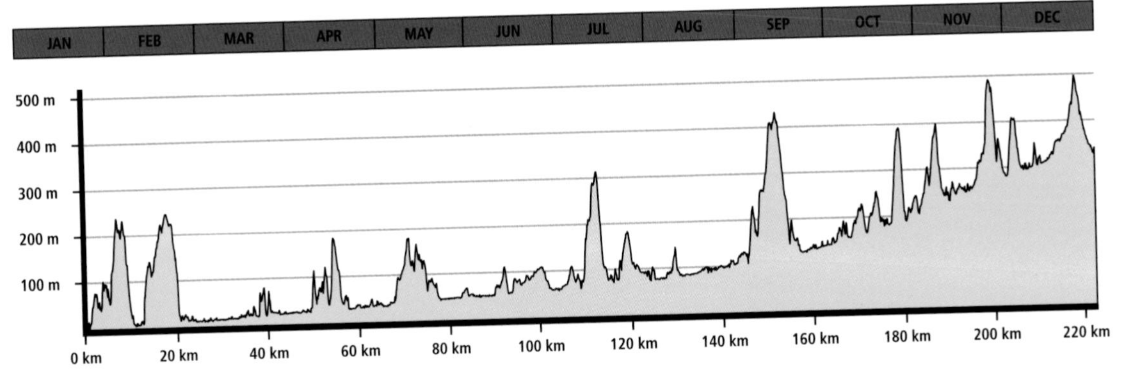

Machynlleth
A470
Montgomery
Much
Wenlock
Church
Stretton
Bridgnorth
Newtown
Caersws
A489
Plynlimon
F
Severn/Hafren
Llanidloes
Bishop's
Castle
A489
Wye/Gwy
Llangurig
A470
Shropshire Hills
AONB
Clun
Craven Arms
A4117
Cambrian Mountains/
Elenydd
Knighton
Teme
Ludlow
A456
A483
Rhayader
A488
A4110
A44
Llanwrthwl
Llandrindod Wells
Lugg
A44
Leominster
A44
Newbridge-on-Wye
Drygarn Fawr
Builth Wells
ENGLAND
A4112
A4111
A483
A470
A49
Llanwrtyd Wells
Merbach Hill
Monnington on Wye
Erwood
Llanstephen
Llowes
Hay-on-Wye
Wye
Hereford
A438
WALES
Ledbury
Mordiford
Llyswen
Glasbury
Llandovery
Capler Camp
A449
A470
Black
Mountains
A465
How Caple
Brecon
M50
Ross-on-Wye
Black Mountain
Brecon Beacons
National Park
Goodrich
A465
Symonds Yat
Wye Valley
AONB
Monmouth
Ebbw Vale
A465
Coleford
A40
Merthyr Tydfil
A449
Wye
Lydney
A465
Tintern
Cwmbran
Severn
S
Chepstow
Port Talbot
M4
Caldicot
M48
Pontypridd
M5
Caerphilly
Newport
M4
N
M4
Bridgend
Cardiff
Bristol
0
20 Kilometres
M5

25

25 YORKSHIRE WOLDS WAY – 124km

The 124-kilometre Yorkshire Wolds Way is a National Trail that leads you from the banks of the wide Humber, in the shadow of its iconic bridge, across the rolling chalk hills and dry valleys of the Yorkshire Wolds. It follows good tracks and grassy paths through pastures, woods and poppied cornfields before reaching the Yorkshire seaside, where it meets with England's Coast Path and the Cleveland Way.

The Yorkshire Wolds Way starts in the shadow of the Humber Bridge, on the banks of the river where a ferry crossing once connected to the opposite shore. When it was built in 1981, the bridge was the longest suspension bridge in the world – it now languishes in eleventh place but its silhouette can still be seen from kilometres out at sea.

You begin the trail by passing under the mighty bridge, and then skirt the Humber Bridge Country Park. The park is nicknamed 'Little Switzerland' because quarrying has carved out steep cliff faces. You pass the now sail-less Black Mill, once used to crush quarried chalk, and continue along the shores of the Humber estuary on a path that forms part of the Trans Pennine Trail from Hull.

At North Ferriby a teenage Edward Wright, already a keen amateur archaeologist, stumbled across wooden planks in the muddy shores of the estuary – this was the first of three Bronze Age boats that Wright discovered between 1937 and 1963. It is at Ferriby, near the memorial to these discoveries, that the Way turns inland – although whether you turn through or past the village depends on the tide.

After a complicated crossing of the busy A63 main road, you follow the tree-lined Terrace Plantation to Welton, the village where Dick Turpin was reputedly finally arrested, for shooting a game cock. A grassy path through Welton Dale and a short road section leads you close to Brantingham – the Way skirts the village and neighbouring South Cave but does visit the Brantingham Church, which dates back to the twelfth century, although it was much restored by the Victorians. You walk around the edge of the Little Wold Vineyard – vines were first planted at Market Place Farm in 2012, and the vineyard now produces seven different wines.

You climb by woods, golden rapeseed and poppy-dotted barley fields through the undulating Comber Dale, East Dale and Swin Dale. Planted in the fields at the top of Sober Hill are the giant turbines of a wind farm. These hillsides are homes to some of England's oldest settlements; you pass the site where more than a hundred barrows where excavated to discover burials from the Iron Age Arras Culture. Personal belongings were buried with the people; four barrows contained chariots.

At Rifle Butts Quarry, you have a choice to make. You can divert, on a disused railway track, towards the shops, pubs and cafes of Market Weighton. The town was once home to the Yorkshire Giant, William Bradley, who at 2.36 metres high was and is the tallest British man ever; a Community Day is held there in memory of him of every year. The other route takes you via Goodmanham, once the site of a pagan temple which was controversially destroyed in AD 627, when Edwin, King of Northumbria, converted to Christianity.

◀ LOOKING WEST TOWARDS MILLINGTON PASTURE BETWEEN NETTLE DALE AND SYLVAN DALE. © AMY HUNT

The two routes meet up near the site of Londesborough Hall. The Duke of Devonshire demolished the Elizabethan hall in 1819, to cover the costs of renovating Chatsworth. The Way takes a country road towards Nunburnholme, eventually tracking across fields. You have panoramic views across the Vale of York and perhaps, on the clearest of days, the distant towers of York Minster. You face an up-and-down path, rolling through green fields to pass Millington – the village is a short detour from the Way.

The Way climbs through the tussocked fields of the undulating Dales. It follows the Huggate Sheepwalk, an old drovers' road. After the dry valleys of Horse Dale and Holm Dale, you reach Fridaythorpe. This small village, which is the highest in the Wolds, marks the halfway point of the Way.

In the green Thixen Dale, artist Chris Drury has created a spiral-banked modern earthwork, Waves and Time; it is one of several artworks commissioned for the Way. A road takes you through the village of Thixendale. You may take a direct route to Wharram le Street, but most take the slightly longer path through Deep Dale to visit Wharram Percy, the deserted medieval village. No one is certain why this once thriving settlement was abandoned, although the Black Death and conversion from arable to sheep farming land probably played their part. Little remains except for a crumbling church, but archaeological excavations have revealed rich details about medieval life.

After Wharram le Street, you walk on bridleway through arable fields to enter woods near Settrington Beacon. The trail descends into Wintringham and after a steep climb through the shady woods of Deep Dale Plantation,

APPROACHING HORSE DALE. © PAULA CONNELLY

you reach Enclosure Rites, another Yorkshire Wolds Way artwork. The Way turns east here to head for the Yorkshire coast. Through woods, hedgerowed fields and farms, you follow an elevated route towards Ganton.

You can enjoy wildflower-fringed paths through the undulating Camp Dale, Raven Dale and Stocking Dale. You may catch your first glimpse of the sea from the dale tops. In Muston, a yellow bike commemorates the 2018 Tour de Yorkshire, which passed through the village. You are soon in the seaside resort of Filey, but the route does not end in the town centre. Instead it climbs up to a clifftop path. The Way ends at the pointed stone sculpture that marks the trail meeting with the Cleveland Way at Filey Brigg.

The Yorkshire Wolds Way is clearly waymarked and may be walked at any time of year, although late spring or early summer – when the wildflowers begin to bloom, before the tourists arrive on the Yorkshire coast and when you might just get to enjoy sunshine between the showers – is the perfect time to attempt it. The Way tends to skirt around or pass close to villages and towns rather than through them – you should not underestimate the additional kilometres that diversions from the route to reach accommodation may add to your daily distance.

Tucked between the moors, the coast and the Dales, the Yorkshire Wolds are Yorkshire's forgotten gem. Every summer, people drive through these green chalk hills on their way to Bridlington, Filey and Flamborough, and never stop to explore the valleys and woods, or the towns and villages rich in history. The Way is an opportunity for you to discover the gentle, rolling beauty of the Yorkshire Wolds as you walk from the wide River Humber to the high cliffs of the Yorkshire coast.

ABOVE: THE WAYMARKER IN COW DALE HEADING WEST BETWEEN FRIDAYTHORPE AND THIXEN DALE. © AMY HUNT
BELOW: HEADING NORTH-WEST OUT OF FRIDAYTHORPE. © AMY HUNT

25 YORKSHIRE WOLDS WAY: ESSENTIAL INFORMATION

TRAIL ESSENTIALS

Start: **Hessle, East Yorkshire, England**
End: **Filey Brigg, North Yorkshire, England**
Distance: **124km**
Ascent/descent: **2,010m/1,970m**

HOW TO GET THERE

Hessle has a train station with direct connections to Doncaster (with its international airport), Hull (with ferry services to the Netherlands and Belgium), and connecting rail services to Leeds, with another international airport.

Filey Brigg is on the clifftops, and you will need to retrace your steps into Filey. Filey has direct rail connections to Doncaster, with its international airport.

TIME TO COMPLETE

Walking: **6 days/34 hours**
Trekking: **4 days/28 hours**
Fastpacking: **3 days/21 hours**
Trail running: **2 days/16 hours**

PROS

- **Wildflowers** – wildflowers love the chalk landscape of the Wolds. You can see yellow birds-foot-trefoil, rest harrow, bindweed, poppies, eyebright, knapweed and gentian, and these flowers attract butterflies. The Wolds Way Lavender farm, with its own wildflower meadow, is a short detour from the Way.

- **Dry valleys** – broad, green tracks along the bottom of dry valleys, formed by rivers that have drained underground into the chalk, make for fine walking. The Way climbs from the valleys to hilltops with wide views over the North Yorkshire Moors.

- **Artworks** – the WANDER initiative set out to install artworks along the route, although only three – the shelter at Fridaythorpe, Enclosure Rites, and Waves and Time – were commissioned. There are also swirling, poetry-inscribed benches and the Secret Art mobile phone app that links poems and paintings to places en route.

CONS

- **Detours** – the Way tends to skirt towns and villages, although there are some links. You will need to detour from the Way if you want to restock supplies, enjoy a pub lunch or stay in a bed and breakfast.

- **Budget accommodation** – there is little in the way of budget accommodation, with no hostels or bunkbarns on the route. While campsites can be found along most of the Way, you may have to rely on kind farmers permitting you to camp in their fields or indulge in a bed and breakfast on some stages of the route.

GOOD TO KNOW

The Arras graves are one of the most remarkable Iron Age burial sites in Europe. First excavated by William Watson in the early nineteenth century, there are more than one hundred barrows, dating from approximately 400–200 BC. Although many of the graves contained grave goods, including animal remains, four were richer than the others. The Lady's Barrow and the Charioteer's Barrow both contained chariots, while the Queen's Barrow was rich in jewellery. The King's Barrow is an extremely rare example of a chariot burial with intact horse skeletons.

FURTHER INFORMATION

www.nationaltrail.co.uk/en_GB/trails/yorkshire-wolds-way

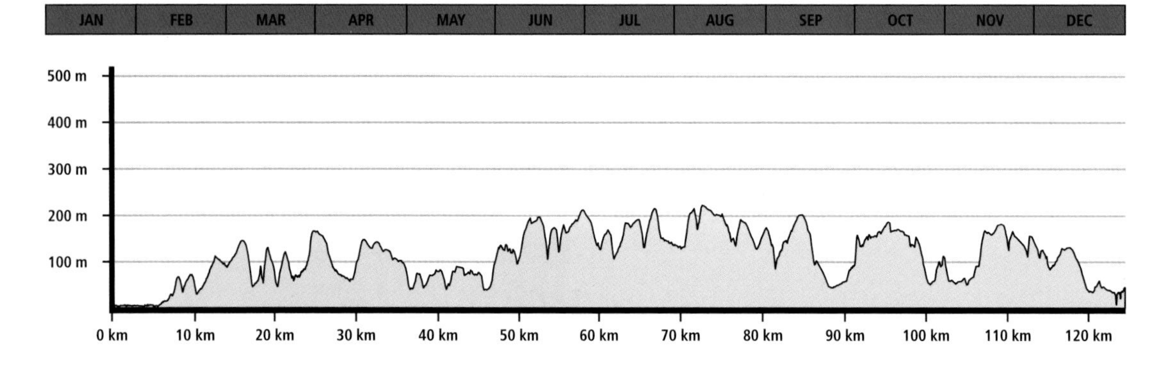

Scarborough
South Bay
North Sea
moorside
A170
Pickering
Allerston
Eastfield
A165
A170
Brompton
Filey Brigg
Filey
A169
Derwent
A64
Flixton
Staxton
A1039
Muston
Filey Bay
Ganton
Sherburn
Hunmanby
Knapton
A64
Rye
Speeton
B1257
Malton
Wintringham
Norton-on-Derwent
Settrington Beacon
A165
Flamborough
The Wolds
B1253
A64
Kirby Grindalythe
Flamborough Head
North Grimston
Rudston
Bridlington
B1249
Wharram le Street
Sledmere
Wharram Percy
Derwent
Burton Agnes
Thixendale
A614
Fimber
A165
Wetwang
Fridaythorpe
Bridlington Bay
Driffield
Garrowby Hill
A166
Bishop Wilton
A614
Skipsea
Huggate
Bainton
Millington
A164
A1079
Pocklington
Nunburnholme
A614
Hornsea
Barmby Moor
Londesborough
Londesborough Park
Scorborough
Siggglesthorne
Goodmanham
A1035
Market Weighton
A1079
Bishop Burton
Beverley
Skirlaugh
Hull
A163
A165
A1034
B1230
A1174
Coniston
A614
A164
ENGLAND
South Cave
M62
Kingston upon Hull
Hedon
Howden
Brantingham
Hessle
N
A63
North Ferriby
A1033
Humber
Goole
Humber Bridge
Barton-upon-Humber
A1077
A1077
Winterton
0
10 Kilometres

BIG TRAILS – AT A GLANCE

	PAGE	COUNTRIES	DISTANCE	ASCENT/DESCENT	WALKING TIME (DAYS/HOURS)	TREKKING TIME (DAYS/HOURS)	FASTPACKING TIME (DAYS/HOURS)	TRAIL RUNNING TIME (DAYS/HOURS)	TRAIL ICONS	WHEN TO GO											
01 Arran Coastal Way	3	Scotland	103km	540m/540m	4/23	3/20	2/15	2/12		J	F	M	A	M	J	J	A	S	O	N	D
02 Beacons Way	9	Wales	155km	5,870m/5,860m	10/58	6/47	5/36	4/25		J	F	M	A	M	J	J	A	S	O	N	D
03 Beara-Breifne Way	15	Ireland	578km	6,790m/6,750m	24/147	15/120	12/90	9/68		J	F	M	A	M	J	J	A	S	O	N	D
04 Burren Way	21	Ireland	80km	1,130m/1,150m	4/22	3/18	2/14	2/10		J	F	M	A	M	J	J	A	S	O	N	D
05 Capital Ring	27	England	120km	690m/690m	5/27	3/23	3/17	2/14		J	F	M	A	M	J	J	A	S	O	N	D
06 Channel Island Way	33	Channel Islands	165km	2,560m/2,560m	10/47	7/38	6/28	5/21		J	F	M	A	M	J	J	A	S	O	N	D
07 Cumbria Way	39	England	115km	2,060m/2,070m	5/32	4/27	3/20	2/15		J	F	M	A	M	J	J	A	S	O	N	D
08 Dingle Way	45	Ireland	182km	2,720m/2,720m	8/49	5/40	4/30	3/22		J	F	M	A	M	J	J	A	S	O	N	D
09 Glyndŵr's Way	51	Wales	217km	6,100m/6,190m	12/72	8/58	6/45	4/31		J	F	M	A	M	J	J	A	S	O	N	D
10 Hebridean Way	57	Scotland	249km	2,750m/2,730m	10/62	7/52	5/38	4/29		J	F	M	A	M	J	J	A	S	O	N	D
11 Isle of Wight Coastal Path	63	England	113km	1,290m/1,290m	5/29	3/24	3/18	2/14		J	F	M	A	M	J	J	A	S	O	N	D
12 Lady Anne's Way	69	England	154km	2,020m/2,010m	7/40	5/33	4/25	3/19		J	F	M	A	M	J	J	A	S	O	N	D
13 Llŷn Coastal Path	75	Wales	158km	2,120m/2,130m	7/42	5/34	4/26	3/19		J	F	M	A	M	J	J	A	S	O	N	D
14 Moray Way	81	Scotland	155km	1,150m/1,150m	6/36	4/30	3/23	3/18		J	F	M	A	M	J	J	A	S	O	N	D
15 North Downs Way	87	England	213km	2,870m/2,930m	9/56	6/46	5/35	4/26		J	F	M	A	M	J	J	A	S	O	N	D
16 Peak District Boundary Walk	93	England	303km	7,610m/7,610m	16/95	10/78	8/58	6/42		J	F	M	A	M	J	J	A	S	O	N	D
17 Pembrokeshire Coast Path	99	Wales	285km	5,040m/5,050m	13/80	8/65	6/49	5/36		J	F	M	A	M	J	J	A	S	O	N	D
18 Severn Way	105	Wales, England	360km	1,550m/950m	13/78	8/65	6/49	5/38		J	F	M	A	M	J	J	A	S	O	N	D
19 Shropshire Way	111	England	345km	4,350m/4,350m	15/89	9/73	7/55	6/41		J	F	M	A	M	J	J	A	S	O	N	D
20 Southern Upland Way	117	Scotland	347km	6,930m/6,870m	17/101	11/83	8/62	6/45		J	F	M	A	M	J	J	A	S	O	N	D
21 St Oswald's Way	123	England	154km	1,150m/1,360m	6/37	4/30	3/23	3/18		J	F	M	A	M	J	J	A	S	O	N	D
22 Teesdale Way	129	England	154km	1,170m/1,000m	6/36	4/30	3/23	3/18		J	F	M	A	M	J	J	A	S	O	N	D
23 Two Moors Way	135	England	172km	3,710m/3,710m	9/51	6/42	4/32	3/23		J	F	M	A	M	J	J	A	S	O	N	D
24 Wye Valley Walk	141	Wales, England	222km	3,620m/3,300m	10/60	7/50	5/38	4/28		J	F	M	A	M	J	J	A	S	O	N	D
25 Yorkshire Wolds Way	147	England	124km	2,010m/1,970m	6/34	4/28	3/21	2/16		J	F	M	A	M	J	J	A	S	O	N	D